Mathematics Teaching in the Early Years:

An Investigation of Teachers' Subject Knowledge

Carol Aubrey

 The Falmer Press

(A Member of the Taylor & Francis Group)
London • Washington, D.C.

UK   The Falmer Press, 1 Gunpowder Square, London, EC4A 3DE

USA   The Falmer Press, Taylor & Francis Inc., 1900 Frost Road, Suite 101, Bristol, PA 19007

First published in 1997

A catalogue record for this book is available from the British Library

Library of Congress Cataloging-in-Publication Data are available on request

ISBN 0 7507 0597 3 paper

Jacket design by Caroline Archer

Typeset in 10/12 pt Times by
Graphicraft Typesetters Ltd., Hong Kong

Printed in Great Britain by Biddles Ltd., Guildford and King's Lynn on paper which has a specified pH value on final paper manufacture of not less than 7.5 and is therefore 'acid free'.

Every effort has been made to contact copyright holders for their permission to reprint material in this book. The publishers would be grateful to hear from any copyright holder who is not here acknowledged and will undertake to rectify any errors or omissions in future editions of this book.

Contents

List of Tables

List of Figures

Acknowledgments

The research project reported in this book would not have been possible without the financial support, first of all, of the Research and Publications Sub-committee of the School of Education and the Research and Initiatives Committee of the University of Durham for the collection of data related to children's informal mathematical knowledge. The Economic and Social Research Council supported later phases, which focused on the processes of mathematical instruction.

Deirdre Pettitt, who co-constructed the assessment procedures and who, with Jennifer Suggate, co-constructed the teacher interview schedule, supplied critical comment. Hazel Hodgson, who assessed many of the Phase 1 children, deserves a special mention. Those who offered critical peer review of journal, seminar and conference papers helped to refine thinking at critical points of the writing. Teachers and children who took part are owed the most. Their honesty and openness provided the basis for this work. Special thanks go to Ann Scott, Susan Metcalf and to Judith Manghan without whose technical and secretarial expertise the presentation and, hence, communication of this project would not have been possible.

KEY PUBLICATIONS

Key publications which have reported the empirical elements of this book are as follows:

AUBREY, C. (1993) 'An investigation of the mathematical knowledge and competencies which young children bring into school,' *British Educational Research Journal*, **19**, 1, pp. 19–37.

AUBREY, C. (1994) 'An investigation of children's knowledge of mathematics at school entry and the knowledge their teachers hold about teaching and learning mathematics, about young learners and mathematical subject knowledge,' *British Educational Research Journal*, **20**, 1, pp. 105–20.

AUBREY, C. (1995) 'Teacher and pupil interaction and the processes of mathematical instruction in four reception classrooms over children's first year in school,' *British Educational Research Journal*, **21**, 1, pp. 31–47.

AUBREY, C. (1996) 'An investigation of teachers' mathematical subject knowledge and the processes of instruction in reception classes,' *British Educational Research Journal*, **22**, 2, pp. 181–97.

AUBREY, C. (1997) 'Re-assessment of the role of teachers' subject knowledge in early mathematics,' *Education 3–13*, (in press).

Summary

The overall aim of the project was to investigate teachers' pedagogical subject knowledge, in particular, through examination of the co-ordination and utilization of teacher and pupil knowledge in the complex environments of reception classrooms.

Phase 1 concerned the design, piloting and revision of criterion-referenced instruments to assess children's informal mathematical knowledge. Preliminary interviews with four reception teachers to consider their pedagogical thinking and decision-making took place in Phase 2. Reported practice was then considered in the light of selected classroom observations. Phase 3 and 4 aimed to capture teachers' pedagogical subject knowledge, exemplified in teacher–pupil interactions, as it moved in varied, yet planned and structured ways towards specific goals. Background biographical information obtained from teacher interviews and measures of children's mathematical knowledge allowed consideration of the relationship of teachers' subject knowledge and knowledge of their pupils' competence to teaching goals and classroom processes.

It was concluded that at the heart of teachers' pedagogical subject knowledge lies subject content knowledge and knowledge of their pupils' conceptions. The observed diversity in practice among the different teachers and their apparent lack of awareness of the rich informal knowledge brought into school – of counting, recognition of numerals, representation of quantity, addition, subtraction and social sharing, appropriate language of measurement and selection of criteria to sort objects – raises some questions with respect to the adequacy of teachers' subject knowledge. The interaction between the processes of assessment of children's prior knowledge and instruction, however, was demonstrated by the way teachers presented tasks and were able to assess the extent to which children could answer questions about content and apply knowledge strategically. This finding poses some challenge to the notion of assessment as a single event or the stable notion of match. Complex views about children's learning were not necessarily translated into practice suggesting that without clear subject content knowledge neither sophisticated theories concerning children's learning nor scaffolded approaches will necessarily lead to effective teaching.

Building up a case knowledge concerning teaching processes which this project has stimulated may be one way to increase our understanding of subject knowledge for teaching and the development of professional practice. Furthermore the interest already generated in the documentation of children's rich informal mathematical knowledge suggests that providing teachers with increased knowledge of children's mathematical thinking may offer another means to enhance their pedagogical subject knowledge.

1   Teachers' Subject Knowledge: Emerging Themes

Introduction

Over the last decade in Britain and in the United States, as noted by McNamara (1991), policy-makers have been promoting teachers' knowledge of subjects and the application of this subject knowledge in the classroom as a key element in the raising of standards in teaching. As policy-makers have sought to increase the effectiveness of subject teaching through educational reform, conceptual and empirical enquiry has contributed to a changing and developing research base concerning teachers' subject knowledge. Although in the early stages of development, new lines of enquiry are generating fresh debate about the nature and substance of teachers' knowledge and the way this knowledge is transformed in classroom teaching. It was this emergent field of enquiry which provided the impetus for the project which forms the basis for this book. In spite of the concern of policy-makers, however, it is too soon to make general statements about what teachers do know or should know about subject content and about its translation into forms accessible to young children. It is still difficult, at this point in time, to characterize or synthesize these new conceptual constructs and research findings, to indicate their scope or to anticipate future trends and developments.

Before reviewing the substantive and methodological issues it is necessary to make more explicit some of the underlying assumptions, understandings and beliefs concerning the teaching of subjects which have helped to shape knowledge production and utilization, to define legitimate problems and, thus, to influence the direction of research and the interpretation of data.

Aims

The aim of this chapter is to offer, first, a brief overview of the relevant political-educational context and, second, to present a brief account of some of the main philosophical and conceptual issues which have contributed to the current debate concerning teachers' subject knowledge. Chapter 2 will then examine, in more detail, changing models and methods of investigating subject teaching. This will provide a context in which to locate the aims and objectives for the present project and set the scene for the consideration of substantive issues in Chapter 3.

Teachers' Subject Knowledge: The Political-educational Context

Of the wide-ranging organizational and practical changes for education, brought about by the *Education Reform Act* (1988), the introduction of a centrally directed National Curriculum is of particular relevance to the discussion of teachers' subject knowledge. This designated three core subjects and seven foundation subjects which must be taught. The core subjects were mathematics, English and science. The foundation subjects were history, geography, technology, music, art, physical education and, at secondary stage, a modern language. (Welsh was a core subject for Welsh-speaking schools and a foundation subject in non-Welsh-speaking schools in Wales.) Religious education was included as part of the 'basic' curriculum, without being subject to the particular conditions attached to the core and foundation subjects.

In the decade before the introduction of the *Education Reform Act* (DES, 1988) a number of policy documents was issued by successive Secretaries of State which showed an increasing interest in the curriculum, for instance, the *Organisation and Content of the 5–16 Curriculum* (DES, 1984) and *Science 5–16: A Statement of Policy* (DES, 1985b). Her Majesty's Inspectors (HMI) also increased their output of curriculum papers of which the *Curriculum from 5–16* (DES, 1985c) stands out as an important example. Whilst the White Paper *Quality Schools* (DES, 1985a) stated that the Government had no intention to introduce legislation redefining responsibility for the curriculum, the move towards a centrally controlled, subject-based curriculum had begun.

The White Paper *Quality Teaching* (DES, 1983) can be identified as a key document which expressed a parallel concern about student teachers' subject matter knowledge. Criteria set out in a circular (DES, 1989) from the Council for the Accreditation of Teacher Education (CATE), moreover, marked a move towards a greater emphasis in training on students' acquisition of subject matter knowledge and on its role in effective teaching. Student teachers were expected to have subject expertise in one or more areas of the curriculum and to receive tuition in the application of their specialist subject, or subjects, to the teaching and assessment of pupils.

Following the introduction of the National Curriculum concern about the adequacy of school teachers' subject knowledge was still being expressed, in particular, at the primary stage. Alexander, Rose and Woodhead (1992), in a discussion document commissioned by the Government, stated:

> The resistance to subjects at the primary stage is no longer tenable. The subject is a necessary feature of the modern curriculum. It requires appropriate kinds of knowledge on the part of the teacher. (Alexander, Rose and Woodhead, 1992, Summary, para 3.2)

In the follow-up to this report the Office for Standards in Education (OFSTED) 1993 concluded:

Improvement of teachers' subject knowledge was widely acknowledged as of central importance if primary schools were to make the looked-for progress with teaching the National Curriculum. (OFSTED, 1993, para 32, p. 16)

The National Curriculum Council (1993), too, recommended a number of changes for primary schools, including the greater use of single subject teaching and of subject teachers, the provision of further guidance and training with respect to teaching methods and subject knowledge, and the revision of initial teacher training which, currently, did not ensure mastery of subject knowledge across the full range of the National Curriculum or focus sharply enough on teaching skills. More recently the call came from the Department for Education (DFEE) Circular 14/93 *The Initial Training of Primary Teachers* for the strengthening of subject knowledge and practical teaching skills which equipped primary student teachers to teach effectively and which were the foundation for further professional development.

The need to strengthen the subject knowledge of class teachers and student teachers has become a recurrent theme. Whilst subject knowledge has been generally accepted as a fundamental component of teachers' knowledge policy-makers and researchers alike have not, until recently, focused so much emphasis on its development. The emerging emphasis on teachers' subject knowledge indicates a fundamental shift in thinking about teaching.

It is difficult, however, to consider policy and practice without first examining the implicit themes underlying the current educational reform movement with its goal to improve the academic quality of teaching and the new research emphasis on the role of subject knowledge in teaching. The next section will attempt to examine and to analyse the theme of subject knowledge in teaching as reflected in educational thinking.

Teachers' Subject Knowledge: The Contribution of Philosophical and Conceptual Analysis

If teaching involves helping others to learn, then understanding the subject content to be taught is a fundamental requirement of teaching. Teachers' knowledge of subject matter provides an example of an essential category of teachers' knowledge which is neither new nor controversial but one which can be separated into a variety of distinct components for examination. One contribution that the philosophical method can make to the debate on teachers' subject knowledge is to re-examine generally held concepts or assumptions which may carry systematic distinctions needing to be made explicit in order to clarify distinct components and to identify ways of reconsidering these.

Activities which are typically associated with the philosophical method include conceptual and logical analysis of argument, examining assumptions, claims, linguistic intuitions about terms, their associations and implications. No clear distinction between philosophical enquiry and other types of investigation exists and discussion which draws on philosophical methods may well draw on other forms of knowledge and enquiry in the social sciences. Furthermore the philosophical method employs logical analysis of language or concepts which underpins all forms of discussion and writing and, hence, a formal statement that it is being used may not always be made. This means, as noted by Floden and Buchmann (1990), that philosophy can make an important contribution to arguments which are not obviously philosophical or even advanced by writers who are philosophers.

Debate concerning the role of teachers' subject knowledge spans the twentieth century. A classic essay of John Dewey (1904–64) argued that knowledge of teaching subjects conferred an understanding of the ways the mind worked. For Dewey knowledge of subjects equated knowledge and enquiry, and knowledge of the educational process as he conceived it. Learning subjects was about learning:

> The fundamental mental attitudes and operations – that indeed, particular scientific methods and classifications simply express and illustrate in their most concrete form that of which simple and common modes of thought-activity are capable when they work, under satisfactory conditions . . .
> (Dewey, 1904–64, pp. 161–2)

Dewey's argument was that subject knowledge *provided* knowledge of teaching method and, moreover, it was a resource which could be more systematically exploited. Some people were good teachers without studying pedagogy. A conclusion which might be drawn from this was that there may be little advantage to be gained from knowledge of teaching method. His argument hinged on a distinction inherent in his theory of learning and knowledge.

People's minds are driven by problems originating in concrete experience. These problems engendered enquiry, and actions resulting from this enquiry, provided the basis for resolving them. Hence, teachers using this 'scientific' method of thought, themselves, were able to, and should be able to teach in ways that supported pupils' own practice of enquiry. For Dewey this mode of so-called scientific thinking was the appropriate model for all thought. Teaching in ways which stimulated pupils' own practice of enquiry transformed teaching into science, thus, required deep knowledge of subjects which, in turn, embodied knowledge of the educational process.

Wilson (1975), a professional philosopher of education, considered that the meaning or logic of concepts used offered guidance for teaching. In attempting to identify what being a teacher logically required he suggested that the concept of being a teacher entailed that people acquired a taxonomy of characteristics. First, the teacher must have knowledge of subject matter in a way that is most useful for the pupils' learning. Whilst this might include relevant knowledge and facts, it required:

> the idea of having a clear understanding of what it is to make progress in the subject – the type of reasoning involved, its logical structure, the

marks of a 'good historian' (scientist, mathematician, etc.) and so forth. (Wilson, 1975, p. 111)

Second, teaching others also involved demonstrating a serious care about, or commitment to share that knowledge. Third, teaching, in the sense of 'getting others to learn', required additional interpersonal knowledge.

Like Dewey, Wilson believed that preparation for teaching involved getting people to know their subjects and to care about them, to be serious and conceptually alert. In other words the acquisition of these three characteristics was a matter of teachers' knowledge and, hence, education. Whilst Wilson was interested in linguistic analysis, common meanings across time for such terms as, 'knowledge' and 'education', cannot be assumed. The important point to note, however, is that the distinctions which were being made allowed consideration of important meanings that were set in long-established usage. Furthermore, such distinctions, once made explicit, provided access to tacit assumptions that the words conveyed.

Enquiry about teaching, however, is seldom purely conceptual and has often combined philosophical argument concerning meanings, concepts and logic with empirical elements. Exemplifying this approach is the work of Gage (1978; 1985) who argued for the relevance of research on teaching through a blend of philosophical argument with empirical claim. By contrast to Dewey and Wilson, Gage argued that weaknesses in teacher preparation resulted from neglect of pedagogy. Moreover, he believed that further study of school subjects was of little value:

> when the teacher might already know far more about that subject than he or she will ever need in teaching third-graders (9-year-olds) or even twelfth-graders (17-year-olds). (Gage, 1985, p. 27)

His argument incorporated a number of empirical claims, for instance, that teacher preparation was inadequate in its attention to teaching method since teachers already knew much subject matter. This carried an implicit argument in favour of *increasing* the importance of teaching method and assumed that teachers needed to know only the subject matter content already learned in their own schooling or acquired in relevant undergraduate study. Moreover, it assumed that sufficient subject knowledge would allow the teacher to deliver the subject effectively and enable pupils to learn it. More convincing, however, was Gage's assertion that teachers needed to learn teaching method as well as subject knowledge, such as structuring coursework, planning a lesson and interacting appropriately with children. Past failure to address teaching technique adequately was attributable, in part, he asserted, to the lack of an appropriate research base. Teaching, however, was more than the appreciation of technique and, in fact, what Gage was advocating was instruction in empirically based skills, united to a view of teaching which included flexibility, judgment and intuition, with a recognition that teaching could not be reduced to mere technical formulae.

Research results, thus, provided a constructive starting point for Gage rather than a prescription for practice. The limitation of this argument lies in its assumption of the existence of a research base to provide or to determine worthwhile or valued kinds of pupil learning. Moreover, there is an additional assumption that the implementation of such teaching skills will lead inevitably to effective learning and that effective teaching, in terms of attainment outcomes, is necessarily *good*, or desirable teaching. Teaching is, thus, judged worthwhile by Gage in terms of gains on achievement tests. This view however, promotes a narrow and instrumental view of teaching which, it might be argued, distracts attention away from other, and equally important educational goals.

Buchmann (1982; 1984), too, used a combination of analysis of meaning and logic with reference made to empirical, educational research. It is significant to note, at this point, however, that neither Gage nor Buchmann based these claims about teacher preparation on investigations of actual teacher preparation programmes. By way of argument, in contrast, whilst Gage argued that teachers needed more instruction in teaching techniques because they already knew more than they needed to know about the subject they would teach, Buchmann argued that subject matter knowledge had been neglected and that professional preparation of teachers placed too much emphasis on classroom technique.

The fundamental basis for the disparity of views between Gage and Buchmann is revealed in Buchmann's discussion of what and how much teachers need to know about subject matter. Buchmann proceeded by a conceptual argument for the priority of subject matter knowledge. She pointed out that teaching means, in part, knowledge of what is to be taught. In other words, subject knowledge is required in order for teaching to take place. She drew on arguments of Green (1971) and Peters (1977) to demonstrate that teaching presupposes teachers' subject knowledge. This argument, however, cannot indicate the nature or extent of subject knowledge which is required.

In support of her view that teachers needed rich and deep subject knowledge Buchmann drew on empirical studies of learning which demonstrated the importance of understanding how pupils developed subject knowledge and how to deal appropriately with pupils' misconceptions and errors. This presupposed knowledge that goes far beyond subject content. It entailed broad knowledge of the children being taught in order to identify and to correct appropriately the confusions and misconceptions that they held. In order to support children's learning, Buchmann argued that empirical studies have indicated that teaching goes further and deeper than presenting subject content and concluded that teachers needed subject matter knowledge of a kind that was not available in current teacher preparation programmes.

Teachers needed flexible knowledge of their subject that included knowledge about its history, organization and methods of enquiry.

> Given the pedagogical requirement for flexible control of subject matter, knowledge of epistemology and history of science is a specific preparation for teaching. Content knowledge of this kind and at this level deepens understanding of knowledge and subject matter, encourages the mobility of teacher conceptions, and yields pedagogical knowledge in the shape of multiple and fluid conceptions. It also contributes to a form of classroom

life in which all participants are seen and treated as the potential source
of thoughts and actions that make sense. (Buchmann, 1984, p. 46)

In contrast to Gage, Buchmann rejected the idea that teaching method or
classroom management needed detailed attention in favour of a view of a greater
emphasis on *substance*. Significantly she drew attention to the fact that where
teachers focused on issues of management this might well result from gaps in
their own content knowledge and from interpretation of unexpected responses
from children as challenges to teaching, rather than as opportunities for learning.
As Doyle (1986) has shown, where children are engaged by content, problems of
management are less likely to arise. The argument being advanced was, thus, supported by reference to empirical studies and, in fact, a number of different arguments for directing more attention to levels of subject knowledge were put forward.
Like Gage, however, Buchmann made assumptions about what sort of learning and
teaching outcomes were desirable and her argument rests upon the assumption that
scholarship in academic subjects is to be the desired, educational goal. Furthermore, Buchmann assumed an association between the type of teacher subject content knowledge she was advancing and the kind of pupil learning that she hoped
would occur. In fact, as yet, there has been little empirical investigation of the
association between teachers' subject knowledge, as understood by Buchmann, and
the type of pupil learning in terms she valued, as Floden and Buchmann (1990)
have noted.

This analysis of Buchmann's work does, however, suggest the need for a
closer examination of the distinct components of teachers' subject knowledge
and, whilst he did not dwell upon the argument for the importance of subject
knowledge, Shulman (1986a) provided a more extended analysis of the domains of
teachers' subject knowledge and other closely related aspects of teachers' knowledge. Distinctions drawn within the domains of teachers' knowledge were used by
him to draw attention to areas in need of further research. Firstly, he distinguished
subject content knowledge from pedagogical content knowledge and curriculum
knowledge. Subject content knowledge involved knowledge of the substance of the
field, the major concepts and procedures, and the relationships between these. It
also involved the syntax of the field, or knowledge of the discourse of the subject
and the major 'tools' or methods of enquiry for establishing truth in the field, or
undertaking new work within it. Subject content knowledge, however, he argued,
had already commanded considerable research attention. Beyond content knowledge, claimed Shulman, lay pedagogical content knowledge. Within this category
were found the topics most commonly taught in one's subject area, the most compelling ways of representing them to children, the illustrations, examples and explanations. Also involved was an appreciation of what young children found difficult
to learn about the subject, their common errors and misconceptions. It was here
that research on teaching and learning most closely interrelated. Understanding
of children's subject knowledge was most pertinent to the consideration of subject content we teach. Furthermore it was difficult to consider ways of representing
specific ideas or concepts in a subject area without recourse to the consideration of

particular curriculum materials which exemplified that content. Knowledge about alternative teaching materials, texts and apparatus available was essential to the preparation of topics for teaching and constituted the third category of content knowledge, curriculum knowledge. It was through the introduction of such resources by the teacher, designed to represent ideas and procedures, that children acquired understanding and mastery of specific content.

Within each of these domains, Shulman distinguished three forms of knowledge: propositional knowledge, case knowledge and strategic knowledge. Propositional knowledge which, he claimed, dominated teacher education, was difficult to remember or to apply to classrooms. Case knowledge, however, could provide rich descriptions or classroom examples to illustrate propositional knowledge, whilst strategic knowledge supported the teacher's moment-by-moment decision-making by informing the choice amongst, or application of principles in specific classroom contexts or situations.

Beyond propositional, case and strategic knowledge lay three types of knowledge in each of these three categories, depending on whether that knowledge was derived from disciplined enquiry, practical experience or ethical analysis. To take one example, the maxim 'don't smile until Christmas' is not based on research but derived from accumulated experience. It is propositional knowledge and drawn from experience. Each sub-category of knowledge could, moreover, be further divided so that, for instance, propositional knowledge could be grouped into principles, maxims and norms, just as case knowledge could be sub-divided into prototypes, precedents and parables, whilst strategic knowledge guided selection of principles, maxims or norms to apply to particular practice.

This elaborate system of categories and sub-categories depended for its power upon the clarity of distinctions made between categories, the particular features which were highlighted, the explanations, illustrations and examples which were presented; and the extent to which these accorded with practitioner knowledge and experience, in order to make a good case for his distinction of the neglected sources of knowledge in research and teaching. Shulman needed to demonstrate convincingly that subject content knowledge was composed of separate categories and sub-categories. If some cases fell into more than one category, the argument being advanced would be weakened.

Floden and Buchmann (1990) noted that propositional knowledge based on scholarly study of the ethics of teaching appeared to fit as both a principle and a norm since it was based on both disciplined enquiry and on ethics. Similarly Valli and Tom (1988), whilst acknowledging that Shulman had gone as far as anyone in thinking about the forms of teacher knowledge, saw a primary problem in the separation of principles and norms. They challenged the forms of knowledge on the basis of applying specific criteria for use in assessing knowledge base frameworks and stated:

> We can think of no principle in teaching which does not have a normative base. He (Shulman) fails to see the moral bases of pedagogical actions. (Valli and Tom, 1988, p. 5)

To take another example, Dewey might have questioned the distinction between practical experience and disciplined enquiry and argued that practical experience might be disciplined.

Even allowing for these weaknesses in Shulman's argument this should not detract from the important distinction he was able to make in identifying a valuable, yet neglected source of knowledge for teaching. If the purpose of philosophical enquiry is to challenge traditional assumptions about teaching by elaborating distinctions, Shulman provided a system with potential for rich, new understanding of teachers' subject knowledge. In so doing, inevitably, particular perspectives and arguments were highlighted, whilst others remained unexamined. Philosophical enquiry allows for the examination of a variety of ideas and insights using a variety of methods. In the particular case of teachers' subject knowledge further philosophical and empirical work will be needed before questions about the extent to which reason or evidence is justified.

The attention drawn by Shulman to the role of subject knowledge in teaching stimulated a range of investigations which attempted to clarify components of pedagogical subject knowledge. Ernest (1989), for instance, developed an analytical model of different types of knowledge, beliefs and attitudes of the mathematics teacher and their relationship to practice which owed much to Shulman's work but drew particular attention to attitudes, which he felt Shulman had neglected. Marks (1990) drew attention to the ambiguities and complexities inherent in the notion of pedagogical subject knowledge and identified four components: subject matter for instruction, student understanding of subject matter, media for instruction and instructional processes. Tamir (1988) drew particular attention to the distinction between general pedagogical knowledge and subject matter specific pedagogical knowledge. He also believed that a clearer distinction should be made between propositional knowledge (Ryle's, 1952, 'knowledge that') and procedural knowledge (Ryle's 'knowledge how'). Furthermore, he posited a distinction between subject content and subject matter, preferring the latter term which he regarded as encompassing both substantive (content) and syntactic (processes) of a given discipline, derived from ideas of Schwab (1964).

Whilst it is now a decade since Shulman's seminal paper was presented it is, perhaps, most fairly judged in terms of the illumination it provided on the components of teachers' subject knowledge and the further enquiry it generated. Investigation of teachers' pedagogical subject content knowledge, however, is still in the early stages.

In summary, at the more specific level, Dewey's analysis of language and taken-for-granted ideas in academic knowledge provoked a re-examination of the notion of subject knowledge and Wilson, too, exposed the implicit systems of meaning in ordinary language for such terms as 'education' and 'teaching'. The arguments of Gage and Buchmann illustrated the way assumptions about what is worthwhile in teaching and learning are related to valued educational goals and, hence, the relationship of teachers' subject knowledge to formal academic learning. Shulman constructed an elaborate category system which he was able to use in order to argue that certain forms of teachers' knowledge had been neglected in research and practice and, hence, has provided a powerful stimulus to research on teachers' subject knowledge.

Conclusion

The intention of this chapter has been to outline some of the philosophical and conceptual themes which have helped to shape and influence the direction of research and practice in the area of teachers' subject knowledge. The studies examined give an indication of the emerging conceptions and the stimulus that these have provided to the search for a knowledge base for subject teaching. The convergence of attention on subject knowledge by policy-makers and researchers has provided an interesting challenge to questions about teaching and subject matter which could result, as argued by Sockett (1987), in a narrow vision of teaching. The signs are that fundamental issues of teaching and teacher knowledge are being re-examined and this is, perhaps, indicative of an enlargement of the vision of teaching and a greater sophistication in the means for illuminating this.

Examination of these issues would be incomplete, however, without reference to the relevant empirical enquiry on teachers' subject knowledge. Serious questions about the nature of subject knowledge and its relationship to teaching can not be addressed without reference to the context in which this knowledge is taught and learned. Chapter 2 will, thus, consider the modes and methods being used to investigate teachers' subject knowledge and set the scene for the formal statement of aims and objectives for the current project.

2 Changing Models and Methods of Investigating Teachers' Subject Knowledge

Introduction

Chapter 1 aimed to make explicit some of the underlying assumptions, knowledge and beliefs that have shaped current thinking about teachers' subject knowledge. It is these underlying assumptions which are likely to influence investigation of teachers' subject knowledge. Enquiry in teaching rarely remains purely conceptual, however, since teaching is a practical activity and, hence, arguments about practice can hardly be divorced from the classroom context. Such assumptions, nevertheless, are likely to affect the research questions which are posed and the methods which are used. More fundamentally and substantively, the nature and type of knowledge which is investigated is likely to be informed, if not determined by views about what is thought to be important by researchers, by those making the policy decisions, or those dealing with the professional issues which are to be found.

Aims

As noted in Chapter 1 many assertions concerning teachers' subject knowledge combine philosophical and empirical elements. The aim of Chapter 2, however, is to focus on the empirical investigation of teachers' subject knowledge and to review the broad types of enquiry which have been utilized in research on teaching. The implications for policy and practice for reform-minded policy-makers and educational researchers alike, where possible, are indicated. The intention is to consider changing models and methods of enquiry which provide a context in which to locate the aims and objectives for the current project.

Teachers' Subject Knowledge: Emerging Concerns in Empirical Enquiry

As noted by Brophy (1991) research on classroom teaching is a relatively recent phenomenon. Early educators, as noted in Chapter 1, tended to address educational issues through philosophical debate rather than through empirical enquiry. Ball (1991) identified three phases of research on teaching in which teachers' subject knowledge has 'figured, faded and reappeared' as key influences on teaching, in this case of mathematics, and cited a quote by Medley (1979) as typifying the first phase:

> Driven by common sense and conventional wisdom about teaching, the earliest research compiled characteristics of teachers whom others perceived as effective. (Medley, 1979, p. 2)

The second phase of research attempted to establish relationships between teacher behaviours and characteristics (processes) and pupil learning or achievement gains (products). Most recently researchers, in the third phase, have attempted to investigate qualitative aspects of classroom teaching and learning, thinking and decision-making in relation to subject matter areas. Largely, but not exclusively, this has been a knowledge base developed in the United States.

Phase 1

As noted by Ball (1991), research on teaching has commonly focused on characteristics of so-called, 'good' teachers and their influence on what children actually learned. Whilst the theme of teachers' subject knowledge may be a current focus for researchers and reform-minded policy-makers, inevitably, the search for quality assurance and teacher effectiveness has been a perennial theme. Early studies of characteristics of good teachers, based on pupils' assessments of their best teachers, reported that good teachers were 'enthusiastic, helpful and strict' as well as knowing their subject matter better (Hart, 1934). These studies did not, however, test empirically the influence of such factors as what teachers actually did in classrooms or what pupils learned.

In response to the perceived weakness of these early studies, over the 1960s, the *National Longitudinal Study of Mathematics Abilities* was carried out which involved forty states in the United States, 1,500 schools and 112,000 children. Of twenty teacher characteristics and attitudes, no single teacher characteristic, including years of experience in mathematics, personal engagement in mathematics and philosophical orientation to learning, was strongly associated with student achievement (Begle and Geeslin, 1972). Begle (1979) concluded that many widely held beliefs about good teaching were false and, in relation to the notion that the more one knows about one's subject, the more effective one is as a teacher:

> the empirical literature suggests that this belief needs drastic modification. (Begle, 1979, p. 51)

Children of teachers who had studied mathematics at undergraduate level, either as a major or minor subject, scored significantly higher on achievement tests in only 20 per cent of cases. In fact the number of teacher credits in college mathematics was *negatively* associated with children's achievement in 15 per cent of cases.

Given these findings Begle concluded that the effects of a teacher's subject matter knowledge and attitudes on children's learning seemed to be far less powerful than had been previously assumed.

Taking account of the philosophical analysis of teachers' subject knowledge undertaken in Chapter 1 it is surprising, perhaps, that few assumptions underlying this research were challenged or alternative interpretations offered. Ball (1991) questioned:

- whether the number of courses in college level mathematics was a reasonable indication of teachers' mathematical knowledge;
- what was actually acquired through 'majoring' in mathematics, in terms of disciplinary understandings or ideas of pedagogy; and
- whether, in fact, some of what was gained in higher level mathematics courses might be *counterproductive* preparation for teaching.

Phase 2

Instead of questioning assumptions which underpinned the existing operational definitions of teacher effectiveness and the associated research design, researchers turned attention away from teacher characteristics and, hence from subject knowledge, towards the study of generic teacher behaviours such as pacing, questioning, explanations and praise, as well as qualities such as clarity, directness and enthusiasm. This work, reviewed in detail by Brophy and Good (1986), became known as 'process-product' or 'process-outcome' research because it attempted to link classroom processes (largely teacher behaviours) with children's gains on achievement tests (products). Most of these studies were correlational and focused on elementary (primary) school teaching of mathematics and reading in the early stages where achievement was regarded as vital and measurement of outcomes was clear. Subject knowledge was, thus, involved as part of the *context* though not the focus for the research. Brophy (1989) has cited three main conclusions to be drawn from this research:

1 Teachers can make a difference. That is, some reliably elicit greater gains in achievement which can be related to systematic differences in teacher behaviour.
2 Classroom differences in children's achievement gains occur in part because of classroom differences in exposure to academic content and opportunity to learn.

Teachers who elicit greater achievement, thus:

- placed more emphasis on developing mastery of the curriculum, in establishing expectations for children, and in defining their own role as learners;
- allocated most available time for activities designed to foster such mastery;

- were effective organizers and managers who established efficient learning environments which maximized time engaged in on-going activities.

3 Teachers who elicit greater achievement gains do not merely maximize 'time on task' but spend much time actively instructing children. In other words, they interpreted content, monitored, assessed, questioned, and engaged in interactive discourse.

Vital to an appreciation of this period of effective teaching research is the recognition of the assumptions about subject content, the goals of teaching and learning, and the role of the teacher and pupil in effective instruction which are made. Where effectiveness is judged in terms of outcomes it is likely to focus on learning or acquisition of facts, principles and procedures and, thus, encourage a narrow or 'technical' view of teaching. Typically, investigators were trained in educational psychology and did not necessarily have experience of teaching subjects in schools.

The nearest British equivalents to this type of research, carried out by Bennett (1976) and Galton *et al.* (1980), attempted to relate particular styles of grouping and teaching strategy to pupil response or outcome.

The perennial theme of quality control appeared to dominate stage 2 research on teaching, with the question of effectiveness usually taking the form of a statement or claim about the relationship between teacher characteristics and practices and the attainment of a valued, educational objective. As noted by Doyle (1990) the existence of such research was, and remains important in legitimating claims to professional competence. As noted in Chapter 1 raising standards in schooling is a recurrent concern of policy-makers and research on school and teacher effectiveness has been prominent throughout this research.

Over the last decade, however, there has been a reaction by some researchers, against this technical view of teaching, or quality control theme, which allowed a small set of generic indicators to be applied uniformly across a broad range of teaching situations. As noted by Doyle (1990), the search for such indicators led to a minimizing of information, a condensing and simplifying of knowledge and an economy of expression and deliberation. In this process, teaching was:

> stripped of its particulars . . . it is all too easy to adopt a fragmented view of teaching and assume that learning from teaching occurs in a unidirectional and mechanistic way. (Doyle, 1990, p. 13)

Phase 3

As time went on classroom researchers increasingly appreciated the complexity of classrooms and practice of teaching. Peterson (1979) noted how consideration of the ways teachers defined their goals, selected material and approaches for a diverse range of children and leading to a variety of outcomes, revealed how inadequate the search was for a single, most effective approach to teaching. Clark and Yinger (1979) observed that:

> the new approach to the study of teaching assumes that what teachers do is affected by what they think. This approach, which emphasises the processing of cognitive information, is concerned with the teachers' judgements, decision-making and planning. (Clarke and Yinger, 1979, p. 231)

A new emphasis in research on teaching was the redefinition of teaching as thought and decision-making which takes place before, during and after the interactions with children. Some researchers increasingly focused on the knowledge teachers used to conduct practice rather than knowledge which could be used to evaluate teaching. Brophy (1991) characterized this trend in recent research on teaching as likely to focus intensively on single lessons, or series of lessons, taking account of the teachers' explicit objectives and recording classroom processes as they unfolded. Often detailed interviewing might be used, on the one hand, to determine the teachers' underlying rationale and, on the other, to probe children's developing understanding. In other words, what has characterized such investigations is the 'thick' descriptions of classroom processes, as well as the qualitative analysis of teachers teaching and children learning. This type of analysis has also been distinguished by the extent to which it has focused on a specific subject area and, more particularly, on the nature and content of subject knowledge involved in teaching and learning. Furthermore it has required subject specialist researchers who appreciated the goals teachers were trying to pursue, the content being selected and the methods being used to achieve the goals set.

In summary, from the earlier studies of teachers' generic thinking and decision-making, subject matter gradually began to assume a greater importance as a critical variable in research on teaching, with an associated attention to the curriculum and to subject discipline as a source for practice. This form of enquiry has been based on the premise that effective teaching requires specialist knowledge related to classroom systems and subject matter content in order to plan classroom teaching, to carry out or to interpret classroom events. Ball (1991) has suggested, however, that subject matter knowledge in current studies is:

> a concept of varied definition, a fact that threatens to muddle our progress in learning about the role of teachers' (mathematical) understanding in their teaching. (Ball, 1991, p. 5)

Ball's conclusions, concerning the development of empirical enquiry, echo conclusions drawn in Chapter 1 with respect to conceptual enquiry. Investigation of teachers' subject knowledge, both conceptually and empirically, is still in the early stages of development. A more detailed examination of relevant aspects of this emerging, empirical knowledge base related to teachers' subject knowledge, however, will be undertaken in Chapter 3.

Teachers' Subject Knowledge: The Changing Context in Research on Teaching

The previous sections of this chapter have outlined some changing concerns in empirical enquiry related to teachers' subject knowledge. This section will attempt to place this enquiry within the broader context of qualitative enquiry on teaching in order that an examination of changing models and methods of enquiry on teaching can be made.

As noted in the previous section over the last decade, reaction of some researchers against the so-called 'technical' approach to teaching research has grown (see Shulman, 1986b; Brophy and Good, 1986). This can be characterized as a new emphasis on the complex thinking processes and decision-making involved in teaching and learning to teach subjects and a recognition that teachers, themselves, should have ownership of this knowledge. Doyle (1990) has described this dual theme as 'knowledge and empowerment' which has led some writers to emphasize a highly personalistic and phenomenological view of teaching. It is a view of teaching which has stressed intuitive and spontaneous responses of teachers and personal interpretations of situations. Smyth (1987) has characterized such 'practitioner' knowledge as tentative, situational and idiosyncratic, and embedded in the particulars of the practice. The problem with this approach according to Tom (1987) is that the rejection of generalized propositions concerning pedagogical knowledge and teaching practice and the lack of normative reference means that the findings have limited use to other teachers.

Rejection of the 'technical' view that emphasized context-free, generic indicators of teaching quality does not, however, necessarily lead to a rejection of generalized propositions about teaching. It is possible to support the generation of theoretical knowledge about classroom teaching without accepting a 'technical' view of teaching. Qualitative enquiry can generate knowledge about classroom practices, uncover patterns and regularities in classroom events and practices that occur in these contexts which lead to an enhanced understanding of such processes. In other words, classroom processes can be codified and systematized in a form which has utility for teachers.

This emerging work is characterized by an appreciation of both the value and limits of generalizing about teaching. It is marked by a recognition that teaching processes cannot be easily divested of particularity without distortion. Furthermore the orderly and thorough analysis of such processes which are not stripped of particulars can provide powerful interpretations of classroom events and explanations for common dilemmas.

According to Doyle (1990) theoretical knowledge about teaching practices is beginning to be developed and important strands can be identified:

- teaching practices are becoming more richly delineated;
- there is a greater concern for ecological validity or verisimilitude according to the judgment of the teachers who participate in the contexts being studied;

- an interest in multiple consequences and in context- and curriculum-specific effects which can lead to identification of specific conditions under which a particular practice might be appropriate;
- an emphasis on principles for practice which serve as guides rather than on generating general prescriptions which apparently apply to all classrooms.

There are fundamental conceptual and methodological differences between these new approaches and the process-product studies where an investigator enters a setting with pre-determined categories to record and where processes serve as variables to be used as predictors of achievements. Such variables are scarcely processes at all and, at best, characterize a teacher's typical processes over time, decontextualized into units which are apparently associated with pupil achievement.

Doyle (1990) has, in fact, suggested there are at least three distinct strands in recent research on teaching: research on teaching practices, research on subject matter content of teachers and research on enactment knowledge.

Important developments in 'knowledge of teaching practices' have been made as such examples as reciprocal teaching (Palinscar and Brown, 1984) and co-operative learning (Slavin, 1983) demonstrate. These practices tend to encompass whole clusters of teaching actions and are delineated at the level of an entire teaching programme.

This focus on teaching practices may, however, lead to a lack of attention to 'subject matter knowledge' of teachers and, in particular, to pedagogical content knowledge which was introduced in Chapter 1 (see Leinhardt and Smith, 1985; Shulman, 1986a and 1987). The shift in focus here is to the organization and management of subject matter rather than simply the management and control of pupils and interpersonal processes that occur between teachers and children. As noted earlier Shulman identified the central role of subject content knowledge in teaching. The teacher must grasp the structure of the subject matter and the principles of its conceptual organization in order to appreciate the important ideas and skills in specific domains. This also requires some appreciation of the methods, or tools of enquiry, which are used for producing new knowledge in the field.

Between subject content specialism and pedagogy lies pedagogical content knowledge which marks out the subject specialist from the specialist teacher by the ability to represent key ideas in a variety of ways by using demonstrations, examples and metaphors to convey meaning to young children. Furthermore, it requires appreciation of pupils' existing knowledge, their common errors and misunderstandings. Finally curriculum knowledge is required in the selection of appropriate materials and resources in order to represent subject content in ways which have meaning for the diversity of young children likely to be encountered. Research on teachers' subject knowledge has provided detailed cases of beginning and experienced teachers which not only attempt to explicate subject knowledge as it is deployed but offer rich descriptions and analyses of the particulars of teaching.

Another strand of recent teaching research, according to Doyle and Carter (1984), consists of formulations about the structures and processes of classrooms that shape the enactment of the curriculum. 'Enactment knowledge' deals with the patterns and regularities that constitute and shape the life of classrooms. This work has tended to utilize ecological, ethnographic and linguistic methods of social enquiry and early research in this area was directed towards classroom organization and management (see, for instance, the work of Kounin, 1970). A central premise is that the classroom is a behavioural setting, or rather an eco-behavioural setting, composed of 'segments' that structure and order thought and action. The central aim of such research has been to explicate the texture of these segments and their influence on classroom processes. One research focus has been classroom activities which involve classroom time, usually ten to twenty minutes, during which children are engaged in a particular way. Activities are, thus, defined by:

- the temporal boundaries of duration and pace;
- the physical setting, including number and type of participants and their arrangements;
- the behavioural format or programme of action for participants;
- the focal content of the segment.

Changes in these features typically signal a change in the nature and context of the classroom. A key feature of an activity is the programme of action, or events for participants, which sequences or structures appropriate behaviours as well as provides direction and momentum to the situation. Activities are partly social and partly substantive or curricular, involving participants in the accomplishment of tasks.

In fact a second focus of enactment research has been classroom tasks. Tasks are embedded in classroom activities. They define the work children are required to carry out by specifying the products for which they are held accountable and the resources which are to be used to generate these products. Tasks define the character of children's contact with the school curriculum and structure their thinking about subject matter. Research on tasks (see, for instance, Doyle, 1986) which attempts to encapsulate the curriculum in action, has provided insight into the way learning effects occur in classroom settings and how subject matter is shaped by classroom events. Enactment research has illuminated our understanding of the teachers' need to obtain co-operation from children in classroom activities as they move them through the curriculum, by simultaneously designing appropriate academic work and engaging them in the conceptual processes required to understand and to carry out the work. The mode of enquiry is not causal in the sense of a search for predictors of successful enactments but rather it attempts to make explicit the implicit knowledge teachers deploy by interpreting classroom events and explicating knowledge of content, pedagogy and management brought to bear in classrooms. Such knowledge informs practice by enabling teachers to carry out curriculum plans and teaching practices and this research has been extremely influential on the work of British researchers such as Bennett *et al.* (1984) and Desforges and Cockburn (1987).

These examples of strands in more recent research on teaching are not mutually exclusive though they represent different analytical and interpretative frameworks.

Pedagogical content knowledge, for instance, incorporates knowledge about teaching practices since the curriculum and instruction are inseparable. Similarly curriculum enactment knowledge includes content represented in tasks and resources and management of classroom actions.

Knowledge about practices is closely bound to knowledge about contexts in which practices are enacted. In fact enactment research is similar in many aspects to research on personal practical knowledge of teachers since it is constructed from the study of thinking and action in classroom settings and what teachers know is assumed to be particularistic and structured by events. The emphasis in enactment research, however, is less on the private and idiosyncratic than on the general and analytic. The aim is to provide a common language about classrooms which will inform teachers' thinking and practical decision-making although it is recognized that the application of that knowledge will be personal and particular in nature.

Doyle (1990) has concluded that these recent approaches to teaching practices, subject content and classroom enactment are providing a codifiable knowledge which is substantially richer than that derived from the previous process-product research.

What such a review does not consider, however, is the contribution such research can make to the development of professional practice, either of beginning or experienced teachers. More fundamentally, it does not consider how teachers learn to teach in the first place, and how such knowledge about teaching might be used to analyse and resolve existing teaching dilemmas.

Current research on class teaching tends to have been informed by a view of learning or knowledge development which stresses an active information-processing approach or sense-making on the part of the learner and a corresponding view of teaching which supports this active role of the learner in constructing meaning. This theme will be developed more fully in Chapter 3. Resnick (1987) has suggested that a 'constructivist' theory of learning and understanding can provide valuable insights into the nature of teachers' own learning about teaching and suggests teachers similarly construct meaning in particular situations in accordance with their own distinctive conceptual and emotional biographies. Knowledge is constructed by the teacher, as by children, through the interaction of prior knowledge with current experience. Such a perspective emphasizes the importance of ongoing teaching experience and the gradual accumulation of practical knowledge from reflection on that experience over time. This constructivist perspective is very compatible with Schon's (1983) notion of reflective practice and the nature of professional 'thinking in action'. Schon described a special 'knowledge in action' which is activated during practice as teachers interpret events and deal with classroom dilemmas. Fenstermacher (1986) suggested that teachers translate knowledge into action, that is, activate existing information about teaching to inform their current classroom decision-making and practical thinking which underpins their actions. He argued that the benefit of research to teaching lies in its potential to improve practical argument.

The assumption here is that knowledge use in teaching depends upon the teacher's ongoing understanding or comprehension of classroom events and situations. The conclusion to be drawn is that both personal understanding and propositional know-ledge contribute to learning to teach, that is, to the deployment of knowledge in practical situations. This suggests that, on the one hand, researchers need to under-stand how teachers construct meaning whilst engaged in professional practice, which must of its nature be personal and particular in nature and, on the other, provide a relevant research base which can make a valid contribution to teachers' craft knowledge and professional practice. If all learning, whether academic subject know-ledge, pedagogy or classroom practice, is constructive in nature the challenge is to provide a research of teaching which represents practice in ways which have significance for teachers' own work. In other words there is a good argument for the construction of a rich and particular knowledge base of teaching which supports teachers' interpretations of classroom events, informs their planning of appropri-ate new strategies, and facilitates their capacity to generate fresh solutions to unen-countered problems.

Shifting Paradigms and Changing Methods in Research on Teaching

Changing Forms of Enquiry

As indicated in previous sections, research on teaching has been, for a long time, concerned with causality, quantification and prediction of achievement. From this perspective teaching behaviours have been regarded as treatment variables or at-tainment predictors, separated from the intentions and purposes of the teachers concerned. Such research has used the methods of social science, in particular, of psychology for measurement, experimentation and statistical analysis. Teaching methods stripped of their original meanings could then be used to derive category systems. Teachers could be observed and 'rated' for such generic skills which were then related to measures of effectiveness applicable to a range of settings. Claims made for the research-based design of the instruments were used to justify the information about effectiveness thus obtained (see reviews by Dunkin and Biddle, 1974; Gage, 1978; 1985). These studies eschewed detailed examination of teaching methods and curricula as implemented in the complex world of classrooms and focused, instead, on one or two teacher characteristics, such as attitudes or aca-demic achievement, or teaching behaviours, of high inference (such as enthusiasm or clarity) or low inference (such as the use of questions or giving praise). Out-comes could then be measured by ratings or by tests of achievement or attitude. Teaching effectiveness, thus, typically followed the process-product research model (see Rosenshine, 1976). Such studies of effectiveness related measures of class-room performances (processes) to measures of outcome (products). Processes and products were measured for a sample of classrooms, in the correlational phase, and then ranked on the basis of mean achievement and differences in teaching processes among ranked classes identified. Processes derived from correlational research could then be taught to a sample of teachers who were observed to check whether the processes were being used in their teaching. The attainments in the classrooms of these teachers were compared with control classrooms to determine whether the intervention had had an effect. The aim was to explain within class differences in achievement in terms of differences in teaching processes, in other words, to identify conditions which positively affected outcomes of teaching. Consistent correlations between teaching processes and attainment outcomes were achieved and, in many cases, for example in mathematics teaching (see Good, Grouws and Ebmeier, 1983), generated principles which were successfully applied to other settings. In fact, Good and Grouws (1979) constructed a model format for Grade 4 (for 9-year-olds) mathematics lessons that identified a sequence and approximate time allocation for specific activities such as review, introduction of new concepts, guided practice, seatwork and review. This work demonstrated that research findings could contribute to the development of professional practice by providing useful guidelines which could then be communicated simply to experienced teachers. Such studies demonstrated that experienced practitioners could make use of the materials provided in order to modify their practice. This shed little light, however, on the circumstances in which the information was used.

Newer forms of enquiry on class teaching led to theoretical and methodological innovation which was required in order to access qualitative aspects of learning and teaching. The shift in emphasis has been towards an understanding of context and situation, with a focus on domain-specific knowledge, rather than on generic processes. Explanations of events and actions have, thus, been made within the context of purpose and meaning of the teacher and pupils.

Devising a framework for the study of teachers' knowledge required the generation of conceptions which dealt with thought and interpretation of context, in other words, how meaning is constructed. Furthermore it required a recognition that interpretation of classroom events will vary and, hence, constructed meanings may differ. To achieve this some researchers have turned to interpretive methods in order to find means to capture the complexity of classroom practice in which, as noted by Lazerson *et al.* (1985), effects are elusive and not reliably linked to outcomes.

In terms of methodology such work has focused increasingly on:

- data collection in naturally occurring teaching situations;
- thick descriptions of classroom processes, in particular, interactive discourse;
- information concerning teachers' subject content knowledge, pedagogical subject knowledge and, in particular, their selection and representation of content;
- consideration of possible relationships between teachers' orientations towards and beliefs concerning teaching the subject and their classroom practice; and in some cases;
- criterion-referenced measures of individual children's understanding related to teaching goals, through in-depth interviewing, the collection of work samples or observations of performance on application tasks.

The Need for a New Paradigm

The fundamental shift in the nature of this research on teaching away from experimental or statistical rigour, emphasizing context-free, generic indicators of effectiveness towards a systematic enquiry concerned with the codifying and systematizing of processes that occur in the natural setting, required a new research paradigm. The new naturalistic enquiry (Guba, 1978), in turn, led to substantive and procedural changes in the way classroom practice was conceptualized and structured.

In fact, as Miles and Huberman (1984) noted, more and more researchers in fields with a traditional, quantitative emphasis (such as psychology, sociology, linguistics and education) turned to qualitative data collection which provided a source of well-grounded, rich descriptions and explanations of social processes observed in normally occurring contexts. With qualitative data, they noted that:

> One can preserve chronological flow, assess local causality, and derive fruitful explanations . . . qualitative data are more likely to lead to serendipitous findings and to new theoretical integration; they help researchers go beyond initial preconceptions and frameworks. Finally, the findings have a quality of 'undeniability'. (Huberman and Miles, 1984, p. 15)

Underlying qualitative enquiry there are common assumptions that social phenomena exist in the objective world and that there are lawful and stable relationships to be found among them. This reflects a belief in social regularities. It does not deny that people may construe these phenomena in common and agreed ways and recognizes that perceptions are essential to our understanding of the way social behaviour takes the shape it does. Furthermore Huberman and Miles noted that people may not construe events in the same way as social scientists which argues the case even more strongly for describing as precisely as possible and defining the range and generality of findings, as well as the contextual contingencies under which they occur. The complexity of the phenomena under investigation are acknowledged as, in fact, are the frames of reference of the participants which are taken to be integral components of the enquiry.

It is important, however, to evolve a set of valid and verifiable methods for uncovering such social relationships, to interpret and explain social phenomena and to have sufficient confidence that others using similar methods, would reach similar conclusions.

The process of illuminating social processes is inductive in character which renders the traditional concepts and approaches of experimental and correlational studies inadequate. Guba (1978) contrasted the naturalistic paradigm with the natural science research paradigm in terms of methods, purposes, philosophical stance, epistemology and assumptions. Qualitative enquiry offered an alternative approach to the positivist, empirical method previously used and characterized by assumptions that experience is objective and testable, amenable to hypothetico-deductive approaches and subject to lawlike relations, capable of description in precise terms and with meaning determined by existing theory.

As Miles and Huberman (1984) noted, more and more quantitative methodologists are using naturalistic approaches to complement their traditional approaches. They concluded, in fact, that it becomes less and less common to find any methodologist working exclusively in one framework. Moreover Hammersley (1993) noted that in many respects the quantitative–qualitative distinction is unhelpful. It does not accurately map differences in philosophical position or in practical methods to be found among researchers. It provides only a crude characterization that can often be misleading and, indeed, ignores and obscures much of the variety of method relating to different facets of the research process. Hammersley suggested that there is a tendency for both quantitative and qualitative approaches to identify a single model research process and product as if this exhausted the ways research is done and what it produces.

He proposed that it was important not to take the particular study as the unit of research but to recognize that the character and products of research might change over the life of a research programme at different stages. An example chosen by him was of a more exploratory orientation in the early stages of a project with a more hypothesis testing orientation later. On the other hand structured data collection and statistical analysis may be concerned with exploring patterns in data and developing ideas. Qualitative case studies may, to offer yet another permutation, be used to test theories.

Five common aspects of the research process can be distinguished: formulating problems, selecting cases, producing data, analysing data and communicating findings. In respect of each of these there are several strategies available to researchers. What Hammersley recommended was a 'methodological eclecticism' with a primary concern for fitness for purpose. Perhaps, as he suggested, it is more accurate to think in terms of iterative cycles of exploration and testing. He concluded that the goals of research vary according to the stage that it has reached and that there is no standardized relationship between qualitative and quantitative method at any particular stage. Research may differ in relation to the products it generates. It is important, in this respect, to distinguish between descriptive, evaluative, prescriptive, explanatory and theoretical conclusions but not to treat some of these as intrinsically more valuable than others.

Whether quantitative or qualitative methods are used, however, what is most important is that planning of methods is explicit and that analysis is rigorous. Many researchers who follow the naturalistic paradigm cite the original work of Glaser and Strauss (1967) or subsequent work (Glaser, 1978; Strauss, 1987; Strauss and Corbin, 1990) as the basis for their research. In contrast to logico-deductive theory, their 'grounded theory' is derived inductively from the study of the phenomena it represents.

> It is discovered, developed and provisionally verified through systematic data collection and analysis of data pertaining to that phenomenon. Therefore, data collection analysis and theory stand in reciprocal relationship to each other. One does not begin with a theory, then prove it. Rather, one begins with an area of study and what is relevant to that area is allowed to emerge. (Strauss and Corbin, 1990, p. 23)

New Methods

Naturalistic enquiry has been described by Lincoln and Guba (1985) as being carried out in a natural context by a 'human instrument' who will be responsive to the situations that will be encountered. This 'instrument' will draw upon his/her own tacit knowledge as well as propositional knowledge, using methods appropriate to such investigation. These are typically interviews, document analysis and observation.

Once initiated the enquiry will engage in successive iterations which comprise: purposive sampling, inductive analysis of the data obtained from the sample, development of grounded theory based on the inductive analysis, and generation of the next stage in a constantly emerging design. Iteration is repeated until redundancy is achieved, the theory is stable and the emergent design complied with, insofar as resource constraints allow.

Throughout this period data and interpretation will be checked with those who have provided sources for the data and outcomes agreed. The study is bound by the nature of the research problems or questions and its trustworthiness is checked against the naturalistic analogues to the conventional criteria of internal and external validity, reliability and objectivity: credibility, transferability, dependability and confirmability, respectively.

This phenomenological approach, thus, involves 'theoretical', or 'purposive' sampling, a process of data collection, coding and analysis which generates decisions concerning what data to collect next and where to find them. In the conventional paradigm the purpose is to define a sample that is representative of a population to which it is desired to generalize. The usual procedure is to obtain a random sample, where every element has an equal chance of being chosen. In naturalistic investigations which are related closely to contextual factors, the purpose of sampling will often be to include as much information as possible. Maximum variation sampling will usually be the chosen sampling mode. Glaser and Strauss (1967) suggested that the criteria for theoretical sampling are applied in ongoing collection and analysis of data associated with the generation of theory. The characteristics are:

- emergent sampling design (no *a priori* specification of the sample);
- serial selection of sample units (the purpose of maximum variation is best achieved by selecting each unit of the sample only after the previous one has been fully analysed to extend, test and 'fill in' the information already obtained);
- continuous adjustment or focusing of the sample (as the investigator develops working hypotheses about the situation, the sample will be refined to focus more particularly on relevant units);
- selection to the point of redundancy, in other words, sampling is terminated when no new information is forthcoming from newly sampled units. (In conventional design the size of the sample is determined by the degree of statistical confidence one wishes to place in it, thus, sampling is planned beforehand.)

This method requires 'constant comparison' of incidents which leads to conceptual labels being placed on discrete happenings, events or instances of phenomena. Concepts are the basic building blocks of grounded theory. The basic analytic procedures by which concepts are generated are: the asking of questions about data; and the making of comparisons for similarities and differences between phenomena. Similar events and incidents are labelled and grouped to form concepts. Concepts are grouped together under a higher order, or more abstract concept, called a category. These categories and their properties emerge from the data. Descriptive knowledge is thereby used to generate grounded theory. Inductive analysis resembles content analysis. It involves the uncovering and making explicit of embedded information through unitizing and categorizing.

Unitizing is a process of coding data into units which allow the precise description of information-bearing units for identification in future analysis. Categorizing involves organizing previously unitized data into categories by constant comparison. This is a method of sorting units into provisional categories on the basis of characteristics. It leads to a propositional statement which serves as the basis for inclusion or exclusion of particular units.

The design is described as emergent since meaning is determined by context rather than preordinate. As noted the investigator engages in continuous data sampling and analysis until redundancy is reached.

Strauss and Corbin (1990) have distinguished 'open coding', the process of breaking down, examining, comparing, conceptualizing and categorizing of data, from 'axial coding', the process of putting data back together in new ways after open coding. This is done by utilizing a coding paradigm involving: conditions, context, action/interaction strategies and consequences. The focus is on specifying a category in terms of conditions which give rise to it; the context in which it is embedded; the action/interaction strategies by which it is handled, managed or carried out; and the consequences of these strategies.

As in open coding and axial coding, through a further process of making comparison and asking questions emerges the 'selective coding'. This is the process of selecting the core category, systematically relating it to other categories and validating these relationships, in other words, explicating the 'story line' about the central phenomenon. The final goal is to provide:

1   a clear analytic story;
2   writing on a conceptual level, with description kept secondary;
3   the clear specification of relationships among categories, with levels of conceptualization also kept clear;
4   the specification of variations and their relevant conditions and consequences . . . including the broader ones. (Strauss and Corbin, 1990, p. 229)

This procedure is in some contrast to the common method of presenting qualitative data which uses thick descriptions to substantiate and illustrate assertions made and to illuminate context and participants. The challenge, however, is to balance providing the reader with a vicarious experience and portraying multiple perspectives without the risk of becoming mundane.

Finally, in order to achieve credibility, that is, increasing the probability that credible findings will be produced, Guba (1981) proposed the major techniques of:

- prolonged engagement, the investment of sufficient time to build trust and to understand the culture of the context;
- persistent observation, to identify what Eisner (1975) described as 'pervasive qualities' and involving the sorting out of the irrelevant to identify the salient;
- triangulation, by using multiple sources, methods, investigators and theories to collect multiple influences, according to Denzin (1978), the risk of distortion is reduced.

Also recommended were:

- peer debriefing, or involving disinterested peers in analytical sessions to reduce the risk of bias;
- negative case analysis, the process of 'revising hypotheses with hindsight' (Kidder, 1981) until all known cases without exception are accounted for;
- referential adequacy, which is a means of holding back some part of the data, for later analysis and review, proposed by Eisner (1975);
- member checking, or taking analysed data to other groups or interested parties, for interpretations to be checked (during the analysis process and at its conclusion).

To establish transferability, thick descriptions provide a specification of the minimum elements needed and the range of information required in order to provide the database.

Finally dependability, or the acceptability of the process of the enquiry, and confirmability, that the findings are consistent with this process, are established through independent auditing, or examination of the accuracy with which the account of the process and products has been kept. This will include the scrutiny of raw data, data reduction, analysis products, process notes and pilot instruments. The purpose of the audit is to increase the probability that the findings and the interpretations will be found credible. The keeping of a reflexive journal is one way in which credibility, transferability, dependability and confirmability are confirmed.

An Evaluation of Naturalistic Enquiry

Although much of the theoretical work concerning naturalistic enquiry and qualitative methods has been completed, aspects are still being developed.

The reliance on the so-called 'human instrument' in design, data collection and analysis, as well as in report writing can be both a strength and a weakness of the process. As Lincoln and Guba (1985) noted unobtrusive, qualitative measures are particularly suitable for the study of complex human interactions but inevitably both tacit and propositional knowledge will be employed in ascribing meaning.

Skrtic (1985), for instance, recognized that a preference for grounded theory does not entail a total rejection of all *a priori* theory. At the planning stage theory from previous research is not discounted although the intention is to avoid allowing it to constrain the enquiry. Similarly, at a later stage in the enquiry, Lincoln and Guba (1985) pointed out that whilst the theory is derived from, or grounded in the data a distinction between *a priori* and grounded theory can be made in the way in which the data are used. Even in the inductive analysis stage unitizing and categorizing is tacitly rule-guided and, thus, propositional knowledge may inform description at this stage of rule-generating.

It is here that qualitative research draws its heaviest criticism, as noted by Skrtic (1985), because typically there is no check on the researcher's interpretation or on the data sources. The user, or consumer of the research, may be asked to depend solely on the researcher's judgments.

It is, thus, in the stage of data analysis that the tacit knowledge and values of the investigator come to bear most on the substance of the study. The researcher's understanding is grounded in the data analysis and in presenting the data to support the overall explanation.

Finally, there are no formal conventions for establishing truth in qualitative research. The task of the researcher is to convince the user of the plausibility of the research, by submitting sufficient evidence to support the assertions made. Lincoln and Guba's (1985) criteria for establishing trustworthiness, whilst remaining to be 'tried and tested' are most persuasive in this respect.

Developing an appropriate reporting style to organize and to communicate data which reflects the multiple realities of participants, makes explicit their own tacit understandings and pulls together a 'story line' from the available information, without undue interpretation is a complex task. It requires validation from the participants and suggests that any wider, or more general application of the findings should be very tentative.

Skrtic (1985) has concluded:

> The literature is not rife with examples of good case studies. It contains even fewer instances of how to best write case studies. There are no conventions for making decisions about what to include or exclude. A case ought to provide thick description, but just what is that? How thick is thick? What are some inclusion–exclusion principles that could be applied by a case study writer? There are presently no answers to these questions. (Skrtic, 1985, p. 209)

The skill, as noted above, is to provide sufficient 'thick description' to illuminate the contexts and participants yet maintain a clear analytic story.

Aims and Objectives for the Project

In Chapter 1 it was noted that both Buchmann (1984) and Shulman (1986a) had drawn attention to the need for a closer examination of the distinct components of teachers' subject knowledge, and in particular, to the distinction between subject content knowledge and pedagogical subject knowledge. Pedagogical subject knowledge, they believed, pre-supposed knowledge that went far beyond subject content to the broad understanding of pupils' own existing knowledge, their common errors and misconceptions, in order to represent key subject content ideas in ways which conveyed meaning to young children and which allowed the identification of common misunderstandings.

In an earlier section of this chapter it was observed that Ball (1991), too, had suggested that definitions of the concept of pedagogical subject knowledge varied and that this was a threat to the progress in research. The need for further empirical investigation of teachers' pedagogical subject knowledge was indicated and the more recent applications of qualitative theoretical and methodological perspectives to classroom enquiry provided the means to implement this. The writer's own work in the area of early years mathematics provided a starting point.

Accordingly the project was designed with the overall aim to explore the co-ordination and utilization of teacher and pupil subject knowledge in reception classrooms. This enabled the informal mathematical knowledge which young children brought into school to be accessed before formal schooling began and allowed consideration of the extent to which reception teachers took account of this in the course of mathematical instruction.

In other words, the project sought to investigate teachers' pedagogical subject knowledge by attempting to establish links between teachers' and pupils' knowledge during teaching. More specifically the objectives were:

1 To investigate teachers' pedagogical subject knowledge and beliefs, in particular in terms of their influence on the content and processes of mathematics instruction in reception classes. (This objective was addressed directly through teacher interviews and indirectly through observation and analysis of classroom discourse over children's first year in school.)

2 To collect data on children's informal knowledge in key areas of mathematics, at school entry, as a starting point for accessing teachers' understanding of the way children think about mathematics, and knowledge about their own pupils' thinking. (This objective was addressed through teacher interview and classroom observation which was considered in the light of children's informal knowledge brought into school as well as through follow-up data obtained from re-assessment towards the end of the reception year).

3 To explore the co-ordination and utilization of teacher and pupil knowledge within the complex world of classrooms. (This objective was addressed through observation and analysis of the content and style of classroom discourse and field notes collected from four reception teachers, taking account of practical and pedagogical considerations.)

4 To consider the implications of the project for a mathematics curriculum for children's first year at school. (This objective was addressed through an examination of findings in terms of learning and teaching mathematics.)

The objectives, thus, set the overall aim to investigate teachers' pedagogical subject knowledge through the collection and analysis of data related to teachers':

- mathematical subject knowledge;
- mathematical content knowledge for teaching and the manner in which topics were taught to young children;
- understanding of children's emerging subject knowledge and their appreciation of what was commonly found difficult;
- representation of mathematical ideas and use of curriculum materials in ways that were compelling to young children;
- beliefs concerning learning and teaching young children in general and particular orientations towards learning and teaching early years mathematics.

Teachers' understanding of children's emergent knowledge was, thus, considered in the light of data collection and analysis related to children's informal mathematical skills and understanding.

Accordingly the project was planned in a number of phases:

- Phase 1 described the construction of assessment tasks designed to incorporate both areas of informal competence young children are known to bring into school and content compatible with the National Curriculum attainment targets. This aimed to examine the current knowledge, strategies and representations held by young children at their start of school. After some slight refinement to the mathematical tasks this phase sought to provide a detailed assessment of the mathematical competences of a group of forty-eight reception-aged children. This will be reported in Chapter 5.
- Phase 2 involved interviews with children's reception teachers which investigated their pedagogical decision-making, in particular, the extent to which account was reported to be taken of such informal mathematical knowledge as children possessed, through consideration of the sequence of topics taught and the active encouragement of children's own construction of knowledge. These were examined in the light of subsequent lesson observations and will be reported in Chapter 6.
- Phase 3 concerned the gathering and coding of data related to the style and content of classroom discourse and focused specifically on a single data handling lesson, as examplar, for each of the four teachers involved in the main phase of the project. This will be reported in Chapter 7.
- Phase 4 analysed the content and style of classroom discourse in the four reception classrooms using categories which emerged in Phase 3 and will be reported in Chapter 8. The core category, teachers' pedagogical subject knowledge, as exemplified in classroom practice, was then exposed with events, incidents and actions of individual teachers over the year providing the source for a clear analytical story. This will be reported in Chapter 9.
- Finally, in a subsequent phase, a further seven reception teachers and sixty-seven pupils were followed through the first year of formal schooling. Particular reference to this phase will be made in Chapter 6.

Teachers' interviews gathered biographical information concerning mathematics subject content knowledge, subject knowledge for teaching, planning and organizational decisions and beliefs concerning learning and teaching clarified processes observed. Children's informal mathematical knowledge gained at school entry and re-assessed towards the end of the school year provided a measure against which to judge teachers' understanding of the way children think about mathematics and, more specifically, their awareness of their own pupils' existing knowledge and competences. In fact both teacher interviews and mathematics assessment provided a source for triangulation. Finally, the educational implications of these findings for the teaching and learning of mathematics in reception classrooms were considered.

Conclusion

It has been the intention of this chapter to outline emerging conceptualizations of teachers' subject knowledge, to review changing methods of investigating the processes of classroom teaching and to consider the implications of this for the design of the current project. Having considered methods of collecting interactive discourse in naturally occurring teaching situations and the possible relationship between teacher knowledge, skills and orientations towards the subject and individual pupil understanding, the next chapter will consider the children's thinking and learning about mathematics and the nature of mathematics teaching.

3 Knowing and Understanding Mathematics: Concerning a Theory of Instruction

Introduction

Chapters 1 and 2 aimed to identify the key issues, conceptual and empirical, which have contributed to the current interest of policy-makers and researchers in the development of teachers' subject knowledge. This provided a context for the presentation of the aims for the current project. Since the overall aim was to investigate teachers' pedagogical subject knowledge in mathematics, through the examination of the co-ordination and utilization of teachers' and pupils' knowledge in reception classrooms this required, first, the detailed investigation and bibliographic review of existing, relevant research on teaching and learning of early years mathematics.

Glaser and Bassock (1989) have suggested three essential components to the progress of research for a theory of instruction:

1 the description of competent performance that it is desired learners should acquire (in this tradition, investigation has relied quite heavily on the consideration of the child as novice and the teacher as expert, just as the investigation of teaching expertise has tended to focus on comparison of novice and expert teachers);

2 the analysis of the initial state of the learner's knowledge and ability (there is now a considerable knowledge base concerning the emergence of subject knowledge of young learners in a number of fields, (see, for instance, Aubrey, 1994); and

3 the explication of the process of learning, that is, the transition from initial state to desired state that can be accomplished in teaching contexts. (Advances in instructional psychology have begun to uncover the higher-order skills underlying basic curriculum areas, such as, problem solving, planning, reflecting, revising and evaluating.)

The work of Glaser and Bassock served to underline the importance of learning theory to the study of teaching and highlighted the need to recognize the role of human cognition and development, in the consideration of both teacher and learner in instructional settings.

Aims

The distinction made by Glaser and Bassock between novice and expert learner and the description of competent performance provided a means for structuring the review of relevant research on learning and teaching. Accordingly the aim of Chapter 3 is to provide an overview of recent research on:

- competent teaching performance and, in particular, the role of mathematical subject knowledge in instruction;
- the role of learning theory in the development of research on instruction; as well as
- the examination of some recent applications to classroom contexts.

Competent Teaching Performance

Introduction

Whatever approach to instruction is adopted or conception of learning underpins classroom practice, teaching is a complex, cognitive activity with shifting, moment-by-moment demands being made which result in a selection of, and reduction in the number and range of stimuli which can be handled at any one time by the teacher (Doyle, 1986). This can lead both to modification of certain established teaching goals and the ignoring of some incoming data which cannot be adequately processed. Jackson (1968) has described this process as a simplification which does not necessarily render the teaching ineffective. Complexity can be reduced, for example, by the selection of only certain incoming information relating to the management and organization of children, from the arrangement of the classroom context to the progressive focusing on a narrower range of goals related to content presentation. If the demands on teaching from handling complex subject matter increase, for instance, this may result in a corresponding lowering of attention to, or management of complex interpretation of the needs of learners and their responses. Borko and Livingston (1990) noted that as the complexity of subject matter increases when children progress through school there may be a corresponding reduction of attention to personal and pedagogical issues. On the other hand, where the demands made by pupils are high, as is the case with young learners or children with special needs, some reduction of attention to subtlety in the presentation and management of subject content may occur.

Failure to deal adequately with some aspects of the multiple demands made by teaching may, of course, lower effectiveness. When the significance of a critical piece of information is misjudged or its implications overlooked, teaching *is* likely to be affected. Attempting to manage too many goals simultaneously rather than prioritizing may reduce the smooth execution of the lesson. Failing to take sufficient account of pupils' social behaviour or becoming too focused on the needs of a few pupils can lead to disruption of plans. Moreover a teacher might lack the appropriate subject knowledge to plan suitable teaching goals or fail to manage the organization of pupils and resources effectively in time. Leinhardt and Greeno (1986), in fact, have suggested that teaching complexity results from:

1　the tension in the management of simultaneous and competing goals in a specific, temporal arrangement;
2　the high information processing demands made by the environment;
3　the strategic action knowledge which must be co-ordinated with semantic knowledge of the subject content.

In this sense teaching is multi-layered, as well as segmented in time. In order to be managed smoothly some layers of thought and action may need to be routinized in order that other layers of thought or knowledge can have more attention or un-expected events can be attended to with flexibility.

There will be different parts of a lesson, for instance, the introduction and presentation of new information, which make particular demands in teaching and some aspects, such as responding to children's errors, checking responses and deal-ing with queries can be unpredictable and require a specific answer which cannot be anticipated in advance. More substantively, the layers will include knowledge of subject matter and its methods (Schwab, 1978; Shulman, 1987). Teachers, as noted already, will need pedagogical subject knowledge in order to introduce a topic appropriately, to produce compelling examples, and to deal with the pupils' misconceptions which may arise. From the point of view of organization general, as well as specific, pedagogical skills of lesson organization and pupil management will be required. In other words knowledge bases which will be available for de-ployment in teaching go beyond knowledge of the subject and the pupils' learning, to knowledge acquired from a range of sources, including development in practical and professional expertise, as well as personal experience. As noted in Chapter 1, this knowledge will range from the inductive to the principled and situated.

The Role of Subject Knowledge in Teaching

Recent investigations of teachers' subject knowledge exemplify Glaser and Bassock's notion of competent performance in instruction. In this tradition of work Lampert (1990; 1992), as teacher and researcher on teaching mathematics, has indicated the central importance of disciplinary knowledge to good elementary (primary) teaching. Leinhardt (1989), too, has investigated teachers' mathematical knowledge while they taught at the same time as they judged knowledge of lesson structure and teaching routines.

In order to investigate systematically the structure, content and style of learn-ing and teaching mathematics in school, as noted above, one must first recognize its complexity and the need for the classroom teacher to draw on many kinds of knowledge. Leinhardt (1987) noted the dearth of studies which document how specific subject matter content is taught and learned and over the last decade she, with a variety of colleagues, has begun to map out the relationship between teacher knowledge of mathematics and instruction, contrasting the competence of novice and 'expert' teachers in teaching particular mathematical topics to particular groups of children.

The classroom environment, as Leinhardt (1989) noted, is complex and dynamic and requires balancing the needs of twenty to thirty young individuals with the need to stay on course so material is covered clearly. The teacher's immediate task is to communicate new information, to review material and to ensure material is accessible or to assess children's knowledge. This is constrained by the need to keep children active, interested and engaged in learning, as well as by the constraints of the particular setting related to time availability and other resources.

Leinhardt (1989) and Leinhardt *et al.* (1991) have suggested that whilst many knowledge systems exist fundamental to teaching and learning, two important core areas are knowledge of 'lesson structure' and knowledge of 'subject matter'. Subject matter knowledge of number, for instance, may include concepts, algorithmic operations, connections among different algorithmic procedures, the sub-set of the number system being drawn upon, understanding of the classes of children's errors and curriculum presentation. Lesson structure knowledge involves knowledge for conducting lessons, general routines for interacting with children, co-ordinating lesson segments and fitting lessons together within the day or within a topic and across days. Subject knowledge supports lesson structure knowledge providing the content to be taught, accessed during planning and in the course of teaching.

This has led to descriptions of lessons in terms of the teacher's *agenda*, or overall dynamic mental plan for the lesson with its goals and actions; the *script*, or outline of content to be presented, carrying the sub-goals and actions built up through teaching the topic; *explanations*, including what the teacher says, does or demonstrates; and *representations* of the mathematical concepts, procedures or ideas, whether physical, verbal, concrete or numerical (see Leinhardt *et al.*, 1991). Included in the agenda would be the main activity structures or 'segments' such as checking completed work, presenting new material and carrying out reviews, guided practice, monitored practice, drill and tutoring.

In terms of structure each segment has its own system of goals and sub-goals that influence the selection of particular teacher–pupil actions. The most significant action segment is the presentation segment since it is in the presentation that teachers introduce new concepts, present new algorithms, review or extend known material and offer explanations. It is the presentation segment which is most closely identified with teaching and in which teachers most heavily draw upon subject matter knowledge. Tutoring, too, is a context where teachers draw on subject matter knowledge. Leinhardt and Smith (1985) suggested tutoring is, in fact, used infrequently and is specifically related to absence, inattention or perceived low aptitude. The explanation or system of goals and actions involved in exposition, has been introduced by Stein, Baxter and Leinhardt (1990) and is usually given during the presentation segment. This will include the identification of the teaching goal, monitoring which signals progress towards that goal, and examples of cases or instances that require its use. Threading through the key moves will be a verbal demonstration, often simultaneous with, and attached to, the numerical and concrete demonstrations, and including parallel representations. Some linkage between representations must be offered as well as an indication of conditions of use and non-use. Finally, there may be some legitimation of the new concept or procedure in terms of known principles and linkage to familiar elements, which may be extended or have new elements added.

The characteristics of these activity structures have much in common with a summary of key instructional behaviour of Good, Grouws and Ebmeier (1983) in the process-produce tradition, in particular, those associated with the teachers' attempts to induce understanding of a mathematics topic which they termed the 'development portion'. Here the teacher would use demonstrations and the manipulation of material and concrete examples to identify salient features and stimulate class discussion. Next the teacher would increase questions to assess comprehension, provide additional support, if necessary, and initiate controlled practice. At this stage teacher monitoring and feedback would still be available.

Leinhardt (1993) has stressed the importance of teachers' introspections about the meaning and nature of teaching in establishing key phenomena of:

- teaching as a process of facing dilemmas, as a web in which multiple paths for next steps are always available, at the same time recognizing that any selection involves trade-offs; and
- teaching as a task in which teachers come to understand the real meaning of a child's response rather than simply establish its correctness.

Appreciation of these phenomena may allow teachers to make classrooms less judgmental, shift responsibility for making sensible contributions to the children, but render the course of instruction less predictable for both teachers and children (Ball, 1988; Lampert, 1985).

As Leinhardt (1993) has noted the research on the role of subject matter knowledge has helped to establish the nature of expertise in teaching. In this tradition researchers have been committed to the study of existing classroom practice generated in part, as noted by Putnam, Lampert and Peterson (1990), by a recognition that improvements to be made will be within the framework of existing classroom practice. Leinhardt has, thus, used existing constructs and methods to study the teaching and learning of mathematics, selecting teachers primarily on the basis of consistent gains in children's achievements. Her work has illuminated important teacher knowledge of mathematical subject matter and the structure and routines for conducting effective, traditional lessons. Although she has advocated different teaching styles and patterns her work has reinforced the criteria used by researchers on teaching effectiveness, emphasized enrichment of concepts and problem solving ability by the provision of concrete experiences, whilst maintaining the value of arithmetic and computation. Furthermore her work has focused on older elementary (primary) aged children, typically 10 years of age.

Few studies in this country have considered the role of teachers' subject knowledge in planning instruction or the extent to which teachers believe mathematics teaching should be organized to facilitate children's construction of knowledge. The study of Tizard *et al.* (1988) of inner city infant schools showed that the amount of mathematical knowledge with which children entered school was the strongest predictor of future progress and given the small amount of mathematics teaching observed during the first year of school this finding did not cause surprise. Only one in five of the infant teachers involved said academic progress was one of their main aims, and marked differences were found in what was taught. Written subtraction was introduced during the first year of schooling in one out of ten classrooms, whilst two had not introduced this even by the third year. Similarly with respect to money, for some, the concept of 'giving change' was introduced in the first year, for others, it was not introduced even in children's third year at school. Some reception teachers believed certain items were too difficult for children, others did not. A conclusion drawn from this study was that children's skills should have been assessed soon after entry to diagnose areas in which help might be needed.

As noted in Chapter 2 the work of Bennett *et al.* (1984) and Desforges and Cockburn (1987) was strongly influenced by Doyle's research on classroom tasks which defined the nature and quality of children's experience of the school curriculum and structured their contact with subject matter. Whilst teachers' curriculum enactment knowledge incorporated content represented in the tasks and resources used the focus, however, was the activities, part social, part curricular which structured behaviour and led to the accomplishment of tasks.

In general studies of British primary classrooms (for instance, Bennett *et al.*, 1984) have drawn attention to an over-emphasis in teaching on four rules, paper and pencil exercises and routine calculations which poorly matched children's existing skills and understanding, just as HMI (1978) and Cockcroft (1982) criticized British mathematics education for its over-emphasis on computation and limited problem solving in real life situations. More recently after the first year of the National Curriculum, HMI (1991) commented that there were signs of a positive effect on classroom practice but that the degree to which schools accepted the new curriculum as a challenge varied widely. After the second year, OFSTED (1993) noted that standards in number were at least satisfactory in 72 per cent of mathematics lessons observed in Years 1, 3 and 6 with wide variations within and between schools. Good standards were characterized by use of a range of methods to teach knowledge, skills and understanding, including direct teaching, questions, explanations and challenging discussion. About four-fifths had reviewed and revised their schemes of work with most effort directed in the newer parts of the curriculum. Fewer than half offered adequate guidance on teaching number, even fewer attended sufficiently to estimation and approximation, or to the development of concepts in general. Whilst almost all classes had access to computers and calculators, few used them effectively to support learning of number.

More recent empirical studies of primary classrooms of Alexander (1992) and Evans, Packwood, St. J. Neill and Campbell (1994) do not suggest classroom practice has changed much since the studies of the 1980s discussed above.

Sources and Outcomes of Subject Knowledge

One focus of studies on teaching performance has been the acquisition of subject matter knowledge and expertise in the practice of teaching. Quantitative and qualitative changes that occur in the course of learning in elementary (primary) or secondary teachers have been investigated by Feiman-Nemser and Buchmann (1986; 1987). Many of these studies, like those of Leinhardt described above, have used teachers' introspection about the meaning and nature of teaching.

A longitudinal study of undergraduate teacher training students at five American institutions at the *National Centre for Research on Teacher Education*, reported by Ball (1990), investigated the mathematical understanding of 252 prospective elementary (primary) and secondary teachers by questionnaire and interview. Both primary and secondary student teachers found it difficult to remember specific mathematical ideas and procedures. These student teachers were unable to show conceptual understanding in explanations of specific terms, procedures and concepts, relying instead on definitions, rules and routines.

Ball (1988) earlier had compared the mathematical subject knowledge of secondary mathematics specialist student teachers with primary specialist student teachers. She showed that the mathematics graduates were able to generate more correct answers for division involving fractions, zero, and algebraic questions than primary school specialists who had difficulty in making sense of division with fractions, relating mathematics to the real world, and using explanations requiring knowledge which went beyond the procedural. She concluded that:

> in mathematics, evidence is mounting that all students, not just those intending to be teachers can meet the expectations for satisfactory work without developing a conceptual understanding of the subject matter the lack of which, we have argued, seriously inhibits a teacher's capacity to help students learn in ways that are meaningful. (Ball, 1988, p. 444)

Other studies of elementary (primary) teachers have produced similar results (e.g., Mansfield, 1985). Knowledge and understanding, however, is shaped by experience both inside and outside formal schooling and, in the case of teachers, this formal experience will include thirteen years of schooling before higher education is begun. The relative influence of teachers' formal schooling in relation to undergraduate or postgraduate training, on subject understanding is yet to be determined. Ball (1988) has suggested, however, that school and the wider community are likely to be a powerful determinant of beginning teachers' subject content understanding.

Since, as the evidence suggests, the benefits of formal schooling and the opportunities of the broader community do not appear necessarily to equip student teachers with the substance and methods of their subjects, or to acquire attitudes towards or dispositions favourable to teaching for meaningful understanding, teaching experience itself has provided another area of investigation for the source of teachers' subject knowledge. Findings of the *Knowledge Growth in Teaching Programme* of Wilson, Shulman and Rickert (1987) at Stanford University, suggested that beginning teachers develop knowledge of children, curriculum, pedagogy and teaching contexts which transforms subject matter knowledge into pedagogical knowledge. Evidence, however, is lacking that knowledge of their subject, its substance and method has increased (Grossman, 1987; Wineburg and Wilson, 1988).

As noted in Chapter 2, there may be parallels between the way teachers learn and, hence, can be taught and the way children learn. Schulman and Grossman (1988) who have focused on how teachers' learn to transform an understanding of subject matter into representations which make sense to children, have suggested seven domains or sets of schemata of teachers' pedagogical knowledge as: subject matter; pedagogical content knowledge; knowledge of other content; knowledge of the curriculum; knowledge of learners; knowledge of educational aims; and general pedagogical knowledge. The first two were the primary focus for their research programme: subject matter knowledge which comprises substantive knowledge of facts, concepts and algorithms; and syntactic knowledge of methods of proof and argument. These domains have much in common with Ball's (1988) knowledge *of* mathematics, or meanings underlying procedures; and knowledge *about* mathematics, involving notions of mathematics as a discipline, where it comes from, how it changes, and how truth is established.

Peterson (1988) building on and modifying Shulman's framework asserted that to be effective teachers needed three kinds of knowledge:

- how children think in specific subject content areas;
- how to facilitate the growth in children's thinking; and
- self-awareness of the teachers' own cognitive processes.

Subject content was not ignored but Peterson believed that it must be held in relation to children's cognitions and teachers' own metacognitions. Unless teachers understood their own thinking in mathematics, mathematical subject knowledge could not be utilized in classrooms.

Leinhardt, described above, used another way of looking at mental organization by considering the way expert teachers differed from novice teachers in the way they solved problems, searched problem space, organized knowledge based on properties rather than rules, and possessed meta-statements to aid decision-making. Leinhardt and Smith (1985), for instance, in collecting data on teachers' understanding of fractions, developed semantic nets of teachers' knowledge by interview, observation and various card sorts. Variations were found in expert teachers who had refined, hierarchical knowledge structures, better integrated and accessible connections among ideas and interrelationships within procedural knowledge. Carlsen (1991) also examined teachers with high and low subject knowledge in science by collecting plans and transcripts of lessons. He suggested that strong knowledge of content must be organized with interrelationship among ideas and mental organization of content which was displayed in teaching, encouraged questioning by pupils and stressed participation and lab-type, or investigative enquiry. Further reference to his work will be made in Chapter 8.

Lampert (1988) as researcher, mathematician and teacher emphasized the importance of teachers' representations in relating new to existing knowledge and the dependence of good teaching upon the teachers' mathematical knowledge as highly related abstractions which used real world situations and concrete representations to facilitate children's understanding. Ball (1990) in her report of nineteen novice teachers examined their ability to develop representation for division of fractions as a story problem or other model. All but two could carry out the procedure but only half could provide a suitable representation.

In fact patterns to emerge from diverse studies of prospective teachers show evidence of the limitations of initial preparation in developing teachers' pedagogical content knowledge and pedagogical reasoning skills. Comparisons of expert and novice teachers have illustrated the interconnectedness among knowledge, thinking and classroom actions in effective practice. Lack of subject matter knowledge and pedagogical content knowledge has been associated with difficulty in making the transition to pedagogical thinking, the inability to connect topics during teaching and a focus on procedural rather than conceptual understanding.

Application of situated knowledge and its acquisition gained in school and out (Resnick, 1987) has provided another framework for understanding teacher knowledge. Out-of-school knowledge acquired in working, social situations to solve ill-defined problems and construct understanding contrasted with the in-school knowledge, where people work alone to memorize rules and rigid concepts and solve well-defined problems in classrooms. Most teachers themselves have had no opportunity to learn in other ways and tend to use pedagogical procedures they also learned in classrooms before training. As Ball (1990) concluded from her analyses of knowledge, beliefs and dispositions held by prospective teachers when they enter training, preparation should help them to *unlearn* as well as learn. Whilst there is, as yet, limited data on the process of becoming a teacher experience in the early stages appears to be critical. Grossman and Rickert (1986) identified a number of sources from which pedagogical content knowledge is acquired: recollections of teachers' own learning, coursework and school experience. Prospective teachers they investigated attributed development of general pedagogical knowledge and concepts of subject matter to college coursework with knowledge of the curriculum and children's understanding of this to school experience.

Whilst it has long been assumed that teachers needed subject knowledge in order to teach it is becoming increasingly apparent that in preparation they need opportunities for growth in subject content knowledge and knowledge of the way children learn mathematics in order to plan teaching, in other words, they need to develop pedagogical content knowledge and pedagogical reasoning.

Ball and Feiman-Nemser (1988) have investigated the knowledge and understanding which may be developed from the use of textbooks by beginning teachers and concluded that this source of knowledge may be misleading. Concepts and procedures may be inadequately developed and few examples provided, according to Romberg (1983). Stodolsky (1988) shared this view and indicated that texts were likely to emphasize hints and reminders about what to do, step-by-step analysis of reasoning and stress on calculation skill.

The possibility of transforming a beginning teacher's subject knowledge is likely to be determined by personal understandings brought to teaching. Teachers, like their pupils, are products of primary and secondary schooling and there is little evidence to support the view that teachers increase subject knowledge from practice of teaching.

The Influence of Attitudes and Beliefs

Teachers' pedagogical subject knowledge will also be influenced, however, by their *beliefs* about the subject: beliefs about learning and teaching mathematics, about pupils and teachers and about subject matter. Grossman, Wilson and Shulman (1989) noted that it was sometimes difficult to differentiate between knowledge and beliefs. Brophy (1991) suggested that it would be difficult to draw a sharp, conceptual distinction since the development of knowledge itself is a process of construction and deconstruction in response to situational demands, thus, unverifiable even by the knower and certainly not distinguishable, unambiguously, from beliefs.

In the specific area of mathematics Ball (1991) has suggested that substantive subject knowledge interacts with assumptions and beliefs about teaching and learning, about children and contexts, to shape the ways teachers teach young children. Similarly children develop assumptions about the nature of mathematical knowledge and activities from their own experience in mathematics classrooms.

McDiarmid, Ball and Anderson (1989) have concluded that mathematics understanding is a product of the interweaving of substantive knowledge, its reasoning and its connectedness, as well as feelings about the subject. Whether they are aware of it or not, teachers represent the subject to children through the teaching tasks they select, the explanations provided, and the kinds of things they emphasize about the substantive nature of mathematics. The tasks teachers set are, thus, a function of feelings and beliefs, interacting with disciplinary knowledge and assumptions about teaching and learning. Such knowledge, beliefs and orientations will both support and limit what teachers do and the flexibility with which they respond to pupils. Even if their views of learning change, however, the scope for teaching topics in new ways will be set by the subject knowledge they hold.

Conclusion

In Chapter 2 process-product research was criticized for its lack of attention to the subject matter being taught, for its lack of attention to the cognitive activities of the teachers and pupils involved, and for its conservatism in focusing on existing practice (Romberg and Carpenter, 1986; Shulman, 1986b). This section has shown, however, that as researchers have responded to this criticism by building new investigations of teaching and subject matter knowledge, of novices and experts, they have maintained a commitment to studying existing practice. The work of Leinhardt, for instance, whilst revealing the importance of teachers' knowledge of mathematics subject matter and classroom routines supporting effective lessons, has continued to affirm traditional, expert teaching. Such work carries assumptions about the nature of knowledge and learning which is defined in terms of existing classroom practice.

The benefits of such work are that since it is derived from teacher observation the conclusions drawn are likely to be practical. It has the inherent weakness of conservatism in seeking to build upon existing practice. This commitment stems, in part, from the assumption that improvements to teaching must be made on the basis of existing practice and, in any case, more radical reform must be built upon rich understanding of current expertise.

An alternative frame of reference lies in transforming the traditional assumptions about knowing and learning and, hence, teaching. The following section will, thus, consider alternative models of learning in order to generate fresh conceptions of teaching.

Models of Learning and Conceptions of Teaching

Introduction

In the acquisition of complex knowledge and skills involved in school subjects over months and years, learning appears to require qualitative restructuring and modification of so-called 'schemata' or ways of knowing. As Glaser and Bassock (1989) noted:

> No single set of assumptions or principles pervades the work of investigators who are conducting studies . . . Rather scientists are working towards principles of learning by bringing ideas from various areas to bear in different ways. Attempts at instruction are based to a limited extent on explicitly stated theory or general conceptions of the processes of acquisition for which specific learning mechanisms are unclear, and on observation of the practice of good teachers or tutors . . . Less consistently, attention is given to shaping the instruction to accommodate the available relevant research on characteristics of the learner's initial state. (Glaser and Bassock, 1989, p. 634)

Recently complex, ecologically valid performance in the school subjects of reading, writing, science and social studies are being described (Glaser, 1986). Anderson (1987) has suggested that work in these areas promises to be a central method for the study of learning. Glaser and Bassock (1989) have noted that concepts that appear essential to the description of complex human behaviour supporting this work are available. Most significant is the influence of knowledge structures and their influence as they interact in competent performance. Furthermore the way knowledge is structured influences its accessibility and, hence, knowledge representation determines understanding and influences problem solving. The significance of executive and self-regulatory processes, or metacognition is also being appreciated (Brown *et al.*, 1983; Bransford *et al.*, 1986).

Too close a focus on mathematical subject knowledge without paying sufficient attention to the role played by children's existing concepts and active constructions, as noted in Chapters 1 and 2, risks the discipline of mathematics being inaccessible to young learners. It is important for teachers to provide contexts in which children's own attempts to make sense of new ideas are valued and supported, and their current understandings acknowledged. Mathematical reasoning and thinking about mathematical ideas from this point of view allow personal sense making rather than depending upon teachers and textbooks. It is a point of view which takes the young learner as a social being actively constructing mathematical knowledge through interactions within the physical and social world.

Theoretical Issues

Two general conceptions in developmental psychology underlie the notions of learning that influence this approach to learning and teaching. These are that:

- conceptual change is self-directed, in the sense that there is an intrinsic motivation to understand the world;
- learning has a social genesis, in other words, conceptual development in children involves internalization of cognitive activities originating in social settings.

According to Glaser and Bassock, from this perspective internal structures, principles or constraints are believed to predispose the young learners' search for causes and explanations of events and situations to extend their knowledge. Failure to generate a satisfactory explanation generates a dissonance or dissatisfaction with existing knowledge which creates mental experimentation to test and modify existing expectations (Gelman and Brown, 1986). The new and more robust explanation is assimilated through restructuring or replacing the initial knowledge organization. The process of creating new explanations by the learner alone, in collaboration, or entirely enacted by others, is believed to be internalized gradually.

Internalization is regarded as a key mechanism in learning by Piaget and Inhelder (1958) and Vygotsky (see Kozulin, 1986). Brown (1978) has pointed out, however, that explication of the mechanisms of internalization, assimilation and restructuring have yet to receive theoretical and empirical analysis. The view of learning in which the social interaction between the experienced adult or 'expert' and the less experienced 'novice' or child, who provides the impetus to, and driving force for, development is derived from the work of Vygotsky. The term 'scaffolding' was first coined by Wood, Bruner and Ross (1976) in conjunction with early mother–child interactions, where the adult simplifies the task and at the same time provides the child with additional support in order to be able to respond independently. Wertsch (1979) described the process as the gradual internalization by the child of the adult scaffold in order that problems solved on the 'intrapsychological' (social) plan move to the 'interpsychological' (individual) plane. In its application to formal teaching situations what has been described as a 'cognitively guided' or 'cognitive mediation approach' is likely to lead to teaching which provides a support or 'scaffolding' to children's incomplete efforts to construct meaning. By such means a temporary and adjustable support is provided to aid the successful completion of a task beyond the child's independent means. Fundamental to the success of this process, as noted below, is appropriate support which takes account of the child's current functioning, of additional information which is required to complete the task, and the way that this will be used to assist the child. The place which such strategies can have in the school curriculum depends on the teacher being knowledgeable about the subject and, as noted by Schoenfeld (1985) in the area of mathematical problem solving, being knowledgeable about the most effective strategies for learning particular subject content and skills.

Work in developmental psychology, according to Glaser and Bassock, suggests that self-regulatory strategies are important for monitoring performance, checking and judging progress and predicting outcomes and that the growth of metacognition is significant in cognitive skills from childhood. The emergence of metacognitive processes has been examined in the context of children's awareness of their own abilities (Flavell *et al.*, 1970) and in the development of instructional programmes in reading, writing and mathematics through supportive modelling of task performance. A notable example has been the programme for reading comprehension of Brown and Palincsar (1984; 1988) which is called 'reciprocal teaching' and which involves the teacher and a group of children taking turns in leading the procedure.

Strategies for monitoring comprehension include:

- posing questions about the main content of a paragraph;
- clarifying or resolving misunderstanding;
- summarizing, or reviewing the text; and
- predicting or anticipating text development.

The teacher acts as model and coach with principles derived from expert scaffolding of Wood, Bruner and Ross (1976). Children observe, gain familiarity with the strategies and through their own active construction are able to assume the role of coach as the teacher transfers the leading role. The motivational as well as cognitive benefits to be derived from group activities have also been recognised in such programmes as co-operative learning (Slavin, 1983).

Vygotskian theory supports a view of individual learning and development as the appropriation of social processes with a role for the adult expert, or more experienced peer, in 'scaffolding' instruction and, thus, creating a 'zone of proximal development' where learners work both within their existing sphere of competence whilst being supported to realize potential and higher levels of performance.

This is an approach which aims to provide scaffolded instruction, where attempts are made to support a class or group of children to carry out a task or solve a problem beyond their independent means. Brown and Palincsar (1988) who reviewed the related research suggested a sequence of stages: assessment, introduction, modelling, and guided practice, independent application and instruction for maintenance and transfer. In the assessment stage the teacher assesses the children's current strategies through questions, observation of problem solving and by setting 'thinking aloud' tasks. The introduction stage provides explicit information on what is to be learned, what problem is to be set and why, or how it will be used. In the guided practice and modelling stage the teacher models 'think aloud' strategies or otherwise demonstrates what is to be done and in the early stages, leads, coaches and provides feedback to children's early efforts, as well as opportunities for transfer (see Scardamalia *et al.*, 1984, for planning and drafting written composition; and Schoenfield, 1985, for mathematical problem solving). It requires of the teacher detailed knowledge of the learning process, provision of appropriate 'scaffolding' which is gradually withdrawn as children gain independence. Attention has already been drawn to the role of the supportive adult in the young child's early learning. Perhaps cognitively guided instruction offers one means of providing a similar instructional mode for the learning and teaching of a subject and has as its goal the children's active construction of mathematical knowledge in social contexts. Subject knowledge is central to both the planning of such teaching goals and to the effectiveness of the procedures used.

All of these recent studies highlight the importance of teachers' mathematical subject knowledge and children's growing competence to use and apply mathematics to their social and physical world. There is some evidence, too, that co-ordination and utilization of teacher and pupil knowledge is best enhanced through a supportive style of classroom discourse which both assesses children's current understanding and extends the children's contributions or scaffolds; a task which would be beyond their independent means.

In these programmes children are found to learn to apply the strategies and self-regulatory procedures used in successful reading, writing and mathematical problem solving as the teacher fades the support.

That children will develop general self-instructive strategies which transfer to other contexts is yet to be established. Furthermore, as noted already, the assumed learning mechanisms of internalization, assimilation and restructuring require further theoretical and empirical explication. Peterson and Swing (1983) have established a number of issues associated with the application of cognitive strategy instruction, to group or class settings which include accommodating individual differences in prior knowledge and current strategies among learners and teaching for independent application (maintenance and transfer), as well as integrating such an approach within the existing curriculum.

Clark and Peterson (1986) suggested that teachers do not base instruction and decision-making in teaching on their assessment of children's knowledge or misconceptions. Putnam (1987) argued that the cognitive demand involved in attempting to keep track of all individual pupils in classroom contexts would be overwhelming and that assessing existing knowledge could not be a primary aim. Furthermore he proposed that teachers followed curriculum scripts in which only minor modifications were made in response to pupil feedback. However Carpenter, Fennema, Peterson and Carey (1988) suggested that attention paid, or not paid, to children's existing knowledge may relate to teachers' specific instructional goals. Aims for teaching procedures involving simple computation exercises, for instance, may be accomplished without reference to children's understanding. Successful solution strategies to problem solving, however, may require the consideration of children's existing knowledge and invented strategies.

The Role of Knowledge Structures and Representation in Learning Mathematics

The previous section has indicated that current cognitive theorists share the fundamental assumption that the individual's knowledge structures and mental representations of the world play a central role in perception of the environment and comprehension. Actions are mediated through these cognitive structures which are actively constructed and modified through interaction. Putnam, Lampert and Peterson (1990) have illuminated the different emphases which have emerged in considering these cognitive structures with respect to mathematics which suggests there are different types of knowledge, for instance, formal and informal, conceptual and procedural as well as interrelationships between them. Furthermore understanding mathematics assumes the learner has the means for representing this knowledge with powerful symbols and systems of symbols.

Representation

The notion of representation is central to both cognitive research and mathematics since all mathematics concerns the representation of ideas to allow the manipulation of information or data. Kaput (1987) suggested that the idea of representation is continuous with mathematics itself. As a basic level, the notion of the learner acquiring knowledge structures implies the learner is developing representation (appropriate cognitive structures). Kaput has argued that mathematical structures are treated as abstractions independent of the material symbols used to represent them. For instance, four is assumed to exist independent of its representation by the word 'four', the number '4' or four objects and so on. Since mathematical structures are abstract they must be expressed in material form or external symbolic representation. These symbols support personal thinking about mathematical ideas and allow communication of thinking about them. Representations include, thus, not only mathematical systems such as the base ten, notational system, but informal systems of representation as well.

Lesh, Post and Behr (1987) identified a number of important systems such as pictures and diagrams, written and spoken languages, manipulable models and real world situations:

Figure 3.1: Lesh's Model for Translations between Modes of Representation

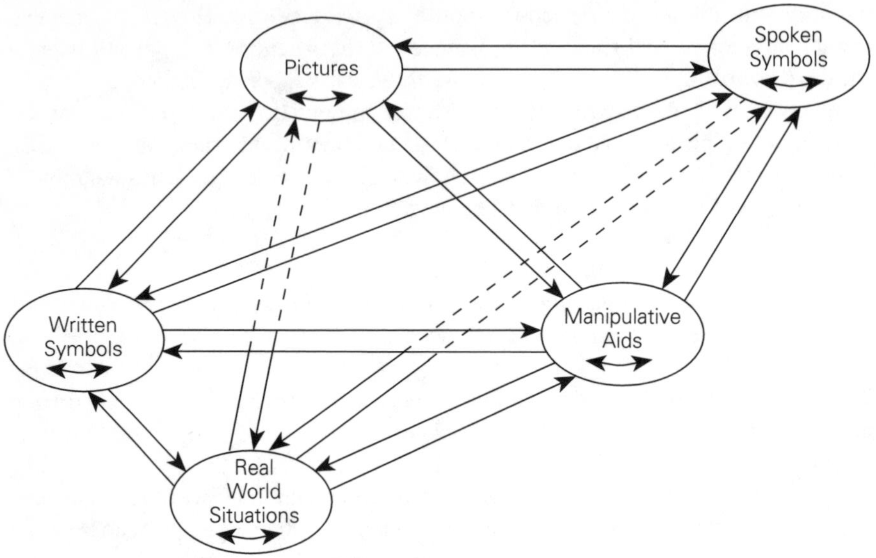

Source: Adapted from Bruner

Manipulative aids may help young learners move from concrete situations and problems to abstract ideas. It is important when learning a new concept for the learner to appreciate a number of perspectives and the diagram stresses the interdependence of these modes. This diagram, in fact, represents a development of Bruner's early work in representation modes (Bruner, 1966). Manipulative aids relate to Bruner's so-called 'enactive' level (use of direct experience), pictures to Bruner's 'iconic' level (use of visual media) and written symbols to Bruner's 'symbolic' level. Lesh added verbalization (spoken symbols) and real world situations to Bruner's model and stressed their interdependence.

A child may, for instance, draw a picture of a manipulative display or construct a manipulative display given a verbal description. Similarly it is possible to make a within-mode translation, for instance, provide alternative verbal representations. Clearly translation between modes cannot take place unless the child understands the concept under consideration and is able to reinterpret it. Similarly this presupposes that the concept is regarded as important and, hence, encouraged in the learning–teaching process. Mathematical problem solving requires movement from real life situations to mathematical systems. Manipulative symbols may be regarded as a half way point between concrete real world or problem situations and the world of mathematical ideas and symbols (written and spoken). Physical materials are, thus, symbols representing real world situations and represent a movement towards symbolic level thinking. Behr (1976) suggested that the gap between manipulative aids and symbols was significant and bridging it complex. The Lesh model suggests mathematical learning and transfer may be enhanced through interaction between different modes. Dienes (1960) believed in three temporally ordered stages of understanding a mathematical concept: first, the informal and preliminary play stage with manipulation of physical contexts and embodiments; second the structured activity stage with structured experiences simulating the concept being learned; and finally the third stage of emergence of the concept with provision for reapplication to the real world.

Munn (1994) in a recent investigation of Scottish nursery children showed how very young children's understanding and representation of quantity, in this case small numbers of blocks in a tin, is highly individual and related to their own purposes rather than adult purposes for similar activities. By the end of the year prior to school entry, however, nearly half of the children used numbers to represent quantity having shifted from iconic to more conventional use of numerals. Their recording of quantity was also used to infer the tin in which an extra block had been added. Furthermore, Munn was able to show a clear association between children's use of verbal counting procedures and the development of their numeral representation.

In summary, representation systems appear to have a dual function like natural language, to support personal mathematical thought and public communication: both personal construction and the product of discourse in the community. This raises pedagogical issues of the match between external representation and the thematic construct it represents and hence, to curriculum materials used to represent mathematical ideas. Janvier (1987) and Dienes (1960) considered the importance of being able to move flexibly within and across representation systems. The implications of this are that learners acquire as personal cognitive tools the powerful ways of representing mathematical ideas that are used in the culture and constructed as particular internal cognitive representations or knowledge structures.

Knowledge Structures

Much attention has been devoted to the consideration and description of knowledge structures assumed to underlie competent performance of mathematical tasks. An important aim of this research has been to specify what that knowledge is and to uncover implicit knowledge underlying understanding. In building models of these knowledge structures two sorts of analysis have emerged:

- detailed analysis of children carrying out mathematical tasks correctly and incorrectly;
- analysis of mathematical content.

This has led to rich descriptions of the way children learn mathematical problems in school as well as appropriate developmental sequences through which children typically pass (Carpenter and Moser, 1984). In fact 'schema' theory (Anderson, 1984) maintained that schemata are forms of knowledge which play a critical role in this constructive process. Schemata are seen as prototypical versions of situations or events which are stored in long-term memory and are built up from many experiences and relevant situations. Schemata provide a framework with which to interpret problem situations. Briars and Larkin (1984) have asserted that comprehension of mathematical word problems requires the learner to bring to bear appropriate knowledge about quantities and relationships among quantities in the form of schemata in particular relationships between known and unknown quantities involved. Their work was built upon extensive empirical descriptions of strategies children use to solve simple addition and subtraction problems and the kinds of problems themselves. They concluded that what is required is available schemata for grasping the relationship among quantities involved, which permits understanding and solving the problem.

In the area of computational skill knowing mathematics may be regarded as acquisition of organized sets of formal rules, correct and incorrect, for manipulating written symbols of arithmetic. Brown and VanLehn (1980) and VanLehn (1983) argued that children infer or construct faulty procedures through incomplete procedural knowledge when they reach the point at which they do not know what to do next. An example would be the subtraction of a large digit from a smaller one in a formal, written algorithm. This depiction of mathematics, however, reduces the knowledge to manipulation of procedures rather than with quantities represented by the symbols, or principles, or problems represented by the calculation (Resnick, 1982). This view of arithmetic contrasts sharply with others so far discussed, with its emphasis on procedures or rules for dealing with written symbols and, in fact, requires no theoretical underpinning.

In terms of problem solving, like representation, this permeates discussion of mathematics. Schoenfeld (1985; 1986) pointed out that general problem solving strategies are not detailed enough to account for mathematical knowledge. These do not distinguish strategies of expert mathematical problem solving from those of novices, nor define their rich organization and available domain-specific knowledge. Underlying interest in all of these approaches is the assumption that knowledge and thinking in mathematics can be specified by explicating knowledge underlying competent performance. Otherwise this can lead to a narrow conception of mathematics and, thereby, cause many unexamined assertions about teaching mathematics.

As the previous discussion has highlighted, a distinction can be made between conceptual and procedural knowledge of mathematics. Furthermore the discussion of representation suggests a further possible distinction between formal, symbolic mathematics learned in school with the rich, informal knowledge developed in out-of-school settings. Moreover as noted above, conceptual knowledge cannot exist or function without some procedural knowledge. In young children's counting, for instance, Greeno, Riley and Gelman (1984) argued that conceptual competence requires implicit knowledge of principles which influence but do not determine procedural performance. Such knowledge guides and constrains counting performance in a wide variety of settings. Greeno and colleagues believed that procedural competence provides the tools for transforming principles into routines and for mapping these procedures to particular contexts. This knowledge is implicit, is demonstrated in practice which is not necessarily flawless, nor unfailingly applied appropriately to a particular situation.

Formal, symbolic knowledge of schools has been contrasted with informal intuitive knowledge acquired in out-of-school contexts as Munn's work demonstrated. This idea is developed in Chapter 4. Ginsburg (1977) and Resnick (1986; 1987) have concluded that a major difficulty for school learning is the lack of account taken of this rich, informal knowledge derived from every-day problem solving situations. In the face of rich informal knowledge, school learning can easily appear arbitrary and meaningless. As noted earlier, if children and adults have implicit principles they do not necessarily draw upon this source. Inventive computation strategies of young Brazilian street traders have been investigated by Carraher, Carraher and Schliemann (1983). Confronting these children with similar problems in written form in school situations, they found them unaware that they could apply these strategies. Peterson, Fennema, Carpenter and Loef (1989) have argued for a better appreciation and use made of children's informal knowledge in school instruction. Their argument rests upon four related constructs that represent fundamental assumptions underlying much contemporary cognitive research into children's learning:

1 Children construct their own mathematical knowledge. (The assumption might be presented on a continuum from active construction to passive reception.)
2 Mathematics teaching should be organised to facilitate children's construction of knowledge. (A contrasting assumption would be that teaching should be organised to facilitate the teachers' clear presentation of knowledge.)
3 Children's development of mathematical ideas should provide the basis for sequencing topics for instruction. In other words, children's informal ideas provide the basis for sequencing instruction. (A contrasting assumption would be to use the structure of mathematics to provide a basis for teaching.)
4 Mathematical skills should be taught in relation to understanding and problem solving. (A contrasting assumption would be to separate mathematical skills and isolate them from understanding and problem solving. Both perspectives assume knowledge and concepts and skills are all important but differ in the goals for teaching them.) (Peterson, Fennema, Carpenter and Loef, 1989, p. 4)

These assumptions are closely related to the constructivist perspective with its emphasis on meaningful learning of mathematics through modifying and building on existing knowledge and thinking.

Learning as Active Construction of Knowledge

Central to current cognitive thought as noted in the previous section is the assumption that the individual interprets his/her environment through existing knowledge structures constructed through adaptation to the environment. The result has been a blurring of the distinction between learning and cognitive development as a separate domain of enquiry. Neither can informal mathematical knowledge learned as a cultural tool in the social environment, for example, counting, addition and subtraction word problems, be separated from formal subject knowledge learned in classroom contexts. Investigation of children's mathematical knowledge demonstrates that they do, in fact, invent or construct new knowledge on the basis of what is already known. For instance, children use different strategies to solve: $a + b = ?$, where a and b are whole numbers between 1 and 10 (Carpenter and Moser, 1983; Fuson, 1982; 1988). In using the ALL (counting all) strategy the child counts a, then counts b more units to arrive at the solution. This may be done mentally, with fingers or with manipulatives. The more efficient MIN (counting from the larger number) strategy starts with the larger of the two addends and counts on the smaller addend. Many children without instruction or even with instruction focused on the ALL strategy invent the MIN strategy to solve problems. An example of an inappropriate or inefficient strategy is the 'buggy algorithm' of Brown and VanLehn (1980) and VanLehn (1983) described earlier, which they attributed to faulty invention of 'repaired' procedures which are constructed when existing knowledge breaks down. These examples demonstrate that children do not simply retain knowledge as presented but actively incorporate new experience to existing frameworks to construct new knowledge. They underline the role of social interaction in presenting accumulated social knowledge in ways which support the individual learner's construction of knowledge. A parent, teacher or more experienced peer may, thus, pass on cultural knowledge of objects of thought to young children (including mathematics).

The basic tenet of all of this work is that learners are active in their learning in a structuring and inventing process. This has important implications for instruction which goes beyond clear presentation of information or modelling procedures.

Applications of Cognitive Theory to Classroom Practice

If learning occurs as a result of the active transformation of new incoming data and meaning is constructed on the basis of what is already known, then there are two major implications for the class teacher. First, the teacher should have access both to children's prior knowledge and their ongoing cognitive processing in order to carry out instruction. Second, in consequence of this, the teacher's goals and, hence, task demands within and across lessons should change and should be adjusted as a result of children's responses. Questions and explanations, demonstrations and modelling, as well as guided support provided will vary within the same learning task for different children and across different learning tasks for the same child. Effective teaching from this perspective thus depends upon the teacher's knowledge of the nature and structure of early years mathematical subject knowledge and knowledge of the way it is acquired by young learners, as well as an appreciation of their common misunderstandings and errors.

Putnam, Lampert and Peterson (1990) have suggested that whilst the constructivist perspective has highlighted the importance of taking into account children's existing knowledge, ideas and procedures, how this perspective should be applied to teaching and instruction is not readily apparent. Clearly much of the research carried out by cognitive psychologists studying the nature of knowledge underlying mathematical performance and the way this knowledge is constructed has been taking place outside the classroom. A number of researchers, however, are working in primary (elementary) classrooms to explore ways of teaching informed by concepts from cognitive theory. In various ways these researchers are trying to bring different assumptions about knowing and learning mathematics into the classroom, which takes account of the real constraints of classroom teaching.

Carpenter, Fennema, Peterson, Chiang and Loef (1989) attempted to change teachers' underlying views of mathematical learning for first grade children (6-year-olds) in the light of cognitive research on children's solving of addition and subtraction word problems. By providing teachers with knowledge about the types of addition and subtraction problems and the strategies children typically used to solve them they found teachers were able to use this knowledge in their instruction. Pupils in 'cognitively guided instruction' were more successful than controls in solving complicated classroom problems and their teachers were more likely to attend to their students' solution strategies than control group teachers.

Kamii (1985; 1989) worked within a constructivist framework attributed to Piaget in first and second grade classrooms (for 6 and 7-year-olds) allowing children to 'reinvent arithmetic' or construct logico-mathematical knowledge through social interaction stimulated by mathematics games. Whilst there were no appreciable quantitative differences between the experimental and control group of 6-year-old children who had received traditional instruction there were striking qualitative differences in the mathematics explanations offered for solutions obtained. The 7-year-olds, moreover, showed higher attainment on standard achievement tests and greater understanding of place value.

Mathematical conceptions have been found by Vergnaud (1982) to be organized in 'conceptual fields' which incorporate problems, situations, relationships, structures, content and operations of thought, built up in daily home and school life and mastery of which may increase over a long period of time, perhaps from three to sixteen years. Addition and subtraction, for instance, are elements of a single conceptual field, the field of 'additive structures'. Furthermore, the teaching of addition and subtraction will require knowledge of which structures and classes of problem children understand most easily and assimilate when taught. Balacheff (1987) set out the framework for such work, known as didactical theory. On the one hand, this assumes that children must actively interpret and make sense of their experience and that knowledge is derived from problems encountered in everyday life; on the other hand, that teaching is a form of 'socializing' children's conceptions. In collaboration with the class teachers, mathematical activities have been designed to elicit children's conceptions through the formulation of problems which require pupils to act upon and evaluate their constructions through class discourse and debate. The soundness of the methods used is then judged in terms of their effectiveness for use in the classroom setting.

Cobb (1988), Cobb *et al.*, (1991; 1992) and Wood, Cobb and Yackel (1990) have also been involved in an ongoing research and development programme which seeks to develop mathematics instruction in second grade classrooms (for 7-year-olds) based on the description and analysis of the mathematics children construct through interaction within the home and school environment, yet which is viable within a traditional classroom setting. Children are encouraged to reorganize their conceptual understanding through activities designed to provide problems solved in a variety of ways with pair work followed by class discussions in which children explain and justify their interpretations and solutions to their peers. Such learning through collaborative dialogue and resolution of conflicting points of view does not usually arise in traditional classrooms. The instructional materials were designed to make sense to children at a number of levels simultaneously, to avoid the arbitrary separation of conceptual and procedural knowledge, at the same time to utilize traditional learning objectives. Cobb worked closely with classroom teachers to establish classroom management and interaction routines which facilitated interactions structured by the materials.

This work was also guided by the constructivist approach to learning attributed to Piaget and to detailed models of young children's mathematical learning of, for example, Steffe, Cobb and von Glasersfeld (1988). From this perspective mathematics learning is seen as a process in which children reorganize their activity to resolve situations that they find problematic. Consequently all teaching activities including those involving arithmetical computation and numeration were designed to be potentially problematic to children at a variety of levels. In this approach children's own conceptions rather than formal mathematics provided the starting point to develop instructional activities.

Two central issues provided a stimulus to this 'problem-centred' approach:

- the extent to which individual interpretations of, and actions on, them aided reflection and, thus, children's construction of mathematical knowledge in problem-solving situations;
- the observation that all representational systems including manipulatives are symbolic and the extent to which this facilitated communication and negotiation of meanings in classrooms.

Representation systems which were found to satisfy these criteria included arithmetical notation, hundreds boards and unifix stored in bars of ten.

In South Africa, Murray and colleagues (1989; 1991; 1993; 1994) conducted research from 1982 to 1987 which culminated in a formal description of the way young children computed and thought about number. It has led to the establishment of a 'problem centred' approach in primary schools by making available to teachers information on how children think mathematically. Participating pupils are reported to have shown much higher performance levels in basic arithmetic and so the experimental phase has led to the implementation across a number of states. Special schools have also been involved.

The 'problem centred' learning is very compatible with a constructivist view of knowledge and learning with stress placed on social interaction among children and attempts by children to make sense of their own and each other's constructions of increasingly sophisticated concepts and procedures. Murray's approach owes much to the work of Cobb and associates. In fact she has a long association with most of the writers described in this section through the international Psychology of Mathematics Education (PME) group. In the experimental curriculum computational procedures have not been imposed on pupils who are encouraged to construct their own conceptually based algorithms. In the first three years of schooling the vertical standard algorithm is not taught and children's self-generated computation strategies are encouraged. Teachers present all mathematical activity as problems to solve, challenging and expecting pupils to solve them in their own way. Negotiation is stressed, as well as interaction and communication between teacher and pupils, and among pupils who are set problems in small groups. Methods are presented orally and in writing with pupils demonstrating and explaining. They are also encouraged to discuss, compare and reflect on different strategies and make sense of other pupils' strategies. The teacher spends much time listening to pupils, accepting explanations and justifications in a non-evaluative manner. She continually assesses knowledge and provides appropriate experiences to facilitate development. Number concept development such as place value is stressed and children's construction of computation encouraged. Like Kamii's teachers, the South African teachers avoid the use of structured apparatus that embodies non-proportional representation of number, for example, Diene's blocks, positional abaci, and Cuisenaire rods. Loose counters and sets of numeral cards (multiples of tens and ones) represent two digit numbers handled as juxtaposition of two numbers from the start.

Direct observation and results of written tests and clinical interviews have shown substantial improvements in learning outcomes of the children in the experimental over the traditional curriculum, as well as higher achievement scores. Positive attitudes towards mathematics and sound beliefs about the activity have also been a result.

By contrast Askew and Wiliam (1993) have noted the dearth of research in Britain on important issues in teaching and learning mathematics. There have been exciting innovations during the 1980s and early 1990s at primary level, however, with the Primary Mathematics project and associated Calculator-Aware Number (CAN) curriculum which explored the possibilities for using calculators to teach number. From the mid-1980s, a variety of CAN projects, launched on a large-scale in close collaboration with practising teachers, were formally evaluated. These were not reported in refereed journals subject to peer review, however, though their impact on teachers and on curricula has been significant. Shuard, Walsh, Goodwin and Worcester (1991) reported one evaluation of free access to calculator utility in twenty schools. Favourable conditions provided in this project did not permit easy generalization but such findings as early confidence with large numbers and operation with negative numbers are promising. One local authority used a standardized test to assess the impact of CAN work on 8-year-olds, who out-performed control children on the majority of test items: CAN children showed flexibility, ease with large numbers, the ability to recognize number patterns and to be aware of their significance, and a willingness to 'have a go' at any problem. Development of a wide range of methods of non-calculator calculation with use made of calculators to check mental calculation for complex calculation, for generating mathematical ideas and processes, as well as for exploring keys and functions were all observed (Shuard *et al.*, 1991).

In the Netherlands between 1980 and 1990, 'realistic' mathematics was introduced to primary schools across the country by the Research Group in Mathematics Education, now called the Freudenthal Institute, after its founder. The realistic mathematics according to Streefland (1991) education stresses rich thematic and concrete contexts, integration of mathematics into other subjects, differentiation of individual learning processes and working together in heterogeneous groups. Theoretically, it owes much to Soviet activity theory (Leont'ev, 1981) which takes people's everyday activity in its societally and culturally mediated environment as both the focus of research and the unit for analysing their mental functioning. In the realistic approach to learning and teaching mathematics is viewed as a human activity arising out of real situations and in which children learn by investigating problems they have formulated. In both activity theory and the realistic approach, the social nature of the knowledge learned and of the teaching process used is central.

Like the work of Murray in South Africa, realistic mathematics eschews the use of manipulative materials. It is in accordance with the constructivist approach in the sense that children are stimulated to construct their own theories and encouraged in social activity: to compare work and methods of problem-solving; to negotiate and to exchange ideas (Gravemeijer *et al.*, 1990). Realistic education theory taps two sources in designing instruction intended to elicit this reconstruction process: 'the history of mathematics', that is, the consideration of ways mathematics as a discipline has developed, moving from concrete tools to abstract form; and spontaneous, self-taught arithmetic methods of children. Materials are regarded as only an aid to solve certain practical problems in specific contexts. Teaching of addition and subtraction to 6-year-olds, for instance, is built around a workbook entitled *The Bus*, which emphasizes the way young children solve problems. Young children play mathematics drama and illustrative scenes about getting on and off a bus. Sums are then presented in drawings of buses linked by arrows which indicate the direction and carry a sign showing how people got on or off. The number is written on the side and the bus is faded as the meaning of the original symbols is learned. Children's own free productions and reflections are valued, including incorrect solutions, and attempts at reasoned arithmetic in arrow puzzles are encouraged as are inventions of other problems in meaningful frameworks. Comparison between the 'Wiskobus' approach and the traditional methods has shown significant differences in the time taken for children to learn arithmetic.

At the level of international comparison, Stigler and Perry (1988) also have shown that differences across cultures in classroom teaching may contribute to superior performance of Asian children (Japanese and Chinese) compared with North American on a range of international achievement tests, including all aspects of mathematical reasoning at Grade 1 and 5 (for 6 and 9-year-olds). Further investigation has shown the whole Asian class working together, talking but not off-task, with public display of errors not to be ridiculed but to be corrected by classmates. Asian children are given more opportunities to solve real life problems and Japanese pupils, in particular, spend a far greater amount of time than either Chinese or American children engaged in reflective verbalization about mathematics. In American classrooms teachers, by contrast, spend more time with individuals than with the class and feel more comfortable praising good performance than discussing errors that occur in the course of problem solving. Like British pupils have been found to do, American pupils spend more time working individually on individual exercises.

In common with the other innovations discussed in this section Asian children spend more time on problem solving, attending to strategies with reflective verbalization and, in particular, analysing errors and misconceptions and, thereby, building up effective strategies.

Conclusion

What does it mean to know and to understand mathematics? Different perspectives on what and how mathematics should be taught and learned have been presented in this chapter. No integrated perspective or comprehensive view has emerged since fundamental issues about the nature of mathematical knowledge and about learning and teaching mathematics remain to be resolved.

Research on competent classroom practice has tended to take mathematical tasks and topics in the traditional school curriculum and seek to explicate the role of subject matter knowledge and classroom routines required to perform these tasks successfully. Attempts to uncover the sources and determinants of novice (beginning) teachers' content knowledge and beliefs have been more successful in demonstrating that existing knowledge, beliefs and orientations both support and set the limits to teaching performance than in identifying clearly the origins of, and influences on, teaching expertise. A number of themes from the psychological literature have emerged concerning the role of representation, the kinds of knowledge structures which are assumed to underlie performance on particular mathematics tasks and the active construction of these knowledge structures by individual learners in particular social and physical contexts. Finally a number of attempts to develop new approaches and innovative practices in classroom mathematics teaching have been described.

On the one hand, socially accepted definitions of mathematical knowledge are available but, on the other hand, there is a need for young learners to construct their own meaning. This is common across the approaches described. Concentration solely on personal knowledge of learners, however, ignores the importance of mathematical conventions which must be learned. Too much emphasis on conventional tools with young children, ignoring the role of individuals' existing conceptions and efforts at meaning, creates the risk that the tools will not be learned in ways that make them accessible to young learners when needed. How, then, is school practice to be developed? If teaching and learning is to be accomplished it must be built around the 'big' ideas that constitute Vergnaud's conceptual fields and which develop over the school years. As noted by Putnam, Lampert and Peterson (1990) these cannot be told by teachers in their complexity but can, perhaps, be created in classroom activities which help children construct them in an ongoing way over the primary school years, refined in a variety of settings.

In addition, symbols and representations must be learned and conventionally used, whilst they may be better remembered if they are learned in meaningful contexts. Mathematical conventions and personal constructions, however, may be by no means clearly distinct. Children cannot learn concepts and procedures unless they actively work to integrate new information within their own existing knowledge and, thus, personally 'sense-make'.

As noted in the previous section, classrooms *can* provide a setting for children's attempts to make sense of new ideas which are valued and explored and where mathematical conclusions are supported by reasoned argument. Mathematical evidence after all is not empirical evidence but requires knowledge that can be shown to derive logically from agreed-upon assumptions. Whilst no one general theory of learning processes or instructional method is common to all the innovative approaches described, talking about mathematics, analysing errors, publicly valuing knowledge which is refined in the classroom setting is common across these settings. Communication of mathematical arguments is learned with external discourse and justification, otherwise much of what is learned is left implicit and, hence, unexamined.

What marks out these approaches is that they centre on examples, focus on strategies, examine errors rather than judge for accuracy. There is much emphasis on activity and discourse focused on real life problems. The importance of talking about mathematics in these contexts is in some contrast to more traditional classrooms where children practice procedures which have been modelled and explained by teachers. By discussing and describing, by participating in mathematical theory children are provided with opportunities to construct mathematics through personal sense-making.

So far the discussion has focused on the context of classroom practice, in terms of the way knowledge of mathematics is learned and represented by the individual child. Turning now to the specific mathematical tasks, to the kinds of mathematical activity in which young children engage, the next chapter will consider in more depth the nature of the early mathematical knowledge which young children learn in school and out.

4 The Construction and Early Learning of Mathematics in School and Out

Introduction

Whilst the previous chapter has emphasized general theoretical perspectives on the young learner actively constructing mathematical knowledge through interactions within the physical and social world relatively brief attention was devoted to the rich empirical knowledge base concerning the development of early mathematics by young children inside school and out.

Reference has already been made in the previous chapter to the distinction between the formal, symbolic mathematical knowledge of school and the rich, intuitive knowledge and problem solving strategies constructed in out-of-school settings which the recent researchers are attempting to address in their innovations to classroom practice.

There is convincing empirical support for the view that schooling and the type of cognitive activity that it encourages is *discontinuous* with everyday activity and practical intelligence or the knowledge-in-practice that it requires. Lave (1988; 1991) has shown how arithmetic activity in the real world does not reflect the formal procedures taught in the classroom. Similarly young street traders in Recife, Brazil, reported by Carraher, Carraher and Schliemann (1985), Saxe (1988) and Nunes, Schliemann and Carraher (1993) displayed a situated construction of arithmetic knowledge through their invented units for calculation which was virtually error-free, as noted in Chapter 3. Clearly a school teacher and pupils, too, are engaged in everyday, situated activity but a long, gradual shift has taken place in the relationship of school-generated and in-school mathematics to ordinary, everyday life. It has led to the production of formal properties, and systems of money, measurement and arithmetic, institutionalized in problem-solving tasks at school with implicit messages that these constitute an objective and universal system of units and relations with which to calculate. The gap between this formally taught system and the strategies needed in the world outside is wide. As Resnick (1987) has indicated that:

> schooling focuses on the individual's performance, whereas out-of-school mental work is often socially shared. Schooling aims to foster unaided thought, whereas mental work outside school usually involves cognitive tools. School cultivates symbolic thinking, whereas mental activity outside school engages directly with objects and situations. Finally, schooling aims to teach general skills and knowledge, whereas situation-specific

competences dominate outside . . . What do these striking discontinuities suggest about the relationships – actual and possible – between schooling and competence in work and daily life? (Resnick, 1987, p. 16)

It may be concluded that children themselves seem to treat school arithmetic as a setting in which to learn rules and, somehow, feel discouraged from bringing to school their informally acquired knowledge about numbers. If schooling does not contribute very obviously to performance outside school, and vice versa, is the reception teacher, for instance, aware of this knowledge acquired before schooling starts, and, moreover, does she look for ways to access and to use it to support in-school learning?

These questions had a particular pertinence to the present project, the start of which coincided with the introduction of the National Curriculum in September 1989 and its attendant changes to curriculum and assessment. At this time there was, in fact, as noted by Stierer (1990) a growing demand for educationally valid methods for recording competence at the start of school in order to establish a baseline measurement, or a national starting point, so that assessments at 7 years could determine educational 'value added' to the children. This concern, of course, had more to do with educational accountability and the need for assessment of the formal school curriculum than with any genuine recognition that children brought into school a rich working knowledge of arithmetic. Furthermore valid assessment at school entry pre-supposes that the teacher understands and has the means to uncover and document this culturally-embedded knowledge and the meanings it holds for young children which may, or may not correspond with conventional school learning.

Aims

This chapter aims to review:

- the rich knowledge base concerning children's construction and early learning of mathematics, in school and out;
- the current National Curriculum and assessment context.

The first task of the project was to construct assessment tasks designed to incorporate both areas of competence young children are known to bring into school and content compatible with the National Curriculum. In order to do this it was necessary first to consult the rich existing knowledge base in this area.

Learning Mathematics Outside School

Long before they enter school children develop a rich working mathematical knowledge from everyday situations. The transcripts from the work of Gordon Wells in the *Language at Home and at School* project (1973–78) provide a rich source for conversations between children and their mothers. Examples abound of activities which give rise to counting and sharing, which make reference to time, money and simple fractional numbers, and stimulate tasks which require sorting to a criterion, use of the language of measurement, position in space and on a line. Hughes (1986), examining the conversations between young children aged from 3 years 9 months to 4 years 3 months and their mothers collected in a previous study (Tizard and Hughes, 1984), by contrast, noted relatively few conversations where the mothers were explicitly using the language of arithmetic. Some examples of this sort, however, were provided. He quoted the instance of a child and her mother singing the traditional song about current buns in a baker's shop, which describes the progressive reduction of five buns as they are sold. Here, and in another similar example related to a discussion of the number of cakes required for tea, the mother involved modelled for the child the use of fingers to represent the number of buns required. Hughes emphasized the point that fingers were being used as a concrete referent, thus playing a crucial role in linking the abstract and the concrete, both representing objects and serving as objects in their own right.

Durkin *et al.* (1986) also documented the relatively high levels of parental input in the learning of number words in informal settings whilst Saxe *et al.* (1987) suggested that such parental help was instrumental in providing children with a framework for understanding quantitative tasks. Munn (1994), however, has demonstrated that such early experience of quantification is highly personal and idiosyncratic and may be interpreted by the child in ways unrelated to those intended by the adult.

It is, in fact, the development of children's early number ideas which has been most extensively delineated in the research literature. Over the years from 2 to 7, which straddle home and school life, children learn to use numbers systematically and to apply them to ordinary, everyday situations. Vergnaud (1982), as noted, has described 'conceptual fields', such as additive structures or multiplicative structures, which require mastery of a variety of highly interconnected concepts, procedures and representations which develop over the years from 3 or 4 to, at least, 14. Denvir and Brown (1987) proposed a framework for describing children's acquisition of number concept and skills and found hierarchical relationships which exist between the acquisition of different number skills. The three most fundamental skills prerequisite to all other items were: comparing collections and stating whether or not they were equal; one-to-one correspondence construction; and saying the number sequence to 20, as well as adding or subtracting by direct physical modelling. Klein and Starkey (1988), in fact, proposed three general types of early arithmetic knowledge present across all cultural contexts: knowledge of the enumerative processes (instant recognition of small group sizes, one-to-one correspondence and counting); computational procedures; and knowledge of the natural number system. These 'universals' are very compatible with Denvir and Brown's foundation skills.

Only a small selection from the main ideas relating to this rich knowledge base can be presented and much of this has informed the innovative practice described in the previous chapter. These will be dealt with as separate topics, number, data handling, measurement, shape and space, which attempt to reflect both areas which have been most extensively investigated and the recent enlargement of the content of the British primary curriculum.

Number

Early Counting

Studies of the last ten to fifteen years suggest that babies may have an inborn sense of numerosity, or quantity, for small sets of items. Sensitivity to numerical displays of arrays for up to three or four items under different conditions has been demonstrated from the first week of life by Antell and Keating (1983). By the age of five months Wynn (1992) has suggested that young infants appear to understand the effect that adding or subtracting one or two items has on quantity. In other words they seem to know that $1 + 1 = 2$ and that $2 - 1 = 1$. At 18 months of age understanding of ordinal relationships for very small values emerges, for instance, that a set of three items is more than two (Cooper, 1984). During the pre-school years use of language to represent numerical information and relationships becomes more and more important as children learn basic number names, the counting system of their culture, as well as the different contexts in which numbers are used. This means that number words are gradually mapped onto their existing understanding of number and deployed appropriately for counting and measurement. The development of basic number skills, in fact, spans the period of 2 to 8 years, that is, the pre-school to early school years. More specifically, this knowledge involves memorizing number words, developing understanding that each one represents a different quantity and, through refinement of counting skills, the growing appreciation of cardinal and ordinal value through a variety of number games, songs and activities, which include informal arithmetic. In the early stages children rely heavily on counting and number knowledge to solve simple arithmetic problems which gradually gives way to formally taught procedures in the school years.

Addition and Subtraction

Pre-schoolers' understanding of natural numbers which continues into the school years up to around 7 or 8 years, includes notions of addition and subtraction. In fact Gelman and Gallistel (1978) showed that children aged 3 to 4 years could accurately solve concrete addition and subtraction problems by learning to recognize one of two plates with different numbers of objects as the 'winner', or describe the transformation in terms of 'you put one on/off'. With a difference of more than one, however, whilst the notion of increasing or adding to the array was recognized they were not so likely to quantify the change which required re-counting of the complete set.

Starkey and Gelman (1982) and Hughes (1981) showed that children aged 3 to 5 years could solve addition and subtraction in a concrete framework, even if the two collections to be combined or separated were never simultaneously visible (the original collection remaining in the researcher's hand or in a box). Many children were able to solve the problems with small numbers within 10 by counting, even if some objects were hidden from view. Fuson (1982) found that between 3 and 5 years most children learned to 'count on' in order to add 1 or 2 to a given number. As noted in Chapter 3, children move from using the ALL (counting all) strategy to solve $a + b = ?$, where a and b are whole numbers between 1 and 10 (counting a, then b more units) to the more efficient MIN (counting from the larger number) often without instruction. This makes fewer demands on working memory (Case, 1985).

A range of researchers have studied children's performance on verbal addition and subtraction problems in order to determine the kinds of meanings children assign to the operations as well as to identify the classes of problems they are able to solve (Carpenter and Moser, 1983; Riley, Greeno and Heller, 1983). To summarize, young children, even pre-schoolers are able to solve a variety of problems although certain problems, such as separating problems, in which the initial set is unknown are available only to older children. Action-oriented problems, such as joining and separating in which the final set is known are easiest to solve. Children pay attention to the structure of problems and select strategies that correspond to the structure. Carpenter and Moser (1983) found that children initially needed modelling strategies with fingers or concrete objects, later they counted on forwards or backwards. Finally children begin to memorize facts, which allows direct retrieval (Siegler, 1986). A similar progression from manipulatives and finger counting, to verbal counting and derived fact strategies is common across cultures though the rate varies according to experience and, to some extent, on language differences in number words (Stephenson *et al.*, 1990; Geary *et al.*, 1992).

Whilst, as noted already, the size of the combinations is critical to children's success Baroody (1984) suggested that number size alone was not the only predictor of ease or difficulty of learning. Kamii (1985) confirmed that small numbers are easiest (up to 4, then up to 6). Suydam and Weaver (1975) and Kamii (1985) found that adding doubles $(2 + 2)$ and related subtraction facts $(4 - 2)$ are easy. Also very easy are 'zero' facts $(3 + 0, 5 - 0)$ and successor/predecessor facts $(4 + 1, 7 - 1)$. Combinations of 10 $(7 + 3, 6 + 4, 10 - 2)$ and doubles, plus one $(5 + 6, 4 + 5)$ are also relatively easy to solve. Other frequently observed strategies, using memorized facts to derive the solution to other problems involving 10 are:

- bridging through 10, $8 + 5 =$ ('8 and 2 are 10, so 3 more makes 13');
- subtraction through 10, $13 - 5 =$ ('13 take away 3 is 10, then I take 2 more away from 10 so the answer is 8');
- 9 is one less than 10, $9 + 6 =$ ('10 and 6 are 16, so the answer is one less or 15');
- compensation, $9 + 7 =$ ('I take 1 away from 9, that's 8 and give it to 7 and that's also 8, $8 + 8$ makes 16').

Children do not necessarily invent such strategies unaided. Kamii (1985) has described the benefits of providing children with opportunities to re-invent such strategies through number games. Steinberg (1985) suggested, however, that even if taught there was no guarantee that children would use the strategies. There is some evidence (Fuson and Kwon, 1992) that decomposition is most reliably used by children who understand the base-10 system. Furthermore this strategy is used earlier and more frequently by Asian than North American children. At this stage processing becomes more accurate, automatic and swift, and provides a model upon which to base more advanced problem solving strategies. Whilst they may manage simple problem solving using counting strategies before school, these more complex strategies are not likely to be used by children until later, and under the influence of formal schooling.

Place value will be experienced in an intuitive way through children's developing knowledge of the counting system. The 'system of tens' convention requires, as Kamii (1989) noted, the child's synthesizing the relationship of order and hierarchical structure. The child has to learn to order the ones mentally but the ones in this system also form units of tens. Kamii (1989) suggested that children must have sufficient experience of constructing the first system of ones in order to provide a firm foundation for the second system of tens which will be constructed over 7 to 11 years.

Clearly place value is one of the 'big ideas' (Putnam, Lampert and Peterson, 1989) which is fundamental to mathematics and mathematics learning. Construction or development of this concept will be an ongoing process, revisited and refined over the primary years.

Multiplication and Division

As with additive fields, multiplicative fields develop over a similarly long period of time. Furthermore, multiplication and division are related in much the same way as addition and subtraction, thus, division is the *inverse operation* of multiplication, for instance $5 \times 3 = 15$ and $3 \times 5 = 15$ but $15 \div 3 = 5$ and $15 \div 5 = 3$.

Just as for addition and subtraction, early multiplication strategies are built on existing knowledge of addition and counting. Initially strategies involve repeated addition, $2 + 2 + 2 + 2$, the value of the multiplicand 2 written out the number of times indicated by the multiplier 4 and 'counting by n', 2, 4, 6, 8, may be used to solve 2×4. Later more mature strategies which involve rules, for example, $0 \times n = 0$ or $1 \times n = n$, will be used and derived, or 'related table' facts retrieved from memory.

Similarly for division problems children use first their knowledge of addition and multiplication (Vergnaud, 1983). For example, to solve 8/2 the child may rely on multiplication knowledge, that is, $2 \times 4 = 8$ or $2 + 2 + 2 + 2$, as above, making use of addition knowledge. Both of these strategies, however, assume some basic awareness that division involves determining the number of subsets of a small number, the divisor, contained in a larger number, or dividend.

Desforges and Desforges (1980), however, proposed that the numerical basis of early social sharing in young children has remained largely unexamined and they were able to demonstrate that young children 4 to 6 years have a powerful grasp of social sharing up to 30 polo mints among 2, 3 and 5 dolls, with and without remainders. A significant increase in the use of checking strategies and a one-set-to-each-doll strategy with age was noted. Predictably, increasing the set size and introducing remainders increased the problems that children experienced. It was concluded that their young children showed a robust number-based understanding and approach to the notion of sharing, especially with small set sizes. It was proposed that division, a mathematical notion, might have its origin in such activities which predate the formal introduction of division, which is generally introduced to children in the final year of infant schooling. Furthermore this foundational understanding of division might *not* be constructed as the inverse of multiplication as mathematicians might suppose.

Kamii (1989) also believed that multiplication and division grew out of real-life situations and sharing problems at around 7 years. Her view was that children invented strategies to solve story problems with small numbers along with all other operations. Such activities became part of children's repertoires as they counted money, for instance, and played games repeatedly. Her expectation was that they would eventually invent faster ways without knowing multiplication tables or being, necessarily, able to create correct answers by using the 'correct' procedure.

Murray *et al.*, (1991) shared the view that multiplication and division grew out of problem solving. In her experimental curriculum children invented powerful, non-standard operations through dealing with unclassified problems. 6-year-old children modelled a problem by drawing in greater or lesser detail and solved it by further drawing the action needed (direct representation). They also used iconic representation, like dots, or repeated addition and subtraction.

Whilst the teaching of multiplication and division in school typically occurs after the formal introduction of addition and subtraction and their symbolic representation, the origins of these operations exist within the practical, everyday situations in which children operate. Anghileri (1995) has suggested it is not division which is a complex operation but when it is learned in school, it must be integrated into children's existing knowledge and be compatible with their expanding everyday experience of number.

As children gradually become more familiar with the different situations that embody the different aspects of multiplication and division, and the different language this involves, understanding of the properties of multiplication and division is gradually developed. In fact less research has been carried out to investigate the strategies that young children use to solve multiplication and division problems.

Knowledge of the properties of multiplication and division, however, is essential for many more advanced mathematics topics, such as area, proportion and algebra. Furthermore real-life problems of division with remainders may provide an introduction to fractions and decimal notation and a recognition that factors always appear as whole numbers.

Data Handling

One of the earliest number concepts which has not yet been examined is classification, the grouping together of objects on the basis of a common attribute. The notion that there is a whole class of things which are alike in some way and which can be distinguished from other things develops from early experience of handling and exploring objects in the natural world, as described by Williams and Shuard (1988). It is from this practical knowledge of classes of things which are like or different, from children's sorting and separating, their combining and relating, that the idea of *set* develops. Whilst the formal language of sets will not be met before school, the child will have experience of activities which build an awareness of the connection between members of a set, that is, the common property which makes it possible to decide whether another new object belongs to the set or not. As children become used to classifying and forming subsets they learn that members of two sets are related together, for example, friends have different pets, shoes have different colours. Through this experience of combining sets into a whole as well as making small, subsets from a large collection, the foundation for mathematics and logical thinking will be formed (see Inhelder and Piaget, 1958). Commercial toys, in many cases, will have extended children's ideas of classification with animals, shapes and colours. Games such as 'one difference', making a line of logiblocs, different by one attribute, provide experience and discussion of sorting, reasoning and deduction.

Once in school, experience of classification using actual objects will be repeated and, at a later stage, diagrams will represent the objects concerned. Sorting shells and seeds, for instance, or plastic blocks and sorting toys will provide the basis for simple Carroll diagrams and Venn diagrams. Through selecting criteria for sorting a set of objects and applying them consistently, and through recording with objects or drawing them, pupils begin to collect, process and interpret data, in other words, to *handle data*.

Whilst Klein and Starkey (1988) have begun to map out generality of processes and development sequences in arithmetic cognition across cultures, the ideas presented in this section do not all fall into that category. Set theory, whilst underpinning much activity in British primary schools has, for instance, no place in the Dutch mathematics curriculum and, as such, would be described by Klein and Starkey in terms of cultural variation rather than universal.

Measurement

As noted above, as children learn number names and counting one of the contexts in which number and ordinal scales will be used will be measurement. In fact assessing relative quantity, length and volume are important strategies for young children in the social context of home and pre-school setting. Whilst many 2 and 3-year-olds seem to have an understanding of measurement to determine equivalence these skills are largely pre-quantitative. Distributive counting – 'one for you and one for me . . .' – discussed above succeeds earlier 'dumping' strategies of a few sweets in each friend's cup which shows little concern for equality, though everyone gets some. Similarly for length, a hot dog cut by a 3-year-old into six pieces and distributed to three friends, will take little account of the length of the piece (Miller, Perlmutter and Keating, 1984).

A relation which children recognize at a very early age is 'bigger than', 'smaller than' and a range of other similar measurement words. In everyday domestic and pre-school contexts, children order bricks, string and sticks of different lengths so from the first intuitive comparison of more and less grows an understanding of both counting and measurement. Comparison of length or weight (mass) begins the process towards finding a suitable unit of measurement and, eventually, to attaching a measurement value to it. Contrast and comparison of two lengths or weights are, at first, qualitative with number only gradually emerging from the process of matching and ordering in a sequence, making way for more quantitative comparison. Ordering in a sequence increases careful observation and encourages estimation.

Sometimes it will not be easy to find out which of two objects is taller or longer and, sometimes, size will change over time as in the case of growth. Children, like adults, will find many ways of devising non-standard measures, using body measurements such as footsteps, strides, handspans or improvised measures, such as cupfuls and spoonfuls. Repeating a unit and making a count emerges from this process and, in any case, conventional measures are already familiar to children in their ordinary, everyday world.

A vast research literature relating to measurement and children's 'readiness' to measure exists, much of which has its origins in, for instance, the work of Piaget, Inhelder and Szeminska (1960). Many studies have been conducted in the style of Piaget and certain, fundamental ideas investigated, such as *transitivity* (if three pieces of string are of different length and $a > b > c$, then $a > c$), *conservation* (if a length of string is cut in half and the two halves are separated, the piece of string still has the same, total length) and *unit of measure* (as noted above, recognising the attribute to be measured and the unit influences the number assigned).

Carpenter (1976) provided a thorough review of the literature concerning readiness for measurement learning. He demonstrated that virtually all 6 and 7-year-olds could respond as effectively to either numerical cues or perceptual cues. Most children, however, focused on a single cue, perceptual or numerical, and showed difficulty in co-ordinating numerical with perceptual information where one type of cue was dominant or unclear. Despite the findings of researchers such as Donaldson (1978) which have shown that alterations to the language and the context of Piagetian tasks can affect their successful completion, conclusions to be drawn are that young children below 7 to 8 years do not competently co-ordinate what they know and what they observe about the attribute with what they know or observe about number assignment.

Shape and Space

Properties of space are familiar to children at an early age, recognition of shape, relative position and size, in fact, precedes awareness of number.

Just as the young child's notion of number and quantity develops slowly, so too does awareness of spatial properties. Topological properties may be noticed first, that is, position such as 'under', 'behind' or 'next to', and general outline and size in shapes. As was the case for measurement, co-ordinating differences is difficult. Whilst it may be appreciated that objects remain the same despite alteration of the position of the observation, at the same time, young children find it difficult to appreciate that a shape drawn in two positions remains the same. Certain differences in shape and size can be distinguished but co-ordinating or combining different kinds of relationships is yet to be developed. At the same time language is developing and simple representational drawing. As noted above, children gain much pre-school experience in sorting, comparing, matching and combining through construction with 3-D household containers, boxes and educational toys. Experience is also likely to be gained in handling 2-D shape tiles, in cutting and folding card. Names for common shapes, such as triangle, circle and square may be familiar and this knowledge can extend to terms for some 3-D shapes, such as cylinder or pyramid. Piaget and Inhelder (1969) suggested that children deal first with 'topological' aspects of shapes between 3 and 4 years; distinguish 'projective' aspects, such as curved or straight-sidedness at 4 to 6 years; and finally, explore 'Euclidean' notions of length, angle, size and area, to discriminate among complex shapes, at 6 to 8 years.

Most of the research in this area relates to the development of formal geometry and geometrical thinking. Some of this material, however, for example the properties of similar shapes, is now being introduced into primary schools. The van Hielēs (1959) proposed levels of thought in which children begin to describe, learn and to engage with geometry. These are:

Level 0 (the visual level) where children perceive figures by their appearance as a whole, rather than specific properties of, or relationship among parts of a figure.

Level 1 (the descriptive level) where children begin to analyse figures and appreciate their properties, though recognizing relationships among figures is not developed.

Level 2 (the informal deduction level) where special relationships among figures and properties of figures such as, a square is also a rectangle, which is also a parallelogram.

Level 3 (the formal deduction level) which begins deduction, reasoning and following lines of argument in proofs of statements presented, or developing sequences of statements to deduce one statement from another.

Level 4 (the abstract, geometric systems level) which is the most rigorous in understanding and justification of mathematic structures.

In the early years, children's geometric thinking is mainly at Levels 0 and 1, according to Burgher and Shaughnessy (1986) and Clements and Battista (1992). At Level 0, 'a square is a square . . . because it looks like one'. There is no reason for it at this global level of understanding. At Level 1, children begin to think about shapes in terms of their parts as they explore and discover properties, such as, 'the square has four sides which are equal and four right-angles'. Language of properties at this level can be used to describe shapes and to explain. Children do not, however, deduce certain properties on the basis of others or consider which properties are essential in defining a shape, which emerges at Level 2 (informal deduction). At this level, they begin to establish why all squares are rectangles but *not* all rectangles are squares. In other words, the square is specified by a definition.

Soviet psychologists Kilpatrick and Wirzup, between 1969 and 1977, investigated the van Hieles' model and confirmed the levels of geometrical thinking. They noted that concepts might be understood implicitly and require effective learning experiences with lower levels as well as familiarization with new ideas in order for these to become explicit.

More recently, Hoffer (1983; 1988), from the United States, has suggested that young children may be familiar with some geometric vocabulary but often have gross misconceptions or incorrect ideas about meanings of such terms. For example, there is a common belief that the only figure which is a triangle is an equilateral triangle. Children, as noted above, may be unduly influenced by the orientation of a shape. For instance a square or triangle, if rotated, may not be recognized. Children at all ages use 'converse' reasoning, for instance, 'a square has four sides, I am searching for a figure with four sides, it must be a square'. Textbooks have been found to be confusing in organization and presentation of ideas which consist largely of naming of shapes and identifying some properties, for instance parallelism, but seldom ask children to reason. Children have been found to idealize a shape and to focus on a particular property as a reference point however dissimilar the figures presented might be. Changes to figures in one aspect may be believed *not* to affect another, for example, a quadrilateral can be transformed into a rectangle with the same perimeter to obtain its area. The van Hieles asserted that such teaching failures result from a communication gap between teachers and children who have different levels of understanding and, thus, talk at different levels. Kilpatrick and Wirzup also confirmed that children working at different levels may be liable to misunderstand each other.

The van Hieles proposed five instructional phases to support progression through the levels:

- information, where two-way conversation establishes what pupils already know and think;
- directed orientation, which engages pupils in a sequence of activities to explore the topic;
- explication, where pupils' awareness becomes more explicit and related terminology is learned;
- free orientation, which produces problem solving that requires use and synthesis of the topic in question; and
- integration, which allows pupils to summarize the topic and to relate this to prior learning.

Certain conclusions can be drawn from these findings which are pertinent to the development of understanding of shape and space of young children. Much more than knowledge of shape vocabulary is required. Solid shapes often do not receive sufficient attention though, as noted above, they relate to the everyday living of young children. Children might benefit from a broader experience in spatial thinking and geometry earlier, with teaching matched to the child's level, yet providing enrichment and extension. Knowledge of basic shape vocabulary can be checked and more specialized shape knowledge reinforced. A terminology associated with solid shapes and an awareness of their properties, can be enhanced from the earliest years.

In all areas of mathematics – number, measurement, shape and space and data handling – children bring into school a rich, informal knowledge learned in everyday, social contexts. To investigate how teachers assess this knowledge and relate it to the framework of the formal curriculum, if indeed they do, was a central aim of the project. The most significant point to note, perhaps, is that this vast range of mathematical knowledge has been exposed through detailed, clinical investigation, observation and practical interview with individual children with a researcher who had the time to negotiate meaning and to ensure perceptions of the task and its purpose were shared by child and adult. Furthermore it should be emphasized that it represents a knowledge base more familiar to researchers, in particular, psychologists than to teachers and educators and, moreover, it is a changing knowledge base as investigation of 'problem-centred' approaches and children's invented strategies expands and may well challenge established sequences such as Denvir and Brown's (1987) hierarchy of mathematics concepts.

Mathematics Learned in School

Introduction

As noted in the previous section, whilst the empirical knowledge base reflects the traditional content of the primary (elementary) curriculum in its focus on arithmetic and measurement, the British curriculum has broadened beyond arithmetic calculation to include emphasis on conceptual understanding, real life applications and under-represented domains such as geometry (shape and space), algebra and data handling. The justification for such a move lies in the perceived need for children to be prepared to become future members of a technological, information-based society. The changes to the curriculum are exemplified by the introduction of the National Curriculum, although the call for a revision to the mathematics curriculum and the overall quality of mathematics instruction to better reflect the needs of an expanding technological society is most closely associated, in this country, with the *Cockcroft Report* (1982).

The National Curriculum Context

The project began in September, 1989 at the time when the National Curriculum was being first introduced to primary schools and, hence, the whole school curriculum

Table 4.1: The Structure of the Attainment Targets in Mathematics

Mathematics – 1989		1991	
Ma1	Using and applying mathematics	Ma1	Using and applying mathematics
Ma2	Number	Ma2	Number
Ma3	Number (Operations)	Ma3	Algebra
Ma4	Number (Estimation)	Ma4	Shape and space
Ma5	Number/Algebra	Ma5	Handling data
Ma6	Algebra		
Ma7	Algebra		
Ma8	Measures		
Ma9	Using and applying mathematics		
Ma10	Shape and space (Shapes)		
Ma11	Shape and space (Location)		
Ma12	Handling data (Collecting and recording)		
Ma13	Handling data (Representing and interpreting)		
Ma14	Handling data (Probabilities)		

was being reformed. The *Education Reform Act* (1988) had set up the framework for a ten-subject curriculum and assessment arrangements as described in Chapter 1. Each subject had programmes of study which defined what was to be taught and attainment targets which represented the knowledge, skills and understanding within the subject. The content, then, was set out and extended within the Statutory Orders and related programmes of study, the former being relatively precise and specific and the latter laid down in general principles and advice. As shown in Table 4.1, which outlines the attainment targets for mathematics, radical changes were introduced to the mathematics Orders in 1991, after two years: the original fourteen attainment targets were reduced to five. This change which regrouped the subject matter, the programme of study remaining the same, was assessed for the first time in 1992 or 1993. (Following the more recent review of the National Curriculum, (Dearing, 1994), new Orders came into force in September, 1995 after the project was completed.)

The National Curriculum specified for each prescribed subject content, concepts and skills to be taught progressively and monitored through an assessment system. This assessment system which measured on a continuous, criterion-referenced scale of ten levels covered the whole period of compulsory schooling, 5 to 16 years. Each level was defined in terms of criteria known as statements of attainment (SOAs).

The content for each subject, the attainment targets and the statements of attainment defining the levels, was determined by subject working parties and, thus, represented the expert judgments of the subject specialist groups rather than any empirical data related to pupils' own knowledge and understanding.

The mathematics programme of study was introduced for 5 to 7-year-old children in September, 1989 as the project started. Whilst reception-aged children were not officially included the need to identify entry skills in order to demonstrate education 'value added' at age 7 years meant that the impact of the National Curriculum was felt in reception classes, as has been noted earlier in this chapter.

Furthermore since the assessment tasks constructed for the current project were designed to be compatible with National Curriculum content, it was necessary to analyse the content carefully, in particular Level 1 content, as well as to consider closely the criterion-assessment system used, based on the statements of attainment.

Nelson and Frobisher (1993) showed that, in general, the statements of attainment in mathematics demanded a particular *action* or behaviour, for example, 'use', 'calculate' or 'solve', which was associated with a particular mathematical *content*. The content might take one of two forms. The first was a mathematical *operation*, for example, 'addition', the second was a description of the content upon which the operations would be carried out, for instance, 'number facts to 20 (including zero)'. Some statements also included a reference to the *context* in which the action would take place, for example, 'using a calculator where necessary'. As the writers noted, the possibilities for inconsistency of interpretation in each of the areas – action, content and context – were numerous. With the revised attainment targets the National Curriculum Council provided a large matrix of statements of attainment, each attainment target presented in the form of 'strands', in order to clarify the new and condensed form. Each of these attainment targets will be discussed briefly in turn as the assessment tasks devised for the project used the statements of attainment at Level 1 as well as relevant elements of the programme of study as a starting point for the design of assessment activities. Discussion here will focus on the revised National Curriculum. As the mathematical content did not change the revision did not have a major impact on the tasks devised.

Using and Applying Mathematics (Ma 1)

Assessment of Ma 1 was intended to ascertain pupils' ability to use and apply the content of the mathematics curriculum in Ma 2 (Number), Ma 3 (Algebra), Ma 4 (Shape and Space) and Ma 5 (Handling Data). The three strands were:

- Applications, choosing the appropriate mathematics and approach for solving problems;
- Mathematical communications, formulating, discussing, interpreting, recording and presenting findings in a variety of ways;
- Reasoning, logic and proof, finding answers, giving explanations, reasons and justification.

Comprehensive assessment of this attainment target would have required practical tasks involving all of the other attainment targets, which would not have been practicable. Furthermore, since children are required to work in groups in a range of tasks across a range of tests, the decision was made to assess only attainment targets 2 to 5 for the project.

Number (Ma 2)

The aim of this attainment was that:

Pupils should understand and use number, including estimation and approximation, interpreting results and checking for reasonableness. (DES, 1991, p. 5)

The statements of attainment at Level 1 indicated that 'pupils should be able to use number in the context of the classroom and school' and 'add and subtract using a small number of objects'. The programme of study indicated that pupils should engage in a range of activities involving:

- counting, reading, writing and ordering numbers to at least 10;
- learning that the size of a set is given by the last number in the count;
- understanding the language associated with number, e.g., 'more', 'fewer' and 'the same';
- understanding conservation of number;
- making a sensible estimate of a number of objects up to 10;
- using addition and subtraction, with numbers no greater than 10, in the context of real objects.

The programme of study, thus, provided more guidance for devising tasks for the project than the very general statements of attainment. The estimation procedure, for instance, displayed two arrays (6 oranges and 10 sweets) for five seconds and children were invited to say how many. The short exposure time was intended to ensure that children would determine numerosity by perception-based rather than by counting strategies.

Algebra (Ma 3)

The algebra attainment target required that:

Pupils should recognise and use symbolic and graphic representations to express relationships. (DES, 1991, p. 9)

There were not so many statements in the revised curriculum and, as was the case for Ma 2, these were very general and lacking in information about the content. The revised Level 1 statement, for instance, required children to 'devise repeating patterns' with the content supplied by the examples, 'a potato print pattern: red, red, blue, red, red, blue . . .' and so on, repeating itself after three elements. By contrast, the old statement required the child to 'copy, continue, and devise repeating patterns represented by objects/apparatus or one-digit numbers'. In this procedure children had the pattern task clearly modelled or demonstrated to them and the opportunity to copy from the model before they were asked to devise their own. This original procedure was the one adopted for the project.

Shape and Space (Ma 4)

This attainment target required that:

> Pupils should recognise and use the properties of two-dimensional (2-D) and three-dimensional (3-D) shapes and use measurement, location and transformation in the study of space. (DES, 1991, p. 13)

In this attainment target, as noted by Nelson and Frobisher (1993), there was much evidence of knowledge and skills introduced in the programme of study being assessed at higher levels. To take an example from Level 1, the statement required that pupils should 'talk about models they have made'. The programme of study specified six types of action: sorting shapes, classifying shapes, building shapes, drawing shapes, describing shapes and describing position. Only the last two actions are relevant to the Level 1 tasks. It was not until Level 2 that children were asked to use mathematical terms to describe common 2-D and 3-D shapes whilst building (construction) and drawing 2-D and 3-D shapes was not assessed until Level 4. At Level 1, it might be concluded, that it was the discussion which took place during the construction which was the focus of assessment but, as noted above, use of mathematical terms to describe 2-D and 3-D shapes was required at Level 2. Naming of shapes and description of their properties, then, was a requirement for attainment of Level 2. For the initial group of children assessed in the project children were provided firstly, with solid shapes for 'open exploration' and secondly, with Poleidoblocs to 'build with a purpose'. As no satisfactory criteria emerged to judge the completed constructions, for instance, complexity or symmetry, scoring was not attempted and the tasks were removed after Phase two. Talking about 3-D shapes, matching faces of 3-D shapes to 2-D shapes and drawing 2-D shapes, elements from the programme of study, were retained in the project assessment, as was use of common words for position in space and on a line and measurement language.

Handling Data (Ma 5)

The aim of this attainment target was that:

> Pupils should collect, process and interpret data and should understand, estimate and use probabilities. (DES, 1991, p. 17)

The three strands included collecting and processing data, representing and interpreting data and probability. As noted by Nelson and Frobisher (1993) in respect of Ma 4, the relationship between statements and programme of study elements was not close. This was particularly marked for probability at Levels 1 to 4, where three of eight elements in the programme of study had equivalent statements of attainment at their own level, three were not directly assessed but were important for later attainment levels and two elements were never assessed at all. A number of attempts was made to devise Level 1 tasks for probability ('recognizing possible outcomes of random events') for the project which were not successful. Bearing in mind that following the Dearing review (Dearing, 1994) the new Orders issued in November, 1994 eliminated probability from Key Stage 1 altogether, the decision taken not to attempt to assess this aspect of handling data in the project was vindicated. The correspondence between Ma 5, Level 1a: 'sort a set of objects, describing the criteria chosen,' and the programme of study: 'selecting criteria for sorting a set of objects and applying them consistently', is described by Nelson and Frobisher (1993) as 'moderate'. Asking children to sort a set of objects and requiring a description of the criteria chosen is more demanding than simply selecting criteria and applying them consistently for sorting a set of objects. For the project children were asked to sort under both conditions.

Issues of Validity and Reliability in National Curriculum Assessment

Some of the assessment tasks devised for the project were criterion-referenced, defined in terms of National Curriculum statements of attainment. Consequently it was important to examine the issues of validity and reliability which such assessment raises and which, in fact, have surrounded the debate concerning National Curriculum assessment. In respect of construct validity this was ensured by checking the logical analysis of subject content in the National Curriculum attainment targets and programmes of study against the empirical analysis provided by the knowledge base related to the development of children's mathematical thinking. This operation provided the means to ensure all appropriate content was included and properly ordered and, hence, content validity was also ensured. Inferences within and outside the domain of assessment, thus, warranted both validity and dependability. Furthermore accurate definition in assessment allowed clear specification of tasks and prolonged engagement allowed trust building with the children concerned. Inferences about the parts of the domain being assessed were also warranted and, hence, reliability was ensured.

The tasks designed for the project, therefore, took full account of issues of validity, dependability and reliability. The feasibility and appropriateness of a busy classroom teacher carrying out this type of assessment will be explored more fully in the next section.

Conclusion

If children's out-of-school mathematical knowledge is best accessed by individual interview, observation and discussion this stands in some contrast to the monitoring and assessment of the formal school mathematics curriculum for a full class of children with all the attendant problems associated with reliability, validity and dependability. As noted earlier, Resnick (1987) referred to the 'actual and possible' relationship between formal schooling and informal, everyday practical competence. As soon as classroom assessment is examined more closely a number of issues is raised which has implications for considering more than just the child as a learner in school and outside, in fact, more specifically the role of the teacher as assessor, the nature of the judgments being made, as well as the context in which the assessment is being made. Most important, as noted by Shorrocks *et al.* (1993) and as demonstrated in the previous section, is that judgments made are based on valid and appropriate evidence in order that well-informed decisions are made concerning what needs to be learned next. This also requires knowledge about the subject matter being assessed, about the nature of assessment and its role in the teaching-learning process.

Merrtons and Vass (1991) suggested that in the past teachers recorded what they had taught and not what children had learned. Effective teaching, however, is less likely to occur if children's learning is not monitored and recorded. Detailed evaluation of learning encourages ongoing formative assessment and, more significantly, leads to planning which takes place in contact with learning needs. Until the introduction of the National Curriculum, as Shorrocks *et al.* (1993) suggested, classroom assessment took place, in Britain at least, in a largely unexamined way. In many cases, of course, changes required were little more than making more explicit and more consistent what was existing good practice. These changes entailed collecting and annotating samples of work more systematically, discussing more carefully and observing classroom processes more closely as the basis for evidence upon which to base judgments about individual needs. In some cases, however, existing practice was not sufficiently rigorous and required a more radical change in curriculum planning and implementation to incorporate appropriate assessment into classroom processes.

A major role identified for assessment has been the monitoring of learning to inform teaching decisions on a day-to-day basis. In this respect assessment is an integral part of the interactions between teacher, pupils and the learning materials. As Harlen and Qualter (1991) pointed out some teachers who practice this formative assessment may not recognize what they are doing as assessment since they see assessment as a formal activity distinct from teaching. In fact assessment will vary from general impressions of behaviour or performance derived from unstructured observations and recollections through more structured observation and discussion with more specific points in mind, to specific activities designed to provide systematic information of a precise kind. It is difficult, as they noted, to conceive teaching which does not use some information about the learners in order to determine the starting point of the intended learning. The information obtained may concern, for instance, what is and what is not known to be used in order to 'fill gaps' and to add to what is 'already there'.

Harlen, Gipps, Broadfoot and Nuttall (1992) suggested that assessment in education is the process of gathering, interpreting, recording and using information about pupils' responses to educational tasks. At one end of the dimension of formality, the task may be normal classroom work and the process of gathering information will involve observation or listening to what a pupil is doing or saying. At the other end of the dimension of formality the task may be a written and timed exercise which is read and marked according to strict criteria.

The danger may lie, as noted by Davis (1995), in an over-emphasis on the satisfaction of the technical criteria of reliability and validity in teacher assessment to the detriment of learning, through insufficient attention paid to proper objectives concerning the development of children's knowledge and understanding. The problem lies in the attempt to characterize the rich and interconnectedness of knowledge which children possess in ways which are simple without rendering them superficial. On the one hand, improvement of consistency and, hence, reliability in criterion-referenced assessment leads inevitably to distortion of such knowledge but, on the other hand, as the first year of Key Stage 1 standard assessment tasks (SATs) showed, complex practical assessment even if it has a spurious validity is, by its very nature, unreliable.

This is not to devalue teacher assessment which is fundamental to good teaching. Rather it is to suggest that the extent to which an assessment is reliable in gaining consistent results over a number of occasions may relate directly to the crudity of information obtained. Sensitive and, thereby, more valid measures may yet be developed but reliability can only be approached as tasks become more and more prescribed and further and further removed from the rich understanding they seek to capture. The argument, as noted by Davis (1995), is conceptual rather than empirical and appeals to empirical research may be futile since the nature of what it is to know and use knowledge in an intelligent and informed manner will be difficult to locate, never mind to access reliably.

Similarly, the notion of match (Bennett *et al.*, 1984) which assumes that teachers can design tasks to introduce new knowledge, to enable children to apply what they know to new situations, to practise skills or to review earlier learning and, moreover, that researchers can judge the success of this, is bound to underestimate the complexity of learning. As noted by Davis (1993), detailed and accurate inspection of current knowledge and skills is unavailable, in principle. Hence, we cannot be 'scientific' about whether a task appropriately encourages the application of such knowledge to unfamiliar contexts.

> Teachers, of course, can make rough and ready yet sensible judgements here. But their answers cannot, and should not be expected to sustain 'accurate' fine-grained measurements of matching. (Davis, 1993, p. 277)

To ensure learning with understanding, teachers must take account of information about existing ideas and skills. If, however, they attempt to become fine-grained in their appraisals of matching:

> they are forced to attempt close-meshed judgements about (a) current knowledge and (b) new knowledge. At this level the notions both of 'newness' and of the pupil's 'current knowledge state' become elusive and problematic. (Davis, 1993, p. 269)

Chapter 2 and Chapter 3 have already indicated the richness and complexity of teaching just as Chapter 3 and Chapter 4 have attempted to describe what it means to know and to understand mathematics from the point of view of cognitive science, from the perspective of research on classroom practice and from empirical investigations of young children learning mathematics. At the beginning of

Chapter 4 it was noted that Resnick (1987) had pointed to the discontinuities between schooling and daily life as well as the relationship between the 'actual' and the 'possible' in teaching. The decision to investigate the pedagogical subject knowledge of reception teachers was made with the full realization that they occupied a pivotal position with a responsibility, on the one hand, to take account of children's existing, practical knowledge of mathematics gained in out-of-school settings and, on the other hand, to prepare to move them forward through the formal school curriculum.

5 Investigating the Mathematical Knowledge and Competences Which Young Children Bring into School

Introduction

Chapters 1 and 2 pointed to a need for further investigation of teachers' pedagogical subject knowledge which lies between subject content knowledge, on the one hand, and pedagogy, on the other, and is characterized by the ability to represent key concepts and ideas in a variety of ways interesting and meaningful to young children. It requires an appreciation of pupils' existing knowledge, their typical errors and misconceptions.

Chapter 3, thus, explored ways of knowing and understanding mathematics from the point of view of classroom practice, from the point of view of instructional theory and from the perspective of the young learner constructing mathematics. Chapter 4, then presented both the rich, empirical knowledge base which has delineated the development of children's mathematical thinking and understanding and outlined the current National Curriculum and assessment context.

The project was designed with the overall aim to consider the co-ordination and utilization of teacher and pupil mathematical knowledge in reception classrooms as described in Chapter 2. Before attempting to establish what knowledge of, and beliefs concerning pupils' existing mathematical understanding teachers had (if any), how they assessed this and whether they took account of it when organizing instruction, it was essential first to establish what mathematical knowledge the children had at school entry. Accordingly the focus of Phase 1 of the project and the topic of this chapter was the investigation of the current knowledge, strategies and representations young children brought into school, as a starting point for accessing teachers' understanding of the way children think about mathematics and knowledge about their own pupils' mathematical understanding.

This chapter will, therefore, investigate the informal mathematical knowledge young children bring into school, accessed before formal instruction began.

Aims

As noted in Chapter 4, the project began at exactly the same time as the National Curriculum was introduced. It was assumed this might lead not only to change in the content of the mathematics curriculum but also in views held on learning mathematics and the nature of instruction. The main aim for Phase 1 of the project was, thus, to examine the current knowledge, strategies and representations held by young children at their start of school. Assessment tasks compatible with key areas of the National Curriculum for mathematics were used to give ecological validity to the situation in which children would find themselves.

Children

Saxe, Guberman and Gearhart (1987) investigated the interplay between social and developmental processes in children's numerical understanding in working and middle class home settings. Four-year-olds from middle class homes displayed greater competence on tasks with more complex numerical goals than did their working class peers. This competence was paralleled at home with variations in the complexity of everyday number tasks carried out with adjustment of goal structure to reflect children's responses by middle class mothers and corresponding adjustment of the goals by children in response to their mothers' efforts. Klein and Starkey (1988) have begun to explore links between mathematics learning and particular social contexts of development in both western and non-western cultures. There is sufficient evidence to show that cultural differences in mathematical learning experiences lead children to construct different levels and kinds of mathematical competence. This evidence persuaded the writer that the sample of children chosen for the project should be as socially and ethnically diverse as possible.

Accordingly schools were selected which represented a mixed social and rich cultural diverse intake. The class chosen to try out the tasks was small as another intake of children was planned for the subsequent term but was represented by English, Turkish, Afro-Caribbean and Japanese children from varied social backgrounds. There were nine boys and seven girls with ages ranging from 4 years and 4 months to 5 years (mean age 4 years and 6 months). Four schools, two urban and two rural, were selected after refinement of the tasks. One of the urban schools which received a mixed social and ethnically diverse intake was used in the pilot phase of the project, the other received a middle class intake from the surrounding private housing estate. Both schools were infant schools with junior schools on the adjoining campus. Of the two rural schools selected one received an intake experiencing high levels of social disadvantage and the other rural school received advantaged, middle class children from the village and surrounding countryside areas. The two rural schools were both combined infant-junior schools. Maximum variation in the schools' intake was sought, therefore, through the involvement of urban and rural schools with high, low and mixed socio-economic intake. Twelve children (six boys and six girls) were selected randomly from each setting for assessment. Their ages ranged from 4 years 2 months to 4 years 6 months (mean age 4 years 3 months).

Tasks

The tasks were constructed to represent Level 1 of the attainment targets and programme of study of the National Curriculum and including the main areas of:

number, algebra, shape and space, and handling data (National Curriculum Council, 1989). As described in Chapter 4, the National Curriculum programme of study was introduced for 5 to 7-year-old children from September, 1989. Although reception children were not officially included the concern to demonstrate educational 'value added' was anticipated to have an impact on reception class teaching and assessment. As already noted, Using and Applying Mathematics (Ma 1) was not included since a comprehensive assessment of this would have required practical tasks using all the other attainment targets with children working in groups over a range of activities.

Assessment of number was also designed to reflect the range of numerical competences that develop in the pre-school years, and where possible existing procedures were taken from the literature, for instance, from Saxe (1987) who, in turn, adapted tasks from Ginsburg and Russell (1981).

The assessment tasks were constructed to form the basis of long, practical assessment interviews with individual children. The assumption was made that if the tasks involved everyday objects and activities familiar to children then they would actively construct meaning with the interviewer, thus, offering an indication of their current level of knowledge and understanding, their strategies and forms of representation. The writer, as researcher, trained as a primary teacher and an experienced educational psychologist carried out most of the interviews. The interviewer sat in the classroom from the end of the children's second week in school, working first with those children most willing and confident. This allowed other and more cautious children to become familiar with the interviewer and the nature of the procedures being carried out. The assessment was lengthy and typically spread over more than a full school day, with breaks. Activities were varied to sustain interest, and assessment discontinued when children lost interest, showed signs of fatigue or flagging interest.

All the assessments took place in the first half of the children's first term in school in order to record informal knowledge acquired in out-of-school contexts rather than mathematical skills and procedures learned in school. Individual assessment schedules were prepared providing both detailed instructions for administration and allowing space for recording each response as well as any noteworthy behaviour. An individual file was kept for each child which included the completed schedule, any written responses of the child and photographs of constructions produced for a shape and space task.

Tests 1 to 9 comprised the number tasks, Test 10 algebra, Test 11 measurement, Tests 12 and 13 shape and space and Tests 14 and 15 handling data.

Test 1   Counting words, based on the procedure of Saxe *et al.* (1987).

The purpose of this task was to determine how far children could say the counting words to a panda puppet in the conventional order. Of the two trials, the highest number the child achieved without violating the conventional number order was used as a measure of the child's rote counting. Any unconventional portion containing omissions at the end was recorded where possible.

Test 2 Counting objects within 10, based on Gelman and Gallistel (1978).

This task was designed to check the child's ability to count, pairing the number sequence with countable items, and governed by the five principles outlined in Chapter 4. Children were asked to count an array of three and seven small wooden horses, first in a line and then a circle, and then to extract smaller sub-sets (4 and 10) from a larger set of 12. In terms of classification the last two items constituted what Carpenter, Fennema, Peterson and Carey (1988) described as 'separate'-type word problem (action of removing a sub-set from a given set), with result unknown. The number of correct responses out of a possible six was recorded.

Test 3 Order invariance, based on a procedure from Baroody (1979), Gelman and Gallistel (1978) and Ginsburg and Russell (1981).

The purpose of this task was to assess the child's understanding that arrays can be counted in different orders and that each order yields the same value. Children were asked to count two set sizes (four and six wooden farm animals), starting first from the extreme left, next starting from the extreme right and finally, starting from the middle. The task, thus, required the child to count objects and understand the cardinality principle (the last number represents the number of items in the set regardless of the order in which the objects are counted). The number of correct responses out of six was recorded as well as any noteworthy behaviour.

Test 4 Reading numbers, based on a procedure of Saxe *et al.* (1987).

The purpose of this task was to assess children's ability to recognize written numerals by presenting pictures of everyday objects or people bearing numbers 1 to 10, 12, 15, and 27. The number of correct responses out of a possible 13 was recorded.

Test 5 Writing numbers, based on a procedure of Hughes (1986).

The child was presented with a large piece of paper and a pencil, arrays of bricks of different quantities (1 to 10), and asked to put something on the paper to show the panda how many bricks there were. Note was made of the correct numerals written, other forms of representation used, for example, dots, dashes or squares, and the child's accuracy in recording the quantity of bricks displayed.

Test 6 Ordering numbers, based on work of Carpenter, Fennema and Peterson (1987).

This suggested that children begin to develop more abstract and flexible counting strategies through counting on forwards and counting backwards.

The purpose of this task was to see whether any of the children had developed strategies for counting on forwards or backwards, possibly indicating the beginnings of 'derived facts' strategies. The child was asked what number came after/before randomly presented numbers 1 to 12, 14, 16 and 20. The number of correct 'forwards' and 'backwards' responses was recorded.

Test 7 Understanding number operations of addition and subtraction based on work of Carpenter, Fennema, Peterson and Carey (1988).

This task involved the very simplest word problems identified by Carpenter *et al.* (1988): 'join' and 'separate' problems, with result unknown allowing the use of direct modelling strategies. The interviewer gave the child a hand puppet and placed a pile of one penny coins on the table. The child was told:

> Puppet wants to buy some icecream so I gave him three pennies. But wait, he says he really needs four pennies. Can you fix it so that he really gets four . . . ? and so on.

This procedure was repeated for $4 + . = 6$, $5 + . = 8$, $6 + . = 10$ and $4 + . = 9$.
A similar procedure was adopted for subtraction, the interviewer saying:

> Puppet wants to buy a bag of sweets so I have given him five pennies. But wait, he says he really needs four pennies. Can you fix it so that he gets four pennies . . . ?

This procedure was repeated for $6 - . = 4$, $5 - . = 2$, $8 - . = 4$ and $9 - . = 4$.
For both addition and subtraction tasks, if the child made no response or made an incorrect response for either an addition or subtraction task one prompt was offered: 'Can you count them?' The number of correct addition and subtraction responses was recorded and any observable strategies or interesting behaviour noted.

Test 8 Division as sharing, adapted from Desforges and Desforges (1980).

The purpose of this task was to investigate children's understanding of social sharing and the strategies they used; in particular, how they dealt with a remainder. Set sizes of 4, 5, 6 and 9 were used and two divisors: 2 and 3. Two or three teddies were set before the child, with a pile of sweets in front of the teddies. The child was then asked to share the sweets between the bears . . . 'so it was fair'.

In order to investigate any possible relationship between social sharing and multiplication as continuous addition, the child was asked two additional questions (without concrete materials being offered): 'How many legs have 2 ducks got?' 'How many wheels are there on 3 cars?'

Scores out of a possible five for social sharing and two for multiplication were recorded as well as any noteworthy behaviour, particularly with respect to the child's treatment of the remainder.

Test 9   Estimation, based on the National Curriculum requirement that children should make a 'sensible estimate of a number of objects up to 10'.

Each child was presented with a bowl of 6 oranges, and a plate of 10 jelly crocodiles, for a maximum of three seconds to avoid his/her counting, and asked how many objects he/she thought there were. The child's response to each item was recorded as well as any other worthwhile observation.

Test 10   Algebra, based on the National Curriculum requirement that children should 'copy, continue and devise repeating patterns'.

In this task the child was asked to copy and to continue first, a pattern of alternative red and green blocks, then a pattern of three contrasting plastic coins, £1, 50p and 2p. Finally the child was presented with a set of objects, contrasting in shape and colour and asked to construct her/his own pattern. Correct responses out of a possible four were recorded and a description of the child's own pattern made.

Test 11   Estimation of measures, based on the National Curriculum requirement that children should 'compare and order objects without measuring'.

For this test dolls, teddies, pencils, paper kites of different sizes were used, as well as bricks of different weight and jugs with different amounts of orange juice. Children were asked to compare items and to match the appropriate item with the appropriate measurement language, for example, longest, thinnest, taller, heavier.

Test 12   Shape and space based on the National Curriculum requirement that children should 'sort and classify 2-D and 3-D shapes,' build and describe 3-D and draw 2-D shapes.

In the first part of this test children were invited to make an open exploration of a set of Dime solids. In the next part of the test children were presented with wooden blocks of various sizes or shapes and two plastic cars. They were asked to make a garage for the cars.

In the second part of the test children were asked to describe faces of solid shapes (a cube, a cuboid, a cylinder, a cone, a triangular prism and a triangular pyramid). In the third section of this test children were asked to match the appropriate face of the same six solids to an outline drawing on a sheet of paper. In the case of two of the solids, the prism and the cuboid, depending on the way the solid was picked up, there was the possibility of the child needing to rotate the solid in order to match it correctly to the outline on the paper. In the fourth section, children were asked to copy each of the set of shapes drawn on the paper (a small and large circle, a small equilateral and a large isosceles triangle, a square and a rectangle).

Test 13   Shape and space, based on the National Curriculum requirement that children should use common words 'to describe a position'.

Children were asked to tell the researcher where a naughty little lamb was hiding from his mother sheep. The intention was to generate position words, in (side), under (below), next to (near/beside), on, above (higher up) and behind.

Since the objective was to determine understanding, where children were unable or unwilling to use position words, the child was invited to hide the naughty little lamb in the appropriate position following the interviewer's instructions, in order that receptive understanding could be determined.

Test 14   Handling data, based on the National Curriculum requirement that children should 'sort a set of objects, describing the criteria chosen'.

Here children were asked to sort, first, a set of dolls and a set of tiny, sorting toys. They were then encouraged to state the basis, or criteria used, for the sort.

Test 15   Handling data, based on the National Curriculum requirement that children should engage in 'recording with objects or drawing'.

For this task the same group of dolls was sorted but this time to given criteria (girl and boy dolls). Children were then asked whether they could represent this sort on paper.

This phase of the project spanned the time when the revised National Curriculum attainment targets were introduced but since this largely reorganized rather than changed the content, as noted in Chapter 4, it did not affect the tasks. Some slight modification to the existing tasks took place after the tasks had been administered to the first class to ensure all number tasks were equivalent to Level 1 attainment of the National Curriculum and to reduce the number of items in one task.

Correct responses for each child were summed, and qualitative aspects of the child's response recorded on a simple masters/non-masters basis.

Results

Counting ranged from one (one child was able to repeat only 'one' and another child only 'one, two') to 101, with a mean sequence length of 21. The majority of children (48 per cent) counted within the range of 11 to 20, 31 per cent within the range of 1 to 10 and 15 per cent within the range of 21 to 30. The rest counted beyond this. In this sample there did seem to be some tendency, as noted by Ginsburg (1977) and Fuson (1988), for children to finish counting with numbers ending in 9 or 0 suggesting early, implicit understanding of the decade structure.

For *counting objects within 10*, 50 per cent of the children were able to count 3 and 7 animals (in a line and in a circle) and another 21 per cent of the children were able to count 3 and 7 animals, in either one or other of these two conditions. A further 21 per cent of children were able to count 3 animals only and 8 per cent had nil scores. Some 31 per cent were able to extract sub-sets of 4 and 10 out of a set of 12, 38 per cent were able to extract a sub-set of 4 only, and 6 per cent were able to extract a sub-set of 10 only. 25 per cent had nil scores.

For the *order invariance* task children were asked to count an array of 4 and 6 farm animals starting from the left, from the right and from the middle. 81 per cent of children scored, 4, 5, or 6 out of a total of 6 items, 2 per cent scored 3, 13 per cent scored 1 or 2 and 4 per cent scored nil. Taken together, the results of the counting tasks (Test 1, 2 and 3) showed that children were learning number words, mapping these onto their existing number knowledge and using them in quantitative situations.

For *reading randomly presented numerals* (1 to 10, 12, 15 and 27) scores were again spread. 25 per cent of children recognized 10 or more numerals, 25 per cent recognized between 5 to 9 numbers, 31 per cent recognized between 2 to 4 numbers and 19 per cent of children recognized none or one. Young children often appear to learn first those numbers which have personal associations, such as their own age and the ages of siblings or house numbers. Findings from a later phase of the project (Suggate *et al.* (1996), unpublished) have suggested that numbers 1 and 4 are memorable and 2 less so, with a sharp drop in accurate responses above 10.

For *writing numbers*, where children were asked to put something on a piece of paper to represent different quantities of bricks (1 to 10), all children were willing to offer some sort of representation for a mean of 8 out of 10 presentations. Some drew round the blocks, some drew circles, some drew squares, some dots and some tally marks, U-shapes and squiggles. 15 per cent of the children could write at least some of the numbers, typically 1 to 4 or 1 to 5, sometimes with 6 and 7 as well. 4 per cent of the children knew how to write all of the numbers up to 10. Children invented ways of representing numbers they did not know from a combination of numbers they *did* know, such as 6 represented as 1, 2, 3. They recorded confidently the numbers they could recall and then swapped to invented representations when formal knowledge was exhausted. One child who wrote numbers up to 4 then added tally marks to number 4 to represent higher numbers. Another child who could write numbers up to 5 wrote 5 5 for 10 and 4 5 for 9. One child started drawing round the blocks but then switched to representing the blocks by circles. One child lined up the blocks on the paper and drew a line exactly the same length to represent them. Reversals of 2, 3 and 7 were common. Some reversed 5 and many had difficulty recalling 4, confusing it with the capital letter A or Y. Whilst some children reversed 6, many had difficulty in recalling 9. There were a number of reversals of 9 and two children who were unsure wrote 6 and 9!

Scores for *counting on forwards or backwards one number* (for numbers within 10) were very spread. 35.5 per cent of children were able to count on forwards one number for 8 to 10 randomly presented numbers, 25 per cent of children counted on forwards for 4 to 7 numbers, 27 per cent of children counted on forwards for 1 to 3 numbers and 12.5 per cent had nil scores. 17 per cent of children were able to count backwards for 8 to 10 randomly presented numbers, 15 per cent of children were able to count backwards for 8 to 10 randomly presented numbers, 15 per cent of children counted backwards for 4 to 7 numbers, 50 per cent

Figure 5.1: Children's Representations of Quantity

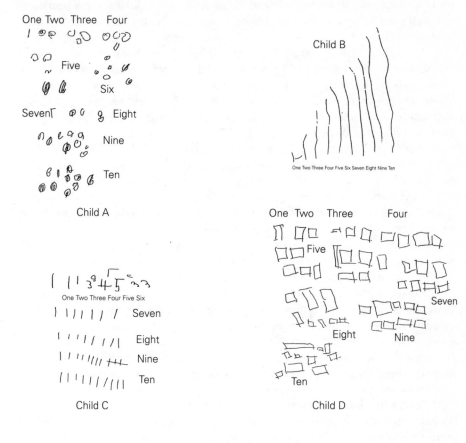

One Two Three Four

Five

Six

Seven Eight

Nine

Ten

Child A

Child B

One Two Three Four Five Six Seven Eight Nine Ten

One Two Three Four Five Six

Seven

Eight

Nine

Ten

Child C

One Two   Three   Four

Five

Seven

Eight   Nine

Ten

Child D

One   Two   Three   Four

Five   Seven

Eight Nine Ten

Child E

One Two Three Four Five Six Seven Eight Nine Ten

Child F

One Two Three Four Five Six Seven Eight Nine Ten

Child G

counted backwards for only 1 to 3 numbers and 19 per cent counted backwards for none of the presented numbers. Results suggested that the children were beginning to develop flexibility in counting on from a given number but found counting back harder.

For *simple addition*, 45 per cent of children scored 5 out of 5, 6 per cent scored 4, 8 per cent scored 3, 25 per cent scored 2, 6 per cent scored 1 and 10 per cent scored nil. For *simple subtraction*, 54 per cent scored 5 out of 5, 9 per cent scored 4, 4 per cent scored 3, 2 per cent scored 2, 18 per cent scored 1 and 13 per cent scored nil. The results showed that around half of the children were able to carry out simple addition and subtraction operations with concrete materials. At least a third, however, had difficulty with both operations.

For *social sharing*, children were asked to share set sizes of 4, 5, 6 and 9 between two divisors: 2 and 3 teddies. 62 per cent of children scored 5 out of 5, 11 per cent scored 4, 19 per cent scored 3, 2 per cent scored 2, 4 per cent scored 1 and 2 per cent scored nil. Children managed this task successfully and distributed sweets fairly. There were no instances of 'dumping'.

For the *multiplication as continuous addition* tasks (without concrete material) scores were spread with 65 per cent of children answering both questions correctly, 12 per cent answering one correctly and 23 per cent answering neither question.

The *estimation* task was difficult to administer as all the children, except the 2 without counting skills, immediately started to count the items when asked to guess and were confused when prompted again to guess and the items were removed. 17 per cent of children correctly estimated the number of 6 oranges in a bowl, with 34 per cent estimating 5, 6 per cent estimating 7. For the estimation of 10 jelly crocodiles on a plate 19 per cent of children correctly estimated 10, 2 per cent estimated 11 and none estimated 9.

For the *algebra* task 25 per cent of children were able to copy and continue a model pattern of simple repeating red and green blocks, 38 per cent of children were able to manage one of the two tasks and 34 per cent of children managed neither.

Other tasks administered in general showed good understanding of the language of measurement (mean score 19 out of 25), position in space and on a line (mean score of 5 out of 6); selecting criteria for sorting (mastery for 85 per cent) and representing these, using the objects concerned (mastery for 96 per cent); exploring and building with 3-D shapes, and matching 3-D to 2-D shapes. No inference was placed on performance of shape and space and handling data tasks beyond noting mastery or non-mastery. For copying forms 94 per cent of children were able to draw a circle, 81 per cent drew a square or rectangle, with only 21 per cent managing to draw a triangle. These results are in line with developmental scales which show most children being able to draw a triangle by 7 years. Descriptions of regular 3-D shapes produced the same mixture of formal and informal responses as other areas:

> . . . it's like a square, like an oblong, like a wheel, like a tent . . . a rectangle, a square, round, a triangle, a witch's hat.

In Test 12, for open exploration and building with a purpose, provisional constructs of complexity and elaboration did not provide a sound basis for assigning a masters/non masters category and the decision was taken to discontinue use of this test after Phase 1.

The children reaching the longest number word sequences in rote counting had consistently high scores across the number and algebra tests, including recognizing and writing numbers, and counting on forwards and backwards one number. Other children with rote counting above the mean had more uneven scores. Some children with rote counting below the mean, however, scored well across the tests. Children with a high performance on either rote counting, or counting on forwards and backwards one number, or both, tended to show competence in other simple number operations such as addition and subtraction and social sharing. Other children, who had a low attainment across the number tests showed competence in operations, such as addition and subtraction and social sharing, with small numbers only. Two 'non-counters' repeatedly gained nil scores for tasks presented, though, as a postscript it can be reported that when the same group of children was re-tested half way through Year 1 one of these children had caught up with peers. The other child still had only very rudimentary skills.

Discussion

The high attaining children were well towards mastery of Level 1 of the National Curriculum Mathematics on school entry. The low attaining children brought into school a range of informal competences and a less stable, conventional knowledge. They might switch from earlier strategies to formal counting procedures when prompted to do so but the concern for precision and accuracy was not always strong. Inaccuracy increased with the size of the numbers involved in the operations, or in the abstractness of the task. The demonstration of such early competences poses challenges to the conventional reception class curriculum which follows a sequence of sorting, matching and classifying, joining and separating of sets, counting and ordering, recognizing and writing numbers 0 to 10, where simple mathematic relationships may be demonstrated through the use of concrete material, and topics such as measurement, shape and pictorial representation run alongside. Whilst they may not possess the formal conventions for representing it, many reception-age children clearly enter school having acquired already much of this mathematical content.

In terms of specific teaching implications as in early reading stages, in early stages of learning mathematics, perhaps too children could be prompted to extend the range of strategies at their disposal so that their natural inventiveness is not undermined by a struggle to find the one single, convergent and acceptable response. Dutch teaching, for instance, encourages problem-solving which has more than one acceptable solution.

An example would be 'How many animals (pigs and hens) can there be if there are 8 legs altogether?' This means building on the range of alternative solutions children, themselves, generate as was commonplace in the innovative practice described in Chapter 3. Later these could be used to compare and consider by children in terms of their utility and their efficiency and accuracy, provided that flexibility in approach has been maintained. Most important would appear to be the opportunity to move gradually through different stages of mathematical representation from personal to formal in real, everyday problem-solving situations, where children can learn the interrelationship among ideas and link their own informal knowledge and strategies to more conventional procedures. Perhaps this calls for the provision of the individualized tutoring in early mathematics which is accepted as prerequisite to the development of flexible reading strategies. It assumes, moreover, that teachers are aware of the informal mathematical knowledge brought into school, children's early invented strategies, and the stages through which these pass. Whilst to provide fully for each child's learning profile in classroom teaching would not be possible, it is important that activities are planned to offer opportunities to use the problem-solving skills children already possess and to extend their knowledge of number facts. The innovative practice described in Chapter 3 has demonstrated this can be achieved in a variety of ways in classroom contexts. With increasing use of calculators and computers in school children continue to need both a facility in mental arithmetic and a number sense to self-check responses made.

There is some evidence from the literature that 'expert' strategies can be taught, for instance, Steinberg's (1985) teaching of 'derived' strategies in addition and subtraction (using known number facts to find the solution to unknown number facts). It may, thus, be equally important for more advanced procedures to be directly taught. Cockcroft (1982) noted that children do not benefit enough from teacher exposition related to mathematical content.

Empirical investigation of young children's construction of mathematical knowledge provides both a starting point for designing an appropriate reception curriculum and a means of critical analysis of existing curricula based on logical analysis of subject content. It remains now for us to consider the development of instruction by the creation of a curriculum content and sequence which both reflects and advances the structure of children's existing forms of representation, problem-solving and knowledge.

Conclusion

The project passed through a number of phases. The overall purpose of Phase 1 was to identify what was salient to the investigation of teachers' pedagogical subject knowledge and to prepare for the more focused investigation of this in the main phases of the project (to be described in Chapters 7 and 8).

Having established the informal knowledge which children brought into school and discussed the possible implications for the reception curriculum the next step was to consider the extent, if at all, teachers themselves were aware of, and took account of, this when planning the reception curriculum. Data concerning children's informal mathematical knowledge, thus, provided a starting point for accessing teachers' understanding of the way children think about mathematics and the way they plan and organise the reception curriculum. Chapter 6 will now present Phase 2 data which related to teachers' reports of their reception class practice. This will then be examined in the light of subsequent lesson observations.

6 Reporting on Teachers' Classroom Practice

Introduction

Phase 1 of the project investigated the mathematical knowledge, strategies and representations that a small group of young children brought into school and after a slight refinement of tasks, provided the detailed assessment of informal mathematical knowledge of a larger group of reception-aged children. These findings were reported in Chapter 5. Since the overall aim of the project was to investigate teachers' pedagogical subject knowledge, Phase 2 sought to investigate teachers' reported planning of the reception curriculum, their pedagogical decision-making and, in particular, the extent to which, if at all, teachers were aware of, and took account of, their children's existing knowledge through topics taught and the active encouragement of children's own construction of knowledge. Accordingly, this chapter will describe teachers' reported classroom practice. This will then be considered in the light of subsequent lesson observations over children's first year in school first, for a group of four reception teachers and second, for a group of seven reception teachers who took part in a subsequent phase.

Aims

The main intention of Phase 2 was to consider reception teachers' planning of the reception curriculum and their knowledge and beliefs concerning teaching and learning mathematics.

Specifically, the aims were to:

- carry out open-ended interviews with reception teachers to investigate their pedagogical decision-making and, in particular, the extent to which account was taken of such informal mathematical knowledge as children possessed;
- consider teachers' reported practice in the light of subsequent lesson observation.

Teachers

The first four reception teachers involved were very experienced and in the 40 to 50-year age range in order to ensure that any differences in reported practice could not be attributed to lack of experience. All four had received three-year college of education training. The second group of seven teachers were, again, experienced, college of education trained and in the 40 to 50-year age range with one, novice teacher, in her early years of experience.

After this phase of the project was completed it was recognized that maximum variation in class teachers' own education and training had not been sought and it became apparent that in order to gain a more comprehensive understanding of teachers' pedagogical subject knowledge it was necessary to include the variety of training routes into primary education.

Teacher Interviews

Interviews carried out with the first four reception teachers were unstructured. Since their current classes had been assessed already teachers knew that the interviewer was interested in children's informal mathematical knowledge. With this in mind, it was explained that the aim of the interview was to find out what sort of teaching and learning of mathematics was planned and took place during the first year of children's formal schooling. It was hoped that by not structuring the interview too closely what teachers construed as important would emerge. Specific questions were asked about one area only. In response to the findings of the study that children bring into school informal strategies for dealing with addition and subtraction problems, teachers were asked whether they introduced addition and subtraction during the reception year and, if so, when and how. This offered one measure of their appreciation of young children's informal knowledge.

The open-ended interview went through a number of stages. These included:

- Introduction and warm up, when the writer as interviewer reminded teachers of the purpose of the project and, as warm up, asked 'What is a typical mathematical activity for you?'
- Delineation of topics, which took place when the teacher was involved and ready to deal with substantive issues. Sample questions like, 'Can you tell me about the mathematical topics that it is important to teach to young children?' reflected the intention of this phase to identify as many aspects as possible of planning, teaching and organizing the reception curriculum.
- Dealing with topics, which took place when the teacher had volunteered as many topics as possible. The interviewer then moved back to explore each topic in more depth.

When all the topics had been explored the interviewer introduced the questions concerning if, when and how simple addition and subtraction were introduced to young children in teaching.

Whilst assessment of children's informal knowledge of these teachers took place at the beginning of the school year, the interviews took place towards the end of the school year, after the summer half term holiday. This ensured that the teachers interviewed actually reported the learning and teaching experiences which assessed children had received.

All interviews were recorded and transcribed. They were analysed in two steps: unitizing and categorizing. The purpose of the unitizing step was to identify and record essential information units. The definition of the unit used was simply: a single piece of information able to stand by itself (understandable outside the context of additional supportive information). It might be a single sentence in the transcript, for example, 'all work is topic-based' or as much as a paragraph. In either case the material in the unit was self-explanatory. The interview transcripts were read carefully sentence by sentence to check whether that sentence carried broad relevance to the aims of this phase of the project. If so it was entered on card which was carefully coded with the designation of the school and teacher interviewed so that content could be traced back to raw transcription data.

The purpose of the categorizing process was to bring these cards relating to the same content together in a loose taxonomy. The process is largely analytic-inductive but also rule-governed, though these rules should emerge as part of the categorization process. At this stage each interview was treated separately to devise a category system which handled the unit cards satisfactorily. The process is in accord with the method of 'constant comparison' described by Glaser and Strauss (1967).

In summary, the categorization process involved sorting unit cards into groupings of similar content and devising a rule to describe the nature of the content included. That is, as Skrtic (1985) noted, tacit knowledge used to judge the cards was translated into propositional language of a rule for classification. As the categorization process proceeded it became clear that there was little disparity across teacher interviews. This was partly because they contained content related logically to established categories that were based on the same professional activity. This is not to say that the contents of the categories were identical. Any differences were considered and the rule and, or content considered for adjustment. The process continued until all categories had been accounted for. These were then translated into tables grouping content under category headings for each teacher in order for comparison between teachers to be undertaken.

Classroom Observations

A more detailed description of classroom observations will be provided in Chapters 7 and 8. Suffice it to say, for the purposes of the current chapter, that once a week over the reception year one mathematics lesson was observed, audio-taped and transcribed each week, for each of the four teachers involved in the main phase of the study and for each of the seven teachers involved in the subsequent phase. The number of lessons for each teacher which included addition and subtraction was identified and the nature of the activity examined, that is, the context in which the operation took place, the representation used (verbal, concrete action, pictorial or diagrammatic) and whether the task was teacher-led or carried out independently by the pupils.

Results

Teacher Interviews

In interview teachers' reports of these young children's curriculum in the first year in school fell into six categories: pre-school experience, curriculum organization, mathematical activities, pupil grouping, use of published material, and introduction of addition and subtraction.

With respect to *pre-school experience*, for children who had attended nursery school, nursery records were available. None of the four teachers mentioned making use of the information in the records as a basis for the planning of their reception class curriculum. Neither was consultation with parents mentioned. In fact, one of the two nursery teachers interviewed on a later occasion claimed that it was a point of contention that the feeder schools did *not* use the information provided. The other nursery teacher stressed the time and care taken in transfer liaison and exchange of information, including detailed records but made no comment regarding the use made of this.

Moving on to *curriculum organization*, all four reception teachers described using a topic approach. Only one mentioned the planning of topics within the school's overall scheme of work; the others stated that topics were selected by the reception teachers themselves.

In terms of *activities* provided the first rural school teacher mentioned 'freedom to choose' in practical activity and the second described her work as 'extended nursery'. The first urban school teacher mentioned 'incidental work' from, for instance, stories, jingles and home corner play. The second mentioned play, construction, sand and water for measurement language, data handling derived from children's own interests, computer games, counting and number songs and jingles and Kim's Game.

With respect to *schemes* used, the first rural school teacher mentioned starting children on SPMG (Scottish Primary Mathematics Group) Infant Mathematics Scheme within the first month of coming to school, stressing that activities took place before and alongside the first SPMG book. The second rural teacher also used the SPMG scheme from about the first half term. Again it was stressed that practical work was used to 'reinforce' the scheme work. The first urban school teacher used the Cambridge Infant Mathematics Programme (IMP) scheme. Alongside practical activities the early IMP workbooks would serve as 'assessment' of what children could do. The second claimed by Easter that children would be using Ginn Mathematics but this would 'depend on ability'.

With respect to *grouping*, the first rural school teacher confirmed that children fell into groups but she tried to 'keep them together and overlap the groups'. The second described 'random' grouping, not based on achievement. By Easter children were grouped, but only for 'number and writing.' The first urban school teacher also claimed random grouping for Term 1 and 2. By Term 3 different groups were formed each with an older child. The second urban school teacher stated that by Easter children were grouped by attainment with 'friends together.'

Finally, with respect to the *introduction of addition and subtraction* the first rural school teacher stated that before Easter some 'September starters' were doing addition and subtraction using apparatus and recording their own numbers. This, in fact, occurred when they reached Book 5 of SPMG. By the end of the year all but one (a special educational needs child) would have done this. The second teacher again said 'when they get to Book 5' stressing at the same time the need for practical activity and sometimes for recording. The first urban school teacher claimed introduction of addition and subtraction depended on progress through the IMP scheme, although in fact it occurred when they got to Book 9, *Continuing Addition*. Children, again, would do addition and subtraction through practical work. The second urban school teacher claimed that the children would do practical 'jobs' first with discussion leading finally to representing the activity (see Table 6.1, pp. 96–99).

Classroom Observations

None of the lessons of the four teachers involved in the main phase of the project was observed to carry out a lesson which involved the operations of addition and subtraction. This is not to say that none was carried out but, rather, that none of the four teachers carried out such a lesson with an observer present. Consequently a more detailed investigation of this aspect of class teachers' work was carried out in the subsequent phase of the project which involved seven teachers. The total number of lessons observed for each teacher and the number of lessons involving addition and subtraction operations is shown in Table 6.2.

Table 6.2: Lessons Involving Addition and Subtraction

Teacher	Total No. of Lessons Observed	No. of Observed Lessons involving Addition and Subtraction
Teacher X	19	Nil
Teacher Y	18	Nil
Teacher Z	16	Nil
Teacher W	20	1
Teacher V	18	3
Teacher U	19	2
Teacher T	18	2

Teacher W

In Lesson 1 she reviewed the setting up of a number table on the theme of 7 with the whole class. Next she proceeded to consider the combining of two sets, 7 + 7, using fingers for counting, before focusing on finding the patterns to be made by partitioning the set of 7 into two smaller subsets, using unifix blocks (5 + 2, 6 + 1, 4 + 3, 7 + 0).

Two small group worksheet activities which followed involved addition. The teacher explained what children should do and they worked independently. Worksheet

Table 6.1: Extracts from Teacher Interviews

	School A	School B	School C	School D
Pre-school Experience	• Most children attend nursery or play group. • Quite a few have knowledgeable professional parents. • Records are available for those who attend nursery school attached to School B. (See School B for details of information received.)	• Nearly all children attend the school's own purpose built nursery. • Records give information on social, physical, language and intellectual development. • Items include building, threading, and copying shapes; matching blocks by colour, shape and size; responding to position words; sorting, ordering, one-to-one correspondence, language of measurement and number recognition.	• Lots go to playgroup and 6–8 or so go to nursery. • Records give information on self-help skills and manipulative skills, co-ordination, drawing and writing. • Intellectual skills include categories for language comprehension, and mathematical skills. • The latter include counting objects and colours, sorting objects; naming colours and shapes; counting to 5 and 10; completing a simple puzzle; language of measurement (big/little, many/few, under/on top, back/front, big/bigger/biggest, small/smaller/smallest).	• Children attend play-group or nursery. • Those who go to nursery attend the same purpose built nursery as children from School C. • (See School C for details of the records.)
Curriculum Planning	• A topic approach is used. Sound, for instance, has been a useful one.	• A topic is used; for instance Harvest, Winter, Christmas, Spring, Seaside and Water.	• All work is topic based, chosen by the reception teachers themselves; for instance, Ourselves, Winter and Weather. • From Ourselves we get non-standard measurement, with body parts, comparison and differences, sets, simple graphs, charts of heights, lengths and sizes, cut-out paper hands and feet, concepts of time, house numbers, eye and hair colours.	• Reception children follow topics which are planned across the school and which last for half a term; for example, Ourselves. • There is scope for progression.

Table 6.1: Cont'd

	School A	School B	School C	School D
Mathematical Activities	• Practical activities are set up and children have freedom to choose. • Mathematical language is stimulated; for example, more/less. • Sand and water is available, balances for weighing, a typewriter and a concept keyboard for the computer. • Children make lots of patterns (bricks/beads). • They play number and card games.	• The reception class is extended nursery. Some know colours, some can count to 10, some further … when they enter school. There is free play and guided practical work. The Maths table provides sorting and counting. There is sand (dry and wet), water and construction toys available. Lots of 2-D and 3-D shapes are used. There is worksheet material for counting, matching and recording numbers. There are number games, but these are only used with an adult. Also there is written, formal Maths…. it is very gradual, so they really know it.	• In the first few days mathematical language arises incidentally from stories, jingles, the Home Corner and from tidying up. There will be sorting and matching by shape, size and colour. Comparison and difference will be introduced, the language of measurement and position, names of shapes, and number vocabulary. One-to-one correspondence is established. Pattern and data handling is considered. There is sand and water and jigsaws, simple to complex. Multilink is used, pegboards and calculators. Number concept 1–6, then 1–10 are learned. Simple diary records and checklists are kept on children.	• Observation and assessment of children takes place through their play, their games, discussion, number, songs, jungles, Kim's Game, shop games, where children wear price tags around their necks. Language of measurement and non-standard measurement is learned through sand and water play. • Data handling using pets and favourite foods takes place, construction and copying 2-D and 3-D shapes. • There is parental help; 3–4 parents help a week.

Table 6.1: Cont'd

	School A	School B	School C	School D
Published Scheme Work	• The *Scottish Primary Mathematics* scheme is used (SPMG), including SPMG Pre-number series *Skittles*. • It depends where they are when this is introduced. • If they have older brothers and sisters they want to start. • Activities run before and alongside the first Scottish Mathematics workbook. • This may be in the first month of coming to school if they have understanding of classification and one-to-one correspondence. • Also used are: *Busy Number Books* (Collins) for discussion; *Exploring Number and Exploring Shape; We Discover Mathematics* (Arnold); *Numbers Around Me*; and *Philograph Publications*.	• The *Scottish Primary Mathematics* scheme (SPMG) is used from about half term. • Practical work reinforces the scheme work. • Before Easter the September children will have finished Book 4. • The Teacher's Book for *Maths Chest* and *Maths Quest* are used. • Introduction is very gradual.	• *Cambridge Primary Mathematics* (IMP) will be started about half term with practical activities. • IMP workbooks are used as a form of assessment. • The first workbooks introduce sorting, matching, numbers 1–5, ordering, introducing 0, numbers 6–10, then ordering 0–10, in Books 1–6, Shape and Space topics too.	• They take the *Bury Infant Screening Test* after 6 weeks in school. • This is particularly helpful with the less able. • *Ginn Mathematics* can be used by Easter. • It depends on ability.
Pupil Grouping	• They fall into groups. I try to keep them together but they overlap.	• Grouping is random by groups of 6. • Children don't stay in groups though they do keep in groups to move around activities. • In Term 3 they are grouped but only for number and writing. • The Christmas ones have finished matching, have one-to-one correspondence by Easter.	• Random grouping in Terms 1 and 2. • In Term 3 differences are not so wide. • Grouping is different: each group will contain older children.	• They are grouped by attainment by Easter, but with friends together.

Table 6.1: Cont'd

	School A	School B	School C	School D
When Addition/ Subtraction is Introduced	• Before Easter some of the September starters are doing addition and subtraction, using apparatus and recording their own numbers. • They want to do it. • When they have reached Book 5. • All but one (i.e., an SEN child) will by the end of the year.	• When they get to Book 5, they do addition and subtraction with practical objects in shopping: numbers of fruit, etc. They do it practically, sometimes recording. It is usually at the end of the reception year. 10 out of 27 may have real understanding and recording. Small numbers are done mentally... addition and subtraction problems? Not in the first few months... Well a few – if any – with brothers and sisters. Number facts are not done in reception but in Year 1.	• It depends on IMP: when they reach Book 9. • Book 8 is *Towards Addition* and Book 9 *Continuing Addition*, e.g., 2 and 4 makes....; more than, less than. • Towards the end of Term 3, 50 per cent of children are at Book 8. • Practical work leads to representation.	• The National Curriculum is not for Reception but it *is* going further ... lower down. • Children do jobs. These are practical with recording at the end. • There is practical work with discussion and later representing the activity. • By the end of the Reception year they show progress.

1, *How Many?* required children to count two subsets of shapes, write the total of the set and colour in the shapes, for example:

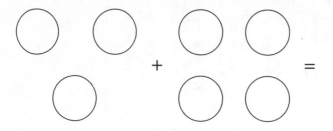

(+ means 'and' and 'plus')   (Write the number here)

There were six examples on each sheet.

Worksheet 2, *Missing Numbers*, displayed arrays where the child was asked to write in the missing number, such as:

$$0 \quad 1 \quad 2 \quad 3 \quad 4 \quad 5$$

$$0 \quad 1 \quad \square \quad 3 \quad 4 \quad 5$$

$$0 \quad 1 \quad 2 \quad \square \quad 4 \quad 5$$

$$0 \quad 1 \quad 2 \quad 3 \quad \square \quad 5$$

Write the missing numbers

On the reverse side, children were required to write the total of a partitioned set:

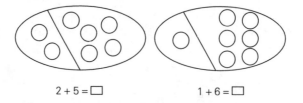

$2 + 5 = \square$ $1 + 6 = \square$

Write how many altogether

Teacher V

In Lesson 1 the class introduction did not concern number but, in fact, dealt with food for the hamster and dental health. Two small group activities which followed focused on number: drawing, colouring and counting sets of 9; and, for three older children who had started school in September, addition work had been prepared in their exercise books. These children worked independently on such examples as:

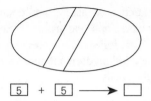

Draw the balls in the two subsets and then count how many altogether in the set.
Write the answer in the box.

In Lesson 2 the same children, again, had an addition exercise prepared in their exercise books. Pairs of coloured squares had to be counted, the number written in the exercise book as well as the total. Unifix blocks which were provided were not needed by the children:

Children were expected to read the sum, for example '2 and 3 makes 5'.

Another group of young children, who had started school at Christmas, were making sets of 3, 4 and 5 in their books.

The class introduction for Lesson 3 did not concern number. One follow-up activity, led by the teacher involved a younger group of children where the teacher used set cards and unifix blocks to introduce the idea of addition. Each child had some blocks in two colours and the intention was to lead to statements such as '3 green and 3 blue makes six'. Children were encouraged to make up sums of their own by taking the unifix blocks and putting them in the split set:

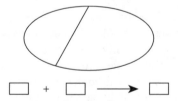

The young children found this activity quite confusing.

As was the case for Teacher W, Teacher V tended to plan two number activities while other children worked on other areas such as language or technology.

Teacher U

In Lesson 1 Teacher U set up a range of activities: two groups were copying and continuing patterns; two children were drawing things 'shorter than yourselves';

another large group of children was reading and counting spots on domino cards and matching with number cards; and one group of 'September starters' was working on an addition activity. This followed the previous day's activity of adding two subsets of blocks. Today the children drew the blocks underneath the numbers, then coloured them and wrote the total:

The class introduction for Lesson 2 focused on reading and ordering numbers up to 10, using the words 'before' and 'after'. This was followed by five different activities: putting unifix blocks into sets labelled 1 to 5; making a threading pattern with three different shaped blocks; completing a 'number before' worksheet, which displayed a number line at the top of the page; making different sets of four, with two colours of unifix blocks, followed by a similar exercise in children's books:

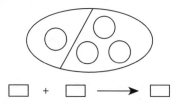

Three older children successfully made up their own addition sums using three numbers obtained from shaking a dice.

Teacher T

In Lesson 1 Teacher T divided the class into five groups: one group was drawing 'Supermum'; one group was using unifix blocks to make matching patterns; one group was doing Sound Lotto with a student; and two groups were working on number with the teacher. One of the groups was reading, ordering numbers and making appropriate sized towers with unifix blocks, whilst the second group was using fingers to work out little addition sums written on cards. This group had already met '+ 1', '+ 2' and '+ 3' in the context of a board game and had shown that they were able to 'read' little written sums. For the game in question, *Dragon's Gold*, a dice was thrown and if the child's counter landed on a blue square on the number track, he or she took a blue card with a sum and moved forward the appropriate number of squares. The children were encouraged to use their fingers for counting and the teacher had been careful to exclude any cards with numbers above 5.

Lesson 2 started with the whole class reading number cards 1 to 10, counting spot cards, matching these to the appropriate number cards and then ordering the numbers 1 to 10. In the follow-up activity one group made 'shape' faces whilst a small group worked with the teacher on addition, using the number balance. This group had played the *Dragon's Gold* game described in the previous lesson three times. The idea now was to link this previous activity to the number balance. The teacher demonstrated the example 4 and 3, encouraging the children to use the 4 and 3 weights, balance with the 7 weight whilst she wrote the equation on the flip chart. Each child then had a turn supported by the teacher's tutoring and 'talking aloud' strategy, to develop understanding of equations as a balance.

Discussion

Interviews

Perhaps one of the most challenging findings from Phase 1 assessment of children's informal knowlege was the sheer diversity of competence and strategies both across mathematical areas and across children involved and the amount of time required to access this. In order for such rich material to be made available to the busy classroom teacher, parents and pre-school personnel might need to be closely involved, both in supplying existing information and taking part in the assessment carried out. Interviews with reception teachers, however, did not suggest that existing knowledge of children's performance was utilized in the planning and organization of the reception curriculum although in most cases records were available. In fact, teachers were at pains to stress that in the first two terms grouping was flexible and not based on achievement. Easter time seemed to be the time when at least three out of four teachers reported that they began to introduce more formality in grouping and introduce formal infant mathematics scheme work. This was not the case for one teacher who described introducing the first Scottish mathematics workbook within the first month of coming to school, though she claimed to try to resist the tendency for children to 'fall into groups'. Both she and another teacher whilst claiming to group 'randomly', clearly construed children's achievement in terms of school entry time, describing the 'September children' and the 'Christmas ones' and grouping accordingly.

All teachers claimed to plan integrated topic work and stressed the importance of play, flexibility and choice of activity. All stressed sorting and matching and counting, and the development of measurement language through the use of sand and water play, constructional activity and 2-D and 3-D shapes. The prominence of such skills in pre-school records and later in children's observed performance in assessment, however, suggested that children enter school with both considerable experience of, and competence in these areas.

In spite of the fact that children entered school with experience and understanding of number word problems, if not the knowledge of the conventions for recording these, introduction of addition and subtraction was determined by its particular position in the sequence of subject content of the scheme in question. Examination of the content and sequence of schemes used, showed that sorting and matching was presented first, introducing numbers up to 10 gradually, sometimes starting with 1 and 2, sometimes with 1 to 5, reading and writing numbers up to 10, joining and separating sets, before the introduction of addition and subtraction.

In this small study of reported practice, the content of existing mathematics schemes and, hence, of classroom teaching was based on a rational analysis of subject content rather than empirical analyses of children's knowledge and strategies under problem-solving conditions. Overall surveys by HMI (1991; 1992) of a similar period following the introduction of the National Curriculum present a comparable picture.

Classroom Observations

Bearing in mind that children brought into school a rich knowledge of counting and a competence in solving simple arithmetic problems in concrete situations, it is interesting to note the absence of addition and subtraction operations in observed lessons for the first group of four teachers and for three of the second group of seven teachers. In line with teachers' reports, the three teachers observed to introduce addition, all did so in March, just before Easter, generally with the older children who had started school in September. Significant in observed practice was the influence of scheme work in the 'discovery of addition' through finding patterns which could be made with sets of things and partitioning into smaller subsets, recorded in addition form. Children were seen to need experience both of partitioning a set into subsets, and of combining two sets into a total set. As noted by Williams and Shuard (1988) 'any addition statement, such as, $5 + 2 = 7$ occurs in a great variety of situations and can be recorded in several ways'.

> At first the action of splitting up a set of seven bricks into the two subsets of five and two bricks is very different from combining a set of five bricks and a set of two bricks. After some experience, these two actions come together in a child's mind, and he realises that $7 = 5 + 2$ and $5 + 2 = 7$ are two statements about the same situation. The actions have become internalised and reversible, an operation has emerged. (Williams and Shuard, 1988, p. 89)

The dominance in observed teaching of sets, relations and structure in number, through its influence on published infant scheme work was marked in the examples presented. Teacher U and Teacher T did, however, draw on children's existing experience with dice and board games. Teacher T, in fact, was seen to draw both on children's early experience of finger counting and board games, and, at the same time, to attempt to map this on to more advanced notions of balance or equivalence in equations. This small sample of reception class teachers' practice serves to underline the wide gap between children's own existing practical ideas and the conventional UK infant curriculum which still reflects ideas and thinking derived from Piaget and theory of sets, relations and mapping, exemplified in curriculum projects of the 1960s.

Conclusion

Whilst the purpose has been to provide a description of practice through the eyes of the participants in the results section, the outline of issues presented in the discussion section must be seen for what they are, as insights based on local experience. Because interpretation depends heavily for validity on local circumstances, broad applications from these findings are inappropriate and generalization must be tentative and depend upon the similarity between the contexts investigated and those to which application is made. It cannot be known if the particular findings are applicable to other contexts. One interpretation of the findings of this chapter is that if reception teachers' practice is to be enhanced, one might conclude that they would need to become more aware of the mathematical understandings and strategies which young learners bring to school, the means for accessing this, an appreciation of both children's common misconceptions and the stages of learning through which they pass towards mastery of mathematical subject matter. From a deeper understanding of children's learning might emerge a teaching practice which placed more emphasis on conceptual development and cognitive change than on play, practical activity and the practice of published scheme work.

The main intention of Phases 1 and 2, however, was to promote an orientation or focus for the main phases of the Project (Phases 3 and 4) which aimed to investigate teachers' pedagogical subject knowledge in terms of its influence on beliefs and on content and processes of mathematics instruction in reception classrooms. In other words, addressing this objective directly through observation and analysis of classroom discourse over children's first year in school, as well as indirectly through interview. Accordingly Chapter 7 will concern Phase 3 of the project which concentrated on the gathering and coding of data related to the style and content of classroom discourse of the teachers involved in the main phase of the project as a basis for exposing the core category, teachers' pedagogical subject knowledge, as exemplified in classroom practice in Phase 4.

7   Teacher and Pupil Interactions in the Course of Mathematical Instruction

Introduction

This chapter will describe Phase 3 of the project which concerned the gathering and coding of data related to the style and content of classroom discourse for each of the four teachers involved in the main phase of the project. It focused specifically on a single data handling lesson, as an exemplar, for each teacher. The intention was to provide a category system which could be used to analyse the teacher and pupil interactions over children's first year at school in Phase 4.

Phase 1 described the construction of a set of assessment tasks designed to incorporate both areas of informal competence young children are known to bring into school and content compatible with the National Curriculum attainment targets in mathematics. The aim was to examine the mathematical knowledge, strategies and representations of one small reception class at school entry. Phase 2 described their class teachers' reported planning and implementation of the mathematics curriculum for the reception year. The aim here was to consider the extent to which account was taken of children's informal competences, through the examination of the nature and sequence of topics taught and teachers' reported encouragement of children's own construction of knowledge. Teachers' reported practice was then examined in the light of subsequent lesson observation.

Phase 1 identified competences brought into school in a range of areas: in counting, recognition of numerals, representation of quantity, simple addition and subtraction and social sharing, appropriate language of measurement, position in space and on a line, and in selecting criteria to sort objects. Reception teachers in Phase 2, for their part, claimed to plan integrated topic work, emphasizing the importance of play, flexibility and choice, with opportunities made for practical activity in areas where children had already demonstrated competence. The content and sequence of the curriculum seemed to be derived from published infant mathematics schemes which provided a rational analysis of subject content. Little account was reported to be taken by class teachers of young children's developing knowledge of mathematics gained in out-of-school, problem-solving situations and little evidence of its consideration in infant mathematics schemes could be found. Examination of reported practice in relation to subsequent lesson observation revealed no discrepancy between observed and reported activity. Whilst this small study of reported practice did not suggest that teachers accessed and deployed children's knowledge strategically in problem-solving situations, Phases 3 and 4 sought to investigate teachers' pedagogical subject knowledge through the close documentation of teacher and pupil interactions and the processes of mathematics instruction in four reception classes over children's first year in school.

Aims

Accordingly Phase 3, the focus for this chapter, aimed to:

- gather and code classroom discourse data; and
- provide a category system for analysis of the style and content of class-room discourse in Phase 4.

More specifically the analysis was intended to allow consideration of:

- teachers' structuring and managing of mathematics teaching, their explanations and representations;
- the children's behaviour and response, where possible, and their attempts to make sense of the teaching;
- relevant teacher–child, child–teacher discussion;
- the roles of teacher and learner as instruction progressed.

Teachers

In line with insights which emerged in Phase 2, maximum variation in class teachers' own education and training was sought for Phase 3. Accordingly the four teachers involved in the main phase of the project (Phase 3 and 4) represented the two main routes into primary education: two were three-year primary trained in colleges of education and two were post-graduate trained. One trained, originally, for secondary science teaching; the second trained for primary science. All of the teachers were very experienced, three were in the 40 to 50-year age range, teacher, and the fourth teacher was in the 35 to 40-year range, more recently trained.

Maximum variation in school intake was maintained so far as possible through the involvement of urban and rural schools with high, low and mixed socio-economic intakes. Some 'trade off' was required between maximum variation of teacher training and variation in school intake. In order to include the second post-graduate science trained teacher a decision was taken to select two reception teachers from one urban school with a high socio-economic intake and to drop one rural school with a high socio-economic intake. The urban school with mixed and the rural school with low socio-economic intake were retained.

This resulted in three schools and four teachers being selected for the main phase of the project. Classroom organizations of the three schools varied widely. The rural school, with a low socio-economic intake, which had its own purpose-built nursery, moved children into a large reception class with one class teacher and an ancillary to support special needs pupils; the urban school with a mixed socio-economic intake grouped children in two, small adjoining reception classes which were team-taught for mathematics, one teacher leading and one supporting follow-

Table 7.1:   Teachers: Their Training and Teaching Context

Teacher	Training	Teaching Context
Teacher A	Three-year primary teacher training	Rural, low socio-economic status of intake
Teacher B	Three-year primary teacher training	Urban, high socio-economic status of intake
Teacher C	Post-graduate secondary training	Urban, high socio-economic status of intake
Teacher D	Post-graduate primary training	Urban, mixed socio-economic status of intake

up activities, and an ancillary providing craft activities; the urban school with high socio-economic intake divided the reception intake into two, small reception classes each with its own class teacher, one having a part-time ancillary for a special needs child and the other making use of regular parental help. This allowed classroom discourse to be collected from four reception classes.

Measures of Children's Informal Mathematical Knowledge

Ten children from each school were assessed using the tasks described in Phases 1 and 2 just prior to school entry. Results for the data handling tasks were used as a measure of children's existing understanding in this area.

Classroom Observations

One day each week at a time agreed with each reception teacher the writer observed and recorded their teaching. Each teacher knew the focus of the researcher was mathematics teaching but it was stressed throughout that no change to existing practice was required or even desired. No view of what should occur was held and the intention of the researcher was simply to record what normally took place. Data collected were of two kinds:

- teacher–pupil interactions were recorded through the teaching period by a small Aiwa tape recorder worn by the teacher in a 'Walkman' belt with a small microphone attached to her collar;
- condensed field notes were taken during the recordings. These were typed up after each session to provide an accurate record of teacher and pupil actions. As field notes accumulated patterns emerged and a more standardized format was produced (see Appendix 4).

No teacher interviews were carried out during the data collection phase of the project and no further information was sought at this time other than topic webs of curriculum content taught, where available. It was felt that the regular presence of the researcher and the continuous tape recording of sessions led to additional time demands being made on the busy teachers involved.

The process of data analysis takes place more than once in qualitative analysis. It is an ongoing process that happens at several levels and for different purposes. It happens in the context or 'field' as data are collected where the purpose is to guide future data collection.

At the second level data analysis serves two purposes. First, like the purpose at the first level of analysis, data are used to guide subsequent data collection at different locations. In the current project, for instance, data handling lessons were obtained from all teachers at the beginning of the year. Thereafter it was essential to ensure that a full range of different mathematical content areas was covered for each teacher and that data collection continued until no new insights were emerging. Second, data analysis serves, partly, to organize the data, to bring them together under a taxonomy. In the case of this project the exemplar data handling lesson obtained for each teacher served to provide the taxonomy and a means for analysing subsequent lessons.

A third and crucially important level of data analysis occurs during the process of report writing. It is at this level that the core category, in this case teachers' pedagogical subject knowledge, is exposed with events, incidents and actions of individual teachers over the year providing the source for the presentation of a clear analytic story.

For the purpose of Phase 3 and, hence, this chapter, data analysis at the first and second level will be described. The intention, as noted in earlier sections of this chapter, was to provide a taxonomy from the first analysis of the data handling lessons which would provide a means for analysing second and subsequent lessons of the four teachers. The third level will be treated in Chapter 9.

Field Notes

A standard format for collecting field notes was generated from an earlier, more general note-making phase through unitizing and categorizing as described in Chapter 5 for teacher interviews, to supplement and to provide a context to each transcription. This included a plan of the classroom showing the main activities and areas, with sections to comment on lesson segments observed, deployment of adults, pupil grouping, role of adults and pupils, activities undertaken, mathematical content involved, materials used, outcomes observed, existing displays, classroom management and any additional comments.

The standard field notes schedule emerged over the first weeks of observation. Preference for grounded theory in this case should not be interpreted as a total rejection of all *a priori* theory. On the one hand, the writer as researcher was not, and could not be a 'naive' observer without awareness of the existing literature. On the other, ways of construing teaching which is goal-driven with a movement towards planned outcomes are not limitless. As suggested by Doyle (1986), this is defined in terms of temporal boundaries, physical setting, the focus or content and the plan of action for the participants. As described in detail in Chapter 6, early notes were analysed in two steps of unitizing, where single pieces of information were identified and stored and categorizing, where individual units were brought together to form a grouping of like content with a rule for classification.

Classroom Discourse

Overall 46 mathematics lessons were observed and recorded over the period between the end of September and the end of May. Once a number of lessons had been observed it became clear that organization and instruction varied little for each class teacher. All the recorded mathematics lessons were transcribed and were, thus, potentially available for analysis. As already reported, a data handling lesson was selected for the first sample, then further lessons for each teacher were selected for analysis until no new information was being generated.

For analysis of discourse the process of unitizing and categorizing was carried out in a different manner from the procedure reported in Chapter 6 for teacher interviews. Raw transcriptions were presented on the left hand side of A3 paper leaving the right hand side free for identifying and commenting on meaningful units of information. As supplementary information from the field notes was available columns 1, 3 and 4 provided contextual information and the last three for generating units and emerging categories. Column 2 allowed examples of discourse to be provided.

Group	Discourse Content	Mathematics	Materials Used	Teacher Activity	Pupil Activity	Comments

The units were revised repeatedly and their relationship to categories re-examined on numerous occasions. This did not turn out to be the simple and elegant process as described by Glaser and Strauss (1967). The final category system which emerged was presented and discussed with peers at both an inter-institutional seminar and at a research seminar at a national congress for mathematics education.

The category system generated was thus grounded in the data derived from the repeated description and reconsideration of emerging patterns from the transcriptions themselves rather than from the imposition of pre-determined categories. The structure of lessons or tasks which emerged from analysis was one of co-ordinating segments and sub-segments. A segment, the basic lesson or task unit, normally consisted of small group work. Main sub-categories comprised supporting: lesson organization and management; instruction; and, less commonly, independent practice or application. Each sub-category had its own general framework which could be analysed into further sub-categories or components. Typically instruction would have an *introduction* when the teacher would tell children what to do, present new learning or demonstrate a new activity, some observation and *assessment* would normally take place as children would be asked to display understanding. At this stage the teacher would observe, *tutor, monitor and guide* individual pupils, prompt and correct and, finally, *review* or *comment on the results* (see Table 7.2). This structure allowed a means for analysing:

Group	Discourse	Mathematics Content	Materials Used	Teacher Activity	Pupil Activity	Comments
Who was involved	Examples given			This will 1 *support lesson organization* and concerns 　A rules/routines relating to materials, movement, organization 　B management and control as the teacher monitors/checks social behaviour of class/individuals; 　C social interaction, conversation; rapport; or 2 *support instruction* where the teacher, 　A introduces concept, procedure, maths term presents new learning, makes links to what already known, informs/tells, elicits (with/without cues), shows, demonstrates, models, 'talks aloud', questions, prepares/introduces material/apparatus; 　B assesses through observing and questioning to check pupils are able to carry out the task, adjusts if necessary, simplifies, adds more steps, reteaches, offers alternative strategies; 　C tutors and guides, repeats questions, 'talks aloud' to pupil actions, leads towards task goal, seeks choral response; 　D helps execute task, assists in tool skills or in preparation of pupil recording of the activity; 　E monitoring/assesses/observes, questions, checks individuals, corrects, deals with errors/misunderstandings, repeats, reminds, asks another pupil, tells, explains, prompts, praised, cross-references to other parts of the lesson, points out conditions of use; 　F reviews/comments on results, suggests another way of representing findings, gives feedback, repeats teaching point; or 3 A *support independent practice/application*, here the teacher introduces, as above, and monitors individual work.	Comments on non-verbal response	*Also note:* • if teacher identifies goal purpose or problems • ensures relevant existing knowledge, skills, experience have been checked, accessed, used • links new concepts through identification of old and familiar • extends or adds new elements • provides verbal demonstrations which run through key moves (so verbal is linked to physical) • gives a parallel representation (verbal, numerical, symbolic) and makes links • provides examples of the case concept or instance, i.e., identifies what it is/is not • presents range of instances and draws attention to salient points • checks impact at key points and decides whether to go on.

Table 7.3: Assessment of Data Handling before School Entry

School of:	Selecting criterion and sorting	Sorting to a criterion	Simple representation
	(Number of children successful, out of 10)		
Teacher A	9	10	10
Teacher B and C	10	10	10
Teacher D	9	10	10
Total:	28	30	30

- the framework of the mathematics lessons;
- the content deployed within the segments, described in terms of National Curriculum attainment targets;
- the style of individual teachers as reflected in the way they conducted routines within segments.

Results

Assessment of Children's Data Handling before School Entry

Informal mathematical knowledge compatible with National Curriculum attainment targets of ten children from each of the target schools was assessed before school entry. Of particular relevance to the present chapter were scores for data handling, where children carried out three simple tasks: selecting criteria to sort a set of small-scale toys, sorting a set of dolls to given criteria and offering a simple representation of this, using the dolls. Nearly all the children assessed could manage these tasks on school entry (see Table 7.3).

Content

Table 7.4 shows deployment of content within the segments of the lessons described in terms of National Curriculum attainment targets. Nearly all children had demonstrated competence in sorting to a criterion (AT 5, L1) before entering school. Teacher B extended knowledge by asking children to sort on the basis of three criteria (size, colour and pattern) and integrated this with counting the pairs of socks (AT 2, L1). Teacher C did not demand a display of this knowledge, she simply told children to sort by colour. Teacher A asked for a display of knowledge (AT 5 L1) in sorting balloons by colour and integrated this with estimating the set size and checking by counting (AT 2, L1), as well as sorting by shape (AT 4, L1). Teacher D drew on children's knowledge of AT 5, L1 and AT 2, L1 in sorting by

Table 7.4: Deployment of Subject Content in Lesson Segments

	AT2 Number Level 1a)	AT3 Algebra Level 1a)	AT4 Shape and Space Level 1a)	AT5 Handling Data Level 1a)	2a)
TEACHER A					
Segment: 1a)	/		/	/	
Segment: 1b)	/			/	
TEACHER B					
Segment: 1	/			/	
TEACHER C					
Segment: 1				/	
TEACHER D					
Segment: 1a)	/			/	
Segment: 1b)	/			/	
Segment: 1c)	/			/	
Segment: 2a)					/
Segment: 2b)					/
Segment: 2c)				/	

colour, estimating the set size and checking by counting and extended this knowledge by recording and interpreting data that had been collected (AT 5, L2). Each of the tasks involved children's prior knowledge of sorting to a criterion, three of the teachers explicitly checked and extended this.

Lesson or Task Structure

Table 7.5 shows the four mathematics lessons structured into segments and subsegments. Activities provided, timing and grouping are indicated.

Teacher A worked consecutively with two groups of five children whilst the rest of the class chose their activity (the play, flexibility and choice described in Phase 2). An auxiliary usually supervised a drawing or painting activity. She sometimes made resources but did not take a teaching role. Activities ranged from wet and dry sand, water and home corner play to book corner, small-scale toys and constructional activity. Table 7.5 shows the task was composed of one segment with two sub-segments, which was repeated once for a second group.

Teacher B worked with one group of four children. The rest of the class sat quietly at tables working on jigsaws, puzzles, constructional toys and a colour matching game. After she had finished working with her group she monitored other children and, in the target lesson, supported a colour matching game. Table 7.5 shows the task had one planned mathematics segment.

Teacher C worked with one group of five children and then monitored other activities. In the case of the target lesson she joined in a picture lotto game. This

Table 7.5: Lesson/Task Structure

Teacher A: sorting balloons (lesson recording: 9.30–10.15am)		Teacher B: sorting socks into pairs (lesson recording: 9.30–10.15am)	
Task Segment 1 Group of five children. **(a) Subsegment** Make a set of blue, yellow, red and green balloons. Estimate who has most and least and count how many colours altogether. **(b) Subsegment** Make a set of round, long and curly balloons. Count how many in each set. Comment on results: which had most and which had least. Children blow up balloons before the next group is called. **Task Segment 2** Repeat of Segment 1 with a second group. Time: Planned mathematics task: 9.30–9.50am Repeated with second group: 9.50–10.10am	**Rest of Class** Play, flexibility and choice of wet/dry sand, water, paint, home corner, small-scale toys, construction activities.	**Task Segment 1** Group of four children sort socks by three attributes: colour, size and pattern. **Task Segment 2** Group of four children play fruit tree game (collecting sets of coloured fruit: green, yellow, orange, purple). Time: Planned mathematics task 9.30–9.45am Number of children involved: 4 (a further four children were involved in the matching game)	**Rest of class** Seated at tables with games, puzzles and construction toys.

Table 7.5: Cont'd

Teacher C: sorting bottle tops (lesson recording: 9.30–10.15am)

Task Segment 1 Group of five children	**Rest of class** Children sit at tables with a choice of number games, jigsaws and various construction toys. Also matching games using shapes, pictures and words.

Sort a set of bottle tops by colour.

Task Segment 2
Group of five children.

Play picture lotto using three attributes: colour, object and number.

Time: Planned mathematics task 9.30–9.45am

Teacher D: sorting children by hair, eye and shoe colour, sorting coloured animals (lesson recording: 9.30–10.30am)

Introductory Presentation Lesson Segment (Whole Class)

(a) Subsegment

Make a set of blue, brown and green eyed children. Count each set (showing the size of the set is given by the last number in the count). Note which set has most/fewest.

(b) Subsegment

Make a set of black, red and blue shoes. Count each set (showing the size of the set is given by the last number in the count). Note which set has most/fewest.

(c) Subsegment

Make a set of fair, brown and black haired children.
Estimate which set has most/least.
Check estimate by counting the sets.

Task Segment 2 Find relations between sets (eye colour and children's names) and record them by linking arrows with teacher.	**Task Segment 3** Construct block graph from data indicating which children have brown, black, fair hair, with teacher.	**Task Segment 4** Sort coloured animals into sets, describing the criteria chosen (children work independently).	**Task Segment 5** Leaf printing with ancillary.

Group size: 4 (all groups rotate once, two tasks undertaken by each child).
Time: Segment 1: 9.30–9.50am.
Segments 2–5: 9.50–10.10am.
All change: 10.10–10.20am.
Number of Children involved: whole class

was not a planned mathematics activity. The rest of the class chose activities from tables of jigsaws, small construction toys, a number fishing game and a simple number matching game on the computer. An ancillary sometimes helped a special needs child. Table 7.5 shows the task was composed of one planned segment.

For **Teacher D** the whole class worked on the introductory segment before moving into four groups. There were two teacher-led and one unsupervised mathematics tasks, whilst one group worked on a painting activity with an ancillary, who generally supported art work.

Table 7.5 shows the lesson had a mathematics presentation segment with three sub-segments in which the whole class took part. This was followed by four tasks which rotated once. Three of these were mathematical and one was an art activity. All children, thus, had a minimum of two mathematics tasks.

Task Components

Tables were produced to indicate the main components of the segments for each teacher's lesson in the first column. For each component there were corresponding columns for the teacher's task and the pupils' response. These gave some indication of the richness and complexity of the task provided. They showed how new knowledge was introduced and existing skills invoked. The teacher's monitoring, assessing and correcting as well as commenting on results were all documented.

Teacher A set up a task for children to carry out independently but questioned to assess what children knew or could do. She monitored, prompted, corrected and reviewed responses. If a response to a question indicated children did not have the knowledge the question was dropped. If a misunderstanding of the nature of her question occurred this was immediately corrected.

Teacher B provided a supportive scaffolding with coaching, monitoring, 'talking aloud' strategies, checking individual children and inviting them all to join in each child's activity. She took part in the activity by modelling and 'talking aloud' through her actions.

Teacher C talked aloud whilst she was engaged in the group's activity. She was frequently interrupted and distracted by other children. She discussed things irrelevant to the activity. Children's responses were not invited, checked or monitored, in fact, contributions were frequently ignored. No comments were made on the results and confusion must have been created through abandoned and ambiguous signals sent.

Teacher D was the only teacher who undertook direct teaching in the formal exposition sense. Individual responses were invited and evaluated and where no children's contribution was forthcoming children were reminded or the appropriate information was supplied. Where possible existing experience was invoked and new vocabulary, new concepts and procedures were introduced. Different verbal and concrete representations were offered and links across segments clearly signalled. Work was intensive and focused and children were kept engaged.

Table 7.6 offers some examples from the lessons of individual teachers.

Table 7.6: Task Components

	Teacher A	Teacher B	Teacher C	Teacher D
Introduction (Goal)	Right. Now what I want you to do is. I want you to sort them. Now I want to see if you can do it. Right.	Well, we're looking for pairs, aren't we? Shall we give David the first turn?	I put the gold ones with the yellow ones because I thought gold was a bit like yellow or orange. I put the orange with yellow as well . . . Can you come and sort with me, right? Well, I was sorting, I was putting the green in that one. Right. Can I just – they are for making – like big ponds to sort things (refers to the pans in the sorting tray).	This morning we are going to sort ourselves into different sets. Lots of different ways to sort ourselves into different groups.
Presents new knowledge				(After children have been sorted into hair and eye colour sets). Now then, with Mrs W and with me you are going to put this information that we've got here – you're different sets – you're going to put it into things called charts or graphs. Okay?
Links to prior knowledge	Main sorting task known (see under Conclusions).	Main sorting task known (see under Conclusions).	Main sorting task known.	Main sorting task known (see under Conclusions).
Monitors/Assesses				
Teacher corrects:	No, Ian, I didn't say how many balloons altogether. How many different colours have you got altogether. Helen was right. How	Oh, Jasminda's chosen one with a pretty edge. There's one bigger than the other? Have a look at Jasminda's. Do you think she's		So how many sets of different eye colours do we have here? Five (in chorus). No. I said how – think. Listen and think. How

Table 7.6: Cont'd

Teacher A	Teacher B	Teacher C	Teacher D
many colours – how many different colours have you got altogether … Seven, that's right.	got the right pair there? I don't think so. I don't either. Cos what does that one have on it? Right, Jasminda, you've got as far as finding two white ones, but they've got different tops so have another look. Same pattern, what about size. Same size. And they're the same colour. Good!		many different sets do we have of eye colours? Three (in chorus). – Two. Are you sure it's two – we've got blue, brown and green – is that two?

Supports

Teacher A	Teacher B	Teacher C	Teacher D
Mm and there's some more. Good. So those are all round ones. Right. Now, let's look at these long ones. Are those all the same shape? I think those are going to be curly ones, aren't they – when they're blown up. So they're all the same.	Right, Emma. What colour does that have on it, Emma? Emma's going to check if she's got her pair. Same? Same size? Same colour? Same pattern? Good girl.		Stand together on one set – altogether on one set. One set of people – one set. We're sorting ourselves into sets, aren't we? One set.

Conditions of Use

Teacher A	Teacher B	Teacher C	Teacher D
What colour have you got? What about you, Ian – Blue. Well, I think we'll call them blue, but it looks a bit like purple to me.	There's two odd ones out. Oh. Look how many odd socks we've got that we can't find the one that matches. We've got one, two, three, four.		I've got one green and one blue! Oh, you've got one of each. Well you can choose your set then. Laura's got one green eye and one blue eye! So she's really in two sets isn't she?

Comments on Results

Teacher A	Teacher B	Teacher C	Teacher D
Teacher A checks children's sorting. She suggests children estimate who has most and least, using language of number. Finally, children count the number in each set.	Teacher B checks childrens sorting. She then encourages children to count how many pairs of socks each has and how many odd socks are left.	Teacher C merely comments on the colours of the tops throughout the task.	Teacher D suggests children count how many are in each set and then asks which set has most and least using language of number. After sorting into hair colour she suggests children estimate which set has most and least using language of number and check by counting.

Discussion

To summarize, analysis of lesson or task segments and sub-segments into components which carried implications for teacher and pupil actions, allowed access to recurrent patterns of teacher instructional moves: introduction, presentation of new learning, linking to children's prior knowledge, supporting of children's actions and responses, monitoring, assessing and correcting, pointing out conditions of use often triggered by pupil questions, and commenting on results. Not all segments contained all of these elements and the four teachers had their own distinctive styles of working. This, in itself, is unremarkable. As noted in a previous section, there are limits to the way the structure and sequence of lessons can be construed and the framework generated has much in common with others in the literature, for example, Leinhardt (1987; 1989) or Bennett and Kell (1989).

Lessons varied, however, in the richness of the moves, the number and quality of verbal and concrete demonstrations and representations used. The 'tutoring' component, supportive of children's actions and responses, characteristic of one teacher's style and used by a second in the informal monitoring of children's self-chosen activities, has been associated with scaffolded teaching and cognitive strategy instruction referred to in an earlier chapter. There are certainly some grounds to suggest that this strategy could be profitably deployed more extensively in small group teaching.

Mathematics content supporting the segments varied, too, in terms of the way prior concepts or procedures were elicited, reviewed or extended and in the way they were linked to new knowledge. As shown in Table 7.2 the results showed that there was a considerable difference in the amount of subject content introduced in lessons as well as in the skill in which this was deployed. Furthermore, the amount of time in which there were opportunities to engage in mathematics tasks varied considerably across classrooms, as well as in the number of children involved, and in the richness and quality of the experiences provided.

Teacher talk and support ranged from the irrelevant and goal-free, distracted by management problems, through modelling, 'talk aloud' strategies with coaching and monitoring, to the more formal exposition within a structure of initiation–response–evaluation (IRE) interactions, described by Sinclair-Coulthardt (1975). This will be developed further in Chapter 8.

In terms of the specific classroom contexts, the classroom structure of Teacher D allowed the mathematics expertise of one teacher to be made available to all reception-aged children through the 'lead', presentation segment which, as noted earlier, is where teachers draw most heavily on subject knowledge as they introduce new knowledge and procedures, review and extend existing knowledge and provide explanations.

Interestingly none of the other three teachers offered a formal presentation or exposition within the data handling lesson in question or in any other lesson observed over the year. Furthermore the use of supporting adults by Teacher D in the follow-up work enabled all children to engage in at least two, adult-led mathematics tasks. By contrast two groups only engaged in a planned mathematics activity in Teacher A's class and one group in the class of Teachers B and C.

In terms of the deployment of subject content, again, Teacher D generated a rich network of connections between concrete situations and representations, verbal, action, numerical and diagrammatic, linked to children's existing knowledge and providing a foundation upon which future experiences could be built. Williams and Shuard (1988) emphasized the danger of reinforcing one connection at the expense of other equally, or more significant connections. One mathematical concept or idea may be used to represent vastly different situations and to avoid one use being over-emphasized and, thus, being regarded as unrelated and arbitrary, children must be helped to make connections into a coherent network. In terms of National Curriculum planning all the children entered school working within Level 1 of the handling data attainment target (selecting criteria for sorting a set of objects and applying them consistently) and were provided by Teacher D with an entirely appropriate lesson which both extended work within Level 1 (creating simple mapping diagrams, showing relationships and interpreting them) and Level 2 (constructing block graphs for discrete data). In fact Teacher D had recently moved from a Year 2 class and so was particularly well placed to have a clear overview of the infant curriculum, its summative assessment in the form of National Curriculum standard assessment tasks and an appreciation of the foundation for this work which the reception class provided.

Of some concern must be the sheer amount of time spent on self-chosen, unsupervised activity. Whilst some of the richest examples of teachers 'scaffolded' instruction were observed in this context, notably by Teacher B, as Wells (1985) has noted, the role of the school is to complement the role of the home in its provision of a more formal and deliberate instruction which seeks to advance subject development rather than simply to support learning in an incidental and, possibly, haphazard way. Within a few weeks of entering school the 4-year-olds of Teacher D were socialized into formal, classroom teaching. The 4-year-olds entering the classrooms of Teachers A, B and C, on the other hand, found a familiar environment for learning which was reminiscent of their pre-school or nursery experience.

The results for Phase 3 raise a number of important questions for consideration. What teacher subject knowledge *is* required to construct and carry out mathematics lessons? How *does* subject knowledge impact on the practice and processes of teaching? How is knowledge and understanding *communicated* and how is it connected to what children already know? Finally, what *does* constitute effective reception class mathematics teaching? Ultimately this last question can only be answered fairly through the consideration of relationships between the effects of classroom processes on children's mathematics learning. Whilst large-scale correlational studies such as those of Good, Grouws and Ebmeier (1983) produced data which identified teacher characteristics associated with pupil achievement, they found it difficult to demonstrate stable relationships across years. Moreover much valuable qualitative data is lost through the use of pre-established category systems. Fine-grained empirical work investigating classroom processes is, by contrast, very much in the early stages of development. A central assumption of such work is that in order to build firm understanding of classroom processes there is the need to develop and draw upon detailed, qualitative descriptions of the way teachers teach mathematics in complex classroom situations. Behaviours which characterize effective teaching will vary from context to context and there is no way to control for all the complex relationships among variables which might affect children's progress in a single year. Studies of crafting and delivery of exemplar lessons, such as this chapter provides, are bound to emphasize the uniqueness of teachers and settings. In this respect there may be good grounds for keeping factors associated with teachers and teaching conditions as stable and uniform as possible.

Data handling is, as noted earlier, a newer and less well-established area of the infant curriculum than some other areas, such as arithmetic. Nevertheless it is one which develops across the whole of children's school years and is of vital importance not only to the mathematics curriculum, but also in its application to other curriculum areas such as science investigations. As such, even in reception classrooms, data handling warrants serious attention with regard to its role in providing a foundation for future learning. In fact since this phase of the project has been completed OFSTED (1995) has commented recently that Handling Data (AT5) is still under-developed in schools even though most teachers recognize this as an important part of mathematics needed for every day life.

Conclusion

This chapter has provided an in-depth analysis of a single example of each teacher's teaching which provides some insight into the different ways a data handling lesson early in the reception year may be tackled. Much more such fine-grained analysis is needed to build up a firmer picture of differences in style among the teachers involved. Having established a workable coding system, the next chapter will consider in more detail variations in style among these teachers which emerged from the analysis of a number of lessons for each teacher.

8 Teacher and Pupil Mathematical Subject Knowledge and the Processes of Instruction in Reception Classes

Introduction

This chapter will describe Phase 4 or the main phase of the project which sought to address the overall aim of the project, to investigate teachers' pedagogical subject knowledge in mathematics, specifically, through the examination of the coordination and utilization of teacher and pupil knowledge in the complexity of ongoing classroom processes. Observation and analysis of the content and style of classroom discourse with field notes collected from the four reception teachers provided the primary means of data collection in this phase, though teacher and pupil subject knowledge was also investigated through interview and assessment.

The knowledge which young children draw upon and which they exploit in their transactions within the social and physical world is learned through and mediated by their interactions with other and more experienced members of their culture. In fact, early mathematics is not only derived from social communicative contexts but is itself a form of discourse, as noted in Chapter 3. Like language development, in the early stages, learning mathematics is a process of being supported by an adult into a particular form of discourse which embodies its own sequence of development, moving from a grounding in practical and social contexts towards a more symbolic and abstract system. Wells (1985) noted language provides the medium of instruction and the chief means through which learning is assessed. As such the study of classroom language justifies the serious attention of anyone investigating educational settings and, in Phase 3 and 4 of the project, provided the main focus for investigation.

Linguistic studies of classrooms such as Sinclair and Coulthardt (1975) and Willes (1983), however, which focused on specifying implicit rules for successful communication in classroom contexts or even the more recent socio-linguistic study of Edwards and Mercer (1987) with its emphasis on joint construction of meaning in classrooms, tended to take little account of the importance of the specific subject content being taught. More recently the role of teachers' subject matter knowledge in influencing teaching activities has been recognized and detailed empirical work linking teacher knowledge to class teaching is expanding this small but growing knowledge base. Brophy (1989; 1991) has demonstrated, particularly in the subjects of science, mathematics and English that where teachers' subject knowledge is rich and better integrated and more accessible they tend to teach more dynamically, represent the subject in a more varied way, encourage and respond more fully to children's questions and comments. Where knowledge is more limited, there is more emphasis on facts, more reliance on subject texts for content, more time spent by pupils in working individually and less interactive discourse.

Carlsen (1991) noted that marked differences in discourse style may be related to teachers' own confidence or competence in the subject being taught. High teacher talk with many questions or talk about irrelevant matters may indicate low subject knowledge. Clearly a high level of questioning with evaluation of responses will lead to correspondingly less pupil talk, less investigation and a growing sense that mathematics subject knowledge is the gaining of approval for a correct response to a teacher question.

Phase 3 analysis of a sample data handling lesson from each of the four reception teachers involved similarly revealed differences in discourse style. The emerging task components (introduces, observes, tutors and guides, monitors and assesses, reviews or comments on the results) were mediated through classroom discourse with different teachers utilizing very different styles and strategies in response to pupils' efforts to complete tasks. Phase 3 provided a category system and preliminary analysis of a small sample of lessons which suggested differences in teachers' styles of discourse. This justified the more sustained analysis of a broader sample of lessons for each of the four teachers involved. This will be reported in the current chapter.

Aims

As stated in the introduction the overall aim of the project was to explore the co-ordination and utilization of teacher and pupil knowledge in the complexities of reception classrooms by following four such reception classrooms through the school year. More specifically, as noted in Chapter 2, the objectives were:

1   To investigate teachers' pedagogical subject knowledge, in particular, in terms of its influence on beliefs and the content and processes of mathematics instruction in reception classes. (This objective was addressed directly through teacher interviews and indirectly through observation and analysis of classroom discourse.)

2   To take existing data on children's informal knowledge in key areas of mathematics, at school entry, as a starting point for accessing teachers' understanding of the way children think about mathematics, and knowledge about their own pupils' thinking. (This objective was addressed through teacher interview and classroom observation which was considered in the light of children's informal knowledge as well as through follow-up data obtained from re-assessment of a sample of children towards the end of the reception year.)

3   To explore the co-ordination and utilization of teacher and pupil knowledge within the complex world of classrooms. (This objective was addressed through observation and analysis of the nature and content of classroom

discourse and field notes collected from the four reception teachers, taking account of practical and pedagogical considerations.)

4   To consider the implications of the project for a mathematics curriculum for children's first year at school. (This objective was addressed through examination of the findings in terms of learning and teaching mathematics.)

Teachers

The teachers involved in Phase 3 and Phase 4 of the project are described fully in Chapter 7. As noted, maximum variation in class teachers' own education and in socio-economic intake was sought. One school (of Teacher A) was rural, serving a depressed mining community with a high rate of unemployment, one school (of Teacher D) was urban, with a mixed social and ethnic intake and one school (of Teachers B and C) was urban, with an intake from a surrounding private housing estate. All teachers were very experienced, three (Teachers A, B and C) were in the 45–55-year age range, and the fourth teacher (Teacher D) was in the 35–45-year age range. Between them they represented a range of routes into primary education: Teachers A and B were three-year trained at colleges of education, Teachers C and D were science graduates who had obtained post-graduate certificates in education. Teacher C had been secondary trained and Teacher D had been more recently primary trained. One means for judging teachers' understanding and utilization of the way young children know and think about mathematics was to access the informal know-ledge these children brought into school as well as to re-assess them towards the end of the year. Accordingly, a group of ten children from each of the three schools involved in the project was selected to provide a small but socially diverse sample.

Measures of Children's Progress

The informal mathematical knowledge of a sample of thirty children had been assessed just prior to school entry in their nursery setting, and it was possible to follow up this sample of ten children from each school who were assessed again towards the end of the school year using the same assessment tasks (see Chapter 5 for details). As Teachers B and C were from the same school and more specific-ally, since Teacher C had a student teacher in her class during the Summer term, a single sample of children from the class of Teacher B was taken. It should be noted, however, that the main purpose of assessment was to consider the extent, if at all, to which teachers made use in their teaching of existing, informal knowledge children brought into school.

Classroom Observations

As noted in Chapter 7 one day each week at a time agreed with each reception teacher the researcher observed and recorded their mathematics teaching. This allowed one free day and enabled the writer to be responsive to the inevitable last minute changes to timetables.[1] Data collected were of two kinds:

1   teacher-pupil interactions were recorded through the teaching period by a small Aiwa tape recorder worn by the teacher in a 'Walkman' belt with a small microphone attached to her collar;

2   as field notes had accumulated in the project a more standardized format was generated. This included a plan of the classroom showing the main activities and areas, with a section to describe lesson or task segments observed, deployment of adults, pupil grouping, mathematical content involved, mathematical displays observed and any additional comments. See Chapter 7 for discussion of the construction of the field notes schedule.

Teacher Interviews

Teachers were interviewed after data collection had been completed and when they had had time to reflect on the year. Questions asked were grouped under a number of headings. The grouping and questions reflected both insights which emerged from Phase 2 interviews but did not reject *a priori* knowledge gained from relevant background literature.

- **'Teachers' mathematical knowledge,'** concerning the teachers' own attitudes towards, beliefs about and sense of competence in mathematics at their own level (subject knowledge and beliefs);
- **'Mathematics that young children should learn,'** related to what teachers regarded were key concepts, knowledge and procedures to be taught to young children (pedagogical subject knowledge);
- **'The way young children learn mathematics, in school and outside'** was concerned with the way teachers accessed this knowledge, dealt with misconceptions and challenged more able children (pedagogical subject knowledge);
- **'Planning and organization,'** concerning the nature of planning carried out by the teachers in the course of reception teaching, their grouping and their use of relevant resources (curriculum knowledge);
- **'General,'** including questions about advice which might be given to a student teacher, and what the reception teachers, themselves, would regard as useful continuing professional development in mathematics teaching.

Analysis

Measures of Children's Progress

Where appropriate, a simple t-test was applied to check whether scores for tasks administered prior to school entry and again towards the end of the school year, were significantly different.

Classroom Observations

As noted in Chapter 7, forty-six mathematics lessons were observed and recorded over the period between the end of September and the end of May. All the recorded mathematics lessons were transcribed and were, thus, potentially available for analysis. The sampling strategy was to select and analyse first a data handling lesson for each teacher. Further lessons were selected to reflect as wide a variation as possible, in terms of subject content, teaching strategy, type of task and spread over the year. Once five lessons had been analysed no new information was generated and sampling was terminated. Five lessons have been analysed in depth for each teacher in this chapter, using the transcriptions of classroom interactions and the field notes. The category system generated in Phase 3 was grounded in the data, derived from the repeated description and reconsideration of emerging patterns from the transcriptions themselves rather than from the imposition of predetermined categories. As noted in the introduction, the structure of lessons or tasks which emerged from Phase 3 analysis was one of co-ordinating segments and sub-segments which, on the one hand, supported lesson organization and management and, on the other hand, served instruction, teacher-directed or pupil-led. A segment, the basic lesson or task unit, normally consisted of small group work. Each segment had its own general framework which could be analysed into sub-categories or components. Typically the lesson would have an *introduction* when the teacher would tell children what to do, present new learning or demonstrate a new activity, some observation and *assessment* would normally take place as children would be asked to display understanding. At this stage the teacher would observe, *tutor, monitor and guide* individual pupils, prompt and correct and, finally, *review* or *comment on the results*, (see Table 7.1 of Chapter 7). This structure allowed a means for analysing:

- the framework of the mathematics lessons;
- the content deployed within the segments, described in terms of National Curriculum attainment targets;
- the style of individual teachers as reflected in the way they conducted routines within segments.

Teacher Interviews

Teachers' interviews were transcribed to allow the consideration of their mathematical knowledge, their views about learning and teaching mathematics and the possible influence of this on their observed practice.

To satisfy trustworthiness requirements, credibility was established through prolonged engagement in data collection (over children's first year in school) with persistent (weekly) observation and high fidelity audio recording of discourse. Triangulation was provided by contextual information obtained from field notes and subsequent teacher interviews, which allowed facts to be checked and outcomes to be negotiated. The opportunity to repeat main phase data collection with a further 7 reception teachers the subsequent year allowed negative case analysis, described by Kidder (1981) as the 'process of revising hypotheses with hindsight'. Two other researchers engaged provided peer review, as did colleagues from other institutions involved in mathematics education and research teams working in similar fields.

Extracts from classroom discourse and selections from teacher interviews presented in the following sections are intended to satisfy three purposes of report writing identified by Guba and Lincoln (1981) to:

- offer evidence, in the form of 'thick descriptions,' for some of the judgments made;
- convey something of the multiple realities captured; and
- provide the reader with a vivacious experience of the settings involved.

All data, raw and coded, were stored with dependability and confirmability strengthened through the scrutiny of draft reports by an external consultant and by the evaluation of papers submitted to refereed journal reviewers.

Results

Children's Progress

Children came into school showing competence in counting, simple number operations, language of measurement, position and position on a line words, copying, continuing and creating patterns, matching 3-D faces to 2-D shapes, sorting to a criterion and selecting criteria to sort items. As other studies have shown, for example, Saxe, Guberman and Gearhart (1987) and Young-Loveridge (1991), the children from the lower socio-economic group of Teacher A and mixed social group of Teacher D showed lower entry scores but had significantly improved by the end of the first year. The provision of extension tests in some areas, however, would have provided a fairer picture of gains obtained. Over the year estimation, ordering, reading and writing numbers and drawing 2-D shapes was emphasized in teaching and improved for all groups. In fact, by the end of the year most children were showing competence at Level 1 in Attainment Targets 2–5 of the National Curriculum in mathematics (1991).

Some tasks, in particular number-related tasks, for some groups of children, specifically those of Teacher A with lowest entry scores, showed most significant change and development over the reception year.

Test 1 **Counting Words** showed significant changes for children in all three schools. Children in the school of Teacher A moved from a mean length for rote counting of 14.7 (range 8 to 29) to 43* (range 12 to 100), of Teachers B and C from 40.7 (range 12 to 99) to 59.1* (range 29 to 100) and of Teacher D from 26.7 (range 10 to 100) to 46.8* (range 29 to 100).

Test 4 **Reading Numbers** also showed significant changes for children in all three schools. Children in the school of Teacher A moved from a mean number of numerals read of 4.8 (range 0 to 10) to 9.7* (range 6 to 13), of Teachers B and C from 9.1 (range 3 to 13) to 11* (range 10 to 13) and of Teacher D from 6.9 (range 1 to 13) to 11.1* (range 8 to 13).

Test 5 **Writing Numbers** also showed an increase in competence of children in all three schools. Children in the school of Teacher A moved from writing a mean of 3 numbers to 10 numbers over the year, of Teachers B and C from a mean of 5 to 10 numbers and of Teacher D from a mean of 2 numbers to 10 numbers. In other words, all children assessed in all three schools learned to write all numerals 1 to 10 over their first year in school.

Test 6 **Ordering Numbers** showed some significant results. In counting on one from a number presented, children in the school of Teacher A moved significantly from a mean of 6 to a mean of 9.1*, of Teachers B and C from 9 to 9.9 and of Teacher D from 8.2 to 10. In counting back one from a number presented, children in the school of Teacher A moved from a mean of 2.7 to 7.9*, of Teachers B and C from 7.3 to 9.5 and of Teacher D from 4.5 to 8.8*. The changes in scores for children of Teacher A and D were significant. The children of Teachers B and C had high entry scores for counting on and counting back one number.

Test 7 **Understanding Number Operations** showed a significant change in addition scores for children of Teacher A, from a mean of 3 to 4.8* out of 5, children of Teachers B and C and children of Teacher D showed high entry scores. For subtraction most children scored highly on school entry, thus, there were no significant changes.

Test 11 **Estimating and Measuring** which involved the use of measurement language showed a significant change in the scores for children of Teacher A, from a mean of 19.1 to 22* out of 23. Scores of children from the school of Teachers B and C and the school of Teacher D were high on school entry.

In Test 12 **Shape and Space** most children from all of the three schools were able to draw a circle on school entry. There was a significant change in the number of children of Teachers B and C able to draw a square (from 5 to 10*), and for children of both Teacher A and Teacher D a non-significant change from 6 to 10. There was not a significant change over the year in drawing a rectangle for children of Teacher A (from 5 to 6) or of Teachers B and C (from 4 to 8). The change for Teacher D (from 2 to 8*) was significant. There was a significant change over the year in the number of children drawing a triangle for Teacher A (from 4 to 9*) and Teacher D (from 4 to 10*) but not for children of Teachers B and C (from 3 to 7).

Test 9 **Estimation** of a set of 6 and 10 items showed some improvement over the year (taking plus or minus one as an acceptable response). Overall, children's accurate estimation of a set of 6 items rose from a mean score of 4.6 to 7.6 out of 10, and for a set of 10, from a mean score of 1 to 4.3 out of 10. A number of tests showed little change over the year since children had good entry scores. Test 12 **Describing 3-D Shapes** did not show a significant improvement over the year. Many children were familiar with the names of 2-D shapes at the beginning of the year and attempted to describe 3-D properties, using such words as 'tent', 'box' and 'ice cream cornet' or, occasionally, 'cone'. More children from the school of Teachers B and C were using terms like 'cylinder' 'cuboid' or 'cube' at the end of the first year. More children from the school of Teacher D were describing 3-D shapes in terms of properties such as 'it's got wide sides and thin sides' but were not using conventional terms for 3-D shapes. Perhaps the most interesting aspect of these results was that, in terms of Van Hieles' five-level theory of spatial development in school geometry which spans basic shape recognition to deductive reasoning and abstract theory construction (see Coxford, 1978), these children entered school with both Level 0 understanding of 2-D shape recognition as well as elements of Level 1 developing awareness of the properties of shape.

Scores for Test 2 **Counting Objects**, Test 3 **Order Invariance**, Test 8 **Division as Sharing and Multiplication as Continuous Addition**, Test 10 **Copying, Continuing and Creating Simple Patterns**, Test 12 **Shape and Space Matching of Faces of 3-D to 2-D Shapes**, Test 13 **Position Words** and Test 14 **Handling Data** all showed good entry scores, thus, significant changes were not observed.[2]

Over the period of Phase 4 of the project, for the measures used, it was not possible to demonstrate an association between teaching behaviours and children's achievement.

Classroom Observations

Content and Structure of Lessons

As shown in Phase 3, **Teacher A** worked consecutively with two groups of five children on a mathematical task whilst the rest of the class chose activities from wet and dry sand, water or home corner play, the book corner, small-scale or constructional toys. Tasks observed provided considerable evidence of deployment and consolidation of existing knowledge in counting, sorting and matching, using language of number, measurement and shape, comparing and ordering objects, with an emphasis on number and worksheet activities. Whilst there was scope inside the classroom and outside for open-ended exploration and practical investigation less opportunity was provided for reflection on this experience, for communicating it to others or for considering its potential in developing mathematical ideas. There was little correspondence between this practical activity and the teacher-directed classroom tasks which did, however, provide connections between language and symbols used and the experience they represented.

Teacher B allocated children to specific tables with specific materials, including jigsaw puzzles, card and board games and constructional apparatus and then circulated informally, leading, encouraging and supporting. This emphasis on activity and discussion was complemented by workbook tasks (Cambridge IMP), worksheet activities and computer games which involved simple matching, ordering, comparing and counting sets and offered an introduction to symbols connected to pictures, as well as simple counting and recording.

Overall, observed lessons suggested that in their reception year these children consolidated the informal knowledge they had brought into school and began to map this onto a more formal language of infant scheme mathematics from their introduction to the language of sets, relations between sets and the beginnings of mathematical structure. In eight out of fourteen lessons observed, however, no specific mathematics task was set. The main drawback to this approach was that as only a small number of children could be tutored closely in any one period much time was spent working without adult support. No practical mathematical investigations took place during the observation period though the teacher did report that simple weighing activities had been carried out in preparation for a specific workbook and simple class mapping diagrams were created to show relationships, as well as block graphs showing frequencies based on data collected.

Like Teacher B, **Teacher C** set a small task or 'job' whilst other children sat at tables with jigsaws, card and board games. The 'jobs' observed did not draw on the wide range of informal knowledge children brought into school and typically required counting, reading and writing numbers within ten or the identification and colouring of simple 2-D shapes in worksheet activities. Although a simple class mapping diagram and block graph was produced which allowed relations to be represented and a junk modelling activity involved children in sorting boxes by shape and size, few opportunities were provided to manipulate objects or consider relations between them which would provide a foundation for mathematical operations or a mathematical vocabulary to support them. Very little formal mathematical language was added to children's own common speech. From the earliest weeks in school Teacher C kept a number line (0 to 10) written on the chalk board. She was observed on more than one occasion to refer children to this, the focus of attention being on the ordinal aspect of number. The zero served to represent the point before one on the number line, in other words, the starting point. The connection between counting words and the number line was emphasized by the teacher leaving other, and equally important connections unexplored and running the risk that the number line would appear to children as arbitrary and unrelated to other important mathematical experiences.

Overall there was little opportunity to develop an awareness of number, shape and pattern or to carry out operations fundamental to dealing with the numerical, quantitative and spatial properties of objects and events encountered by children.

Teacher D worked with the combined reception intake on an introductory mathematics task before moving children into four groups which provided two teacher-led, and one unsupervised mathematics task, as well as one ancillary-led craft activity. Groups rotated once allowing all children to engage in at least two mathematics activities.

Teacher D's lessons showed that in terms of content she drew widely across the areas of number, shape and space, measurement and data handling. Throughout the emphasis was upon practical investigation, class and group discussion and the use of diagrams to record activities carried out and to express relationships which had been established. Noteworthy, too, was the extent to which teacher-led tasks utilized children's prior, or informal knowledge as a starting point for building upon and extending subject knowledge.

Counting skills brought into school were deployed within mathematical tasks, reinforcing the notion that the size of a set was given by the last number in the count, and as a means of checking the estimation of sets to be 'most', 'least', 'biggest', 'smallest' or the 'same'. By term two, children were being encouraged to check their counting of objects within one hundred by regrouping of items into tens and units. This helped to make explicit children's implicit understanding of the decade principle long before regrouping strategies were required for formal addition and subtraction of tens and units. This also led to counting in tens and, thus, to the consideration of number patterns.

In data handling Teacher D quickly built upon children's entry skills to sort objects to a criterion, through the introduction of the language of sets and relationships between them. She moved on from distinguishing members of a set from those which were not to the use of more than one attribute in classification and to the means for displaying such relationships with Venn and Carroll diagrams, arrows for mapping and simple block graphs. Children's existing knowledge of the names of common 2-D shapes was accessed, reinforced and extended through the discussion of the faces of 3-D shapes. The names of common solids were introduced as well as similarities and differences among 2-D and 3-D shapes being highlighted, for instance, in the number and length of sides and 'edges' or number of 'points'. Children's existing language of measurement was immediately extended through the introduction of comparison and ordering in weight and height, as well as by the use of non-standard measures in length, weight and time.

In terms of National Curriculum content, children were working under the guidance of a supportive adult within Level 1 and Level 2, thus, beyond their independent means and always towards the next stage of development. Throughout the year children's mathematical ideas were developed through teacher-designed activities aimed to increase awareness of spatial properties, the structure of number and the measurement of quantity, as well as to introduce sets, relations and logical thinking, with interconnections always emphasized. (Table 8.1 shows deployment of National Curriculum content with lessons.)

Table 8.1: Deployment of National Curriculum Subject Content in Segments

Teacher A

Segment	Using and Applying Mathematics			Number			Algebra		Shape and Space				Data Handling	
	Level 1		**(L1)**	**L1**		**L2**	**L1**	**L2**	**L1**			**L2**	**L1**	**L2**
	a)	**b)**	**c)**	**a)**	**b)**	**a)**	**a)**	**a)**	**a)**	**b)**	**c)**	**a)**	**a)**	**a)**
Lesson 1 Segment 1		/							/				/	
Lesson 2 Segment 1		/											/	
Lesson 3 Segment 1					/									
Lesson 4 Segment 1		/							/		/		/	
Lesson 5 Segment 1				/							/			

Teacher B

Segment	Using and Applying Mathematics			Number			Algebra		Shape and Space				Data Handling	
	Level 1 a)	b)	(L1) c)	L1 a)	b)	L2 a)	L1 a)	L2 a)	L1 a)	b)	c)	L2 a)	L1 a)	L2 a)
Lesson 1														
Segment 1				/									/	
Segment 2				/									/	
Lesson 2														
Segment 1				/										
Lesson 3														
Segment 1				/										
Lesson 4														
Segment 1				/										
Lesson 5														
Segment 1				/										
Segment 2				/										
Segment 3												/		

Teacher C

Segment	Using and Applying Mathematics			Number			Algebra		Shape and Space				Data Handling	
	Level 1 a)	b)	(L1) c)	L1 a)	b)	L2 a)	L1 a)	L2 a)	L1 a)	b)	c)	L2 a)	L1 a)	L2 a)
Lesson 1														
Segment 1				/										
Lesson 2														
Segment 1													/	
Segment 2				/										/
Lesson 3														
Segment 1				/								/		
Lesson 4														
Segment 1		.		/										
Lesson 5														
Segment 1									/					

Teacher D

Segment	Using and Applying Mathematics			Number			Algebra		Shape and Space				Data Handling	
	Level 1 a)	b)	(L1) c)	L1 a)	b)	L2 a)	L1 a)	L2 a)	L1 a)	b)	c)	L2 a)	L1 a)	L2 a)
Lesson 1														
Segment 1				/									/	
Segment 2													/	
Segment 3														/
Segment 4													/	
Segment 5														
Lesson 2														
Segment 1												/		
Segment 2												/	/	/
Segment 3									/					
Segment 4									/					
Segment 5									/					
Lesson 3														
Segment 1								/						
Segment 2			/					/						
Segment 3			/					/						
Segment 4			/											
Segment 5				/								/		
Lesson 4														
Segment 1					/			/						
Segment 2				/				/						
Segment 3								/						/
Segment 4								/						
Segment 5								/						
Segment 6								/						
Lesson 5														
Segment 1					/									/
Segment 2													/	
Segment 3*														
Segment 4*														
Segment 5*														

* No mathematics

Lesson Components

Teacher A did not instruct formally or make explicit links to children's prior learning. Each lesson was introduced by telling children what to do and, where necessary, introducing the materials to be used.

> Now what I want you to do is, I want you to sort them out ... Right, now you all have a set of multilink. I want to see if you can make me another set which is exactly the same ...

Can you find number one? Can you find where number two is? Right, can you draw a line in from number one to number two?

The fish is done for you. The fish is matched with the fish. What's this one? (A frog.) Can you find another frog?

Once children were working she observed, questioned and assessed, where necessary simplifying or modifying the task by adding smaller steps or suggesting alternative strategies for individual children. At this stage questioning and cued elicitation played an important diagnostic role in establishing what children knew or could do.

Are all the balloons the same? No? How are they different? They are different shapes. That's right. What different shapes have you got?

Making a matching set of multilink cubes was simplified by ordering the cube model in a line so that children could construct their own set by one-to-one correspondence. For another child the model was placed on a sheet of paper then he was instructed to draw round one cube, find the matching cube and place it in the same circle. Whilst children worked the teacher continued to monitor individuals, coaching, supporting and correcting misunderstanding.

Is that a circle? It doesn't matter about the colour. Now what comes after 10? (11.) 11. 11 is two 1s.

Finally, she would review and comment on results as a group though still extending individual responses. In one lesson, for instance, a child who had been asked to make a set of the biggest shape tiles was told to put them in a line and check the size by placing one tile on top of another. This procedure was repeated for the 'smallest' and 'next biggest' set. In another lesson after making multilink train models, the teacher read aloud the activity card instructions and supported children's efforts by commenting, questioning and providing strategies.

Right, it says which trains are longer than this blue line. That one? Any more? Put it along there. It's not longer?

No, it says which trains are shorter so that one's shorter. What about that one? Is it longer or shorter? Try and see . . .

With two children the task was extended even further.

Which one of yours is the longest, Martin? What about the next longest? Do you know how much longer? It's got more hasn't it?

This went beyond visual comparison of length of two items to numerical comparison. For Martin she supplied the answer and for a second child she persisted with questions until the correct response was secured.

In **Teacher B**'s classroom, too, very little direct instruction of mathematics took place and children's independent activity provided early, informal experience of shape, size, comparison, number, pattern and relationship. Much of her work was incidental and resulted from informal monitoring rather than from pre-planned tasks. In so doing she would lead games, encourage pupils to support one another or help generate their own solutions. Set tasks were clearly introduced with children informed, or reminded what was to be done.

> What are we looking for? (Pairs.) Pairs. Right. We'll have a go. They are asking you to put two ducks in a set. Do you remember? You have to go carefully round 2 ducks then you have a set.

> Let's start with the 8 first . . . then we take some away to form the other numbers. Right, Anna, so it's knives to go with forks . . . Now it says, How many are in each row?

Support for children's games was marked by her style of tutoring and guiding, or 'scaffolding' of their attempts. Her strategy was to 'talk aloud' to the actions being carried out, thus, making explicit the player's intentions and offering a model of self questioning which provided the steps for the procedures required.

> Oh, he's putting them together very carefully . . . They are the same size, aren't they? Are they the same pattern? . . . and are they the same colour?

Furthermore she involved the rest of the group by inviting them to monitor or 'shadow' the moves being made.

> Oh, David . . . can you see what you've done there . . . Would you like to check it again. I think Alex has spotted what happened (He's done 5!) Instead of . . . ? 4! (chorus)

At all points checking was encouraged and corrections used to provide further challenges.

> You've put 5, so how many less than 5 do we need on that one? (4.) Yes, we need 4, so we need one less.

> That one has 4. How many in that row? You only had to leave one out of that one . . . Just one too many because . . . how many? 1, 2, 3. Good.

On other occasions children were encouraged to work together and then check with her whether they had the same answer. Games supplied a context to connect cardinal to ordinal aspects of number, as well as a purpose for setting early number problems.

Who is going to be first . . . second . . . let's see who is going to be third?
How many more do you need to fill your fruit tree?
(In other words how many more must be added to 2 to make 5.)

Anna's got only 2 so how many more than Anna have you got?
You've got 1 more than Anna and you've got 2 more to get.

It (multilink staircase) goes from 1 to 10. Watch. 2, 4 . . . (6!)

By contrast, with workbook exercises the teacher checked each stage before giving instructions for executing the next. There was more telling and instructing in procedures than tutoring and guiding of children's own ideas which marked the assistance given in independent activity. Self-checking and giving peer support, however, was still encouraged.

Much of **Teacher C**'s classroom discourse provided support to organization, concerning rules and routines related to materials, management and control, rather than support to mathematics instruction. Little mathematical instruction took place. The most supportive discourse recorded took place in conjunction with the tutoring of a small group for a game of picture lotto and, on another occasion, in conjunction with use of the computer. This teacher's most sustained and supportive classroom discourse was incidental, unplanned and fortuitous in nature. Comments made, concerning her own recollected experience of learning arithmetic through games at home, bore some resemblance to the environment she created for her young children.

Children don't seem to play as many precise games as they used to, like ludo, snakes and ladders, and dominoes. Very few have ever done them or card games. I don't understand because as soon as I sat upon the floor we had dominoes to play with. The dominoes were wonderful for counting.

Attempts to take account of children's interests in, for instance, the 'secret picnic job' resulted in understatement of mathematical points. Here children were asked to draw a number, between 1 and 9, of different sandwiches, ham being triangles and cheese being squares, on a paper printed with a circular plate. Children counted the sandwiches drawn and placed the number in the box provided. Little description, comparison or discussion of 2-D shapes took place during the task which was stimulated, in fact, by a sandwich-making activity which had taken place the previous day.

A 'cherry job' which involved counting three cherries on a worksheet, tracing over the numbers 1 to 3 and colouring the cherries, was introduced briefly.

. . . you sit down to do your cherry job. You can do your counting with your cherries and matching.

More discussion, however, focused on children's number formation and name writing. A bottle top sorting activity started without a clear goal being stated by the teacher who, instead, simply talked aloud about what she was doing. Most of this self-talk focused on deciding the colour of the top rather than on the purpose of the activity. She did, however, explain how to use the sorting tray.

> I want the yellow over the yellow and the red over the red . . . I was putting green in that one. Right . . . they are for making, like big ponds, to sort . . .

The tasks observed lacked mathematical purpose, distorting children's developing understanding of the number system as well as ignoring important mathematical elements of sets and relations between sets, shape and space and measurement of quantity. Children were not provided with a formally stated goal or a summary of the results and instructions which were given typically emphasized execution of the task, providing assistance with tool skills or preparation for recording the activity.

For **Teacher D** each lesson had a clear agenda and on each occasion children were provided with a clear and simple goal.

> We are going to sort ourselves into lots of different sets . . .
> We are going to talk about shapes this morning . . .

Throughout different verbal and concrete representations were offered.

> Lots of different sets – different ways to sort ourselves into different groups. I'm putting this piece of wire . . . and it's separating into two circles . . . and we're going to make those two sets . . .

Cross-referencing from the class introduction to subsequent group work was used to link key moves, to draw attention to salient points, new elements to be added or parallel representations to be supplied.

> Now then, with Mrs W and me you are going to put this information that we've got here, your different sets, you're going to put it onto things called graphs or charts.

Questions were used throughout class discussion to establish what was already known and to remind children of prior experience. They were used to involve children in a teacher demonstration and to encourage prediction. Self questions were used to accompany both the teacher's and children's actions as a means of teaching new strategies. Since this teacher introduced new concepts, new terms and new procedures in every lesson, however, attempts to link to what was already known were not always successful and led to an increased reliance on elicitation (with and without cues), on telling or informing, and on showing and demonstrating.

> Now then, does anyone know what shape this is?
> Think of something that you put in your fridge to get cold, to pop in your drink.

Look at the shapes and see something that's different about them. (A set of nothings.) We've had a set of nothings . . . What are we going to have a set of what . . . ? We haven't done . . . is that a big or a little square? There you are then . . . a set of big squares and a set of little squares.

Where new procedures were involved children were simply told what to do.

You are going to write your name on these pieces of card . . . and then with felt pens you're going to draw a line, an arrow, between your name and whichever colour your hair is.

OK, so you put the sugar at the top. Then the marvel. Now which is going to be heaviest, your marvel or your coffee? Weigh them and see . . . Good, the marvel. Put it next then . . . Now the coffee and apples.

Teacher D designed all her own lessons, making no use of published scheme work to provide structure to her planning. This led to errors of judgment in two of the observed lessons. In the example above from a weighing lesson over-estimation of children's understanding of measurement resulted in her planning an activity which required children to order eight masses from heaviest to lightest, using a balance bar to compare two items at a time. Since arranging just three masses in sequence, requires that the third mass must be compared with each of the other two masses before the order can be decided, the ordering of eight items was conducted entirely through the teacher's directions. Furthermore the children were asked to predict the sequence on the basis of visual and manipulative comparison of items, *before* using the balance bar and *without* recording the predicted sequence. Since the items included both small, heavy items and large, light ones there was some discrepancy between the predicted and actual results. This lesson took place before children had had the opportunity to develop the idea of quantity through experience of simple comparison of pairs of items, thus, even the ordering of three masses might have been inappropriate. In another observed lesson inaccurate instructions and misleading apparatus was compounded by a reluctance on the part of the teacher to inform children how to carry out a simple sorting task. Children were provided with a pile of shape tiles and a set hoop twisted into two. They were told to make two sets when, in fact, the teacher wanted them to make one set in order to distinguish between members of a set from those which were not (squares/ not squares). Even when children failed to understand the teacher persisted with cued questions in an attempt to 'elicit' the response which she had determined in advance. In the case of the earlier lesson the teacher simply told children which items to weigh and, thus, conducted the activity. In the later lesson her unwilling-ness to inform children how to carry out the task served at first to increase their misunderstanding but led eventually to her modelling a self-questioning strategy. When introducing a new group activity Teacher D usually worked through one or two examples with children, then she withdrew leaving them to work alone. Once children had attempted the task independently she observed, assessed and retaught.

Like Teacher A, she modified by simplifying and adding more steps and, like Teacher B, used questioning or 'talk aloud, self-questioning' in order to make her decision-making explicit. When children were introduced to a Carroll diagram she demonstrated by breaking the task into a series of step-by-step questions.

> Now this says red/not red and down the side, here, it says triangle/not triangle . . . So let's pick up this. What is this and what colour is it? (Red.) So where does this go? (Beside red.) Well done. Straight away you knew. It goes beside red and beside triangle. Now . . . what shape? (Oblong.) A blue . . . oblong or rectangle. Does it go here? (No! chorus) So it goes 'not triangle', Is it red? (No! chorus) No, so it goes in 'not red.' See if you can sort these shapes into the right compartments for me.

In both class and group work Teacher D used step-by-step, closed questioning to elicit a choral response whilst she provided a simultaneous concrete demonstration as a means of scaffolding. This linked the verbal to the physical demonstration and, at the same time, made explicit the sequence of decisions being made. Following this, one or two children would carry out the action whilst the teacher led the group through the same step-by-step sequence of questions and choral response, this time linked to the child's actions. Finally she would leave the group to continue independently and then review, comment, give feedback and repeat teaching points, where necessary.

Teacher Interviews

With respect to the four teachers' own primary mathematics education the emphasis had been on formal teaching and systematical calculation with little basis provided for ideas derived from practical experience. Teachers B and D, however, remembered enjoying this. Teacher C mentioned that her father had involved her in mental calculation, for instance, with respect to money and weight. Less enthusiasm for secondary mathematics had been generated though Teacher B made positive comments about geometry and algebra. Teacher D reported taking her general certificate of school education (GCSE) as an adult and enjoying it. She noted that her experience as a parent had been an influence on her views of learning mathematics just as Teacher C referred to the impact of her experience as a grandparent. Teachers A and B, who had trained for primary teaching in the 1960s recalled receiving little mathematics teaching on their courses. Teacher C who had trained for secondary schooling had received none. Teacher D regarded her more recent training as practical and informative with relevant mathematical ideas identified. Teachers A and B had gained the view at college that practical experience was important but did not appear to have learned at this time how to map this onto a body of interrelated mathematical ideas.

In terms of what children should learn Teachers A, B and C stressed the importance of direct teaching, in particular, of early number concepts. Teacher D thought all mathematical concepts were relevant with an emphasis on exploration and talk. In fact all four teachers were in agreement that there should be directed practical experience and also that formal teaching had an important place. Advice which would be given to students focused for Teachers A, B and C on identifying children's current understanding, whilst teacher D stressed practical work. The importance of repetition, reinforcement and revisiting of themes was underlined. Teachers A and B interestingly expressed an interest in further professional development in early years mathematics.

Teacher A remembered that in primary school 'you would just get a page of sums and do them, it was very formal'. In secondary school she had 'coped' with mathematics. She 'didn't get a fantastic pass at ordinary level but passed'. She could not remember doing much mathematics at college. It was not her main subject and 'no powerful people, events or textbooks came to mind'.

She believed young children should learn basic number concepts. These 'were very important, especially in the reception class because if children did not grasp them there would be problems further up the school'. She did a lot of work on numbers, 'probably more than shape'. This 'came in but, perhaps, it was not stressed as much as it should be'. Her children needed 'lots of work on arithmetic' because one 'could not assume that they got it at home'. They 'definitely needed a *lot* of practical experience' which was *not* the case when she was at school. There were 'always maths things around for them to use. Children did need to discover but for some it would take for ever'. They also needed to be *told* facts, as she had been at school. In fact, they needed both.

She tried to ensure all groups covered a mathematics task within a day, ideally every day but certainly at least three times a week. Groups were of mixed attainment since there were special needs children in the class. If all the low attainers were together 'there was very little feedback from them'. Sometimes in a mixed group 'they would spark off from another child. If you had them altogether it was hard work'. Records from the nursery were available and she would carry out her own simple assessment of number and colour recognition, building a tower and pattern sequences. She also 'filled in a National Curriculum report which made sure you were going in the right direction'. She would *not*, however, fill in 'knows' only 'has experience of' or 'has covered'.

Teacher B's primary experience had also been 'very, very formal with no practical experience at all' but she had enjoyed it. She thought that some children must have dreaded arithmetic, 'not getting anything right'. At secondary school she took mathematics to ordinary level but 'in no way would have taken it any further'. She did, however, enjoy algebra and geometry. Like Teacher A, she 'did not get a lot of mathematics at college' and noted, 'you hoped that when you went on practice you got a good teacher and that was, more or less, where you picked a lot of it up'. In terms of what mathematics was important to young children, 'relationships, sorting, matching, ordering, counting . . . it almost leads itself on from one topic to another'. Questioned about her style of tutoring children's games, she agreed that 'it just becomes such a natural process in reception. They all come in at such different levels, it is an ongoing thing . . . sets, then much later, recognizing and writing numbers'. The IMP workbooks were 'really an assessment, almost consolidating . . . not the *work* that they were doing'. Workbooks 'were useless without what had gone before . . . well, not *useless*, but you could get so much more from them'. If children found them difficult she would just 'slot in some extra little worksheets'. The IMP scheme was useful in providing 'the exact concept' and the activities gave a 'little prod, another idea that you had not thought of, which might be, related to your theme'.

Often what children found difficult was ordinal numbers. They were given lots of practical experience 'getting them in lines, for instance, almost from the moment they started school . . . you're first, you're second, you're third . . .' and so on. Some children still found it difficult. Also difficult was the stage when they could see a problem in practical terms but they needed a numerical answer, in other words, the move from concrete representation to number facts. Talking aloud about what they were doing was important. To assess 'you observed and questioned indirectly, so they could answer while they are still playing a game in a group'.

Should children discover for themselves? Yes, they should but it had to be directed. They needed practical experiences but they also needed direction and organization. The National Curriculum provided a useful framework and the programmes of study were consulted when a new theme was being planned for half a term. Abler ones could be challenged through the topic, 'to take it that step further'. Not much whole class mathematics discussion took place 'just five or ten minutes for grouping or counting, like, how many in the class, how many absent? One child, she remembered, could always answer and this had triggered off others. Planning for mixed attainment groups was difficult in reception, especially when the 'Christmas starters came in'. By the Summer Term, 'children would be working together on the same sort of thing, in a more structured way'.

Teacher C could not remember much about her own experiences of learning mathematics at school. Her experience as a parent had been an influence on her teaching . Her own primary classes had been 'big . . . 45 . . . and were streamed A and B'. Mathematics and, in fact, all learning was formal. She had had the same teacher for four years and her class 'just worked through sums set on the board. If you finished A sums, you just went on to B sums'. There was 'lots of practice of operations'. Her mother died when she was young and her father brought up the children while he ran his own business. He had been 'good at mathematics'. There was no 'equipment' to help with calculation so mental arithmetic was important. He would ask his children real problems like, 'how much will x cwt of potatoes cost at x per cwt?' She noted, 'children do appreciate links to their own experience'.

At secondary school she was also placed in streamed classes, 'A or B'. In some ways, she felt, the B stream had received more careful teaching and gained 'better reasoning'. Her brother, who had gone to the secondary modern school, helped her with mathematics. He was 'pretty good' and without his help *she* would not have been. She had 'liked geometry, especially working out the proofs'. She had a science degree and went into secondary teaching. Her best training for primary schooling had been under a teaching head teacher. 'She had given sound, practical advice, particularly in mathematics, which is not just figures. She looked at how you could relate mathematics to English and to the topic'. This teacher approached teaching from the point of view of 'children thinking for themselves. Then she would ask herself, do they know, do they understand?' Teacher C noted, 'you listen to how they explain it back to the teacher and build on that . . . It is difficult to explain how and why if you do not understand. Children learn from watching each other, how the high achiever grasps it, for instance. They listen'. She felt peer observation was a powerful source for learning. She also felt children worried more about mathematics than English and that there was a 'need to give back confidence'. 'Planning *must* be in a cross-curricular way.' If mathematics was *not* part of the topic she thought how it could be linked, how it could be introduced to the child so that it meant more.

Teacher D enjoyed mathematics and was good at it in the primary school. She became less interested in the secondary school where she let 'mathematics slip'. A Cambridge extension course reinforced her view of the importance of explaining well. Her own learning, thus, made her aware of the importance of teaching mathematics effectively and her own experience as a parent had been a powerful influence, too. She had gained a science degree but was interested in the way children learned, 'It all hinges on the way it is put over at the beginning'. At college her mathematics tutors had been extremely informative. 'It was a very good course, very practical but there was thinking of the ideas behind it.'

What should young children learn? She thought of all the mathematics concepts which were relevant and dealt with them in a practical way. Nursery records were available and she did her own 'little assessment of number, colour and so on'. She always put lots of things out, talked about them and allowed children to explore, to remember. She 'began in a practical way and reinforced all the time'. There were lots and lots of different ways of exploring something practically, and recording in different ways. She believed in teaching, *not* in children finding out for themselves.

Direct teaching had a place. Her children 'always started with carpet time to introduce new work but concentration varied. The National Curriculum 'kept them on target'. Her work was based on her PGCE (Primary) course which she extended with her own ideas and with teachers' resource books. Scheme work was not used. A variety of mathematics equipment was essential: solid and textured shapes, multilink and unifix cubes with number hats, cards for sequencing, apparatus for weighing and lego for sorting, sequencing and shape and space concepts. Her observed way of working had allowed the researcher to see what might be done. This would not be possible with large groups of children and one member of staff. What she had been observed to do in one lesson would take a week to do alone, rotating the activities. Sometimes an activity would be spread over two to three days. Children would be grouped at separate tables and she would give them appropriate tasks. She would watch and listen. 'There's probably someone there who can't read and is not interested in writing but actually very quick at maths.' To challenge the bright ones she would 'try to get them separately and talk to them a bit more'.

Appendix 4 provides extracts from teachers' interviews. The interviews have been presented in some detail in order to provide an indication of the complex interactions among teachers' mathematical subject knowledge, views and beliefs about learning and teaching, personal biographies and educational histories. Moreover, as the subject knowledge of generalist teachers interacts with attitudes and beliefs about teaching, learning and classrooms so too will young pupils in their classrooms develop similar assumptions about the nature of mathematical knowledge based on the experience they have had in primary classrooms.

Whilst it may be helpful to identify disciplinary knowledge as a distinct component of the generalist teacher's pedagogical subject knowledge, as the interviews demonstrate, teachers are themselves products of thirteen years of formal schooling and have developed assumptions about the nature of mathematical knowledge, about learners and teaching, which continue to exert a powerful influence on subsequent learning in higher education and in continuing professional development. Furthermore, whilst views on learning and teaching and the curriculum may continue to change in ways which impact upon practice, subject knowledge may continue to influence the content of tasks designed and set a limit to the flexibility with which teachers can respond to the challenges that they encounter in teaching. In this regard it is entirely appropriate that the current educational debate concerning subject knowledge and specialist teaching should target initial teacher training as the focus for change and improvement.

The intention of this section has been to present a full and accurate description and overview of the empirical findings in order to allow a judgment to be made about the adequacy of the research process. This paves the way for a consideration of the theoretical findings, or theory building, derived from the data represented. Hence the next section will focus on the core category, pedagogical subject knowledge, and relationships with the sub-categories of pupils' mathematical knowledge, teachers' subject knowledge, knowledge of learning and teaching, and curriculum knowledge. The three main components of qualitative research – data, analytic procedure and theory – will then be reviewed in the final chapter.

Discussion

The analysis of data in this chapter led back towards the progressive focusing on teachers' pedagogical subject knowledge. Figure 8.1 attempts to identify the relationships among pupils' informal knowledge, teachers' subject knowledge, knowledge and beliefs concerning learning and teaching, and curriculum knowledge which constitute pedagogical subject knowledge, and which are exemplified in classroom practice.

Both the lessons observed and the interviews carried out served to emphasize the importance of subject content knowledge in teaching and the impact of this on practice even at this early stage of schooling. Teacher D's knowledge of mathematical content and pedagogy had given her confidence in setting up explorations in number, classification, in spatial properties and measurement of quantity, in bringing out the mathematical relationships involved, and in displaying these in pictures, diagrams and models. Teacher C, by contrast, recognized the importance

Figure 8.1: Classroom Practice Exempifying Pedagogical Subject Knowledge

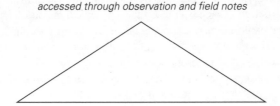

accessed through observation and field notes

Children's informal
knowledge

(accessed through assessment)

Teachers' mathematical
subject knowledge

Knowledge and beliefs
concerning learning and
teaching mathematics

Curriculum knowledge, or
use of appropriate
resources/materials
(accessed through interview)

of exploiting children's interests but lacked a firm grasp of subject matter knowledge without which she was unable to develop explanations or question effectively. Consideration of the interviews in the light of the observations illustrated the way in which knowledge of mathematics was interwoven with assumptions about the way young children learn. These assumptions, in turn, were apparently derived from teachers' own learning experiences. The belief in the value of practical experience of Teacher A, for instance, translated into classroom practice, which, in some cases, lacked a clear understanding of the mathematical ideas behind the material being handled. Teacher B, by contrast, who both provided practical experience and introduced scheme workbooks early, was supported in her choice of early mathematical content which she was able to link skilfully to children's informal knowledge to support their learning. Only Teacher D used formal class presentations to introduce systematically new mathematical ideas and attempted to develop these through children's own activities, by reflecting on, and communicating, the results of investigations. She showed awareness of the importance of explanations, providing explicit links among representations used, verbal, concrete, numerical and symbolic. Accessing prior knowledge and making links to new learning, however, tended to take place in whole class introductions which, perhaps, did not provide the best context for exploring individual responses. In all aspects of her work, however, she displayed precisely those teaching behaviours associated in the effective instruction literature with higher achievement scores, as well as providing her children with most opportunity to engage in academic content over the year. The significance she attached to concrete representations of mathematical ideas was reflected, too, in the detailed response given in her interview to the question of classroom resources. The free practical exploration provided by Teacher A was not guided in order to develop specific ideas or to build them into an organized structure. Teacher B did, through her extension of children's games, allow both free exploration of, and guidance in, making connections to a more formal mathematics of number, sets and relationships. She was the only teacher observed to access and extend children's informal knowledge of simple addition and subtraction word problems known to be brought into school. Teacher C encouraged practical activity on the one hand and the building up of numerical notation on the other, but was less aware of the need for children to experiment with the way the number system was built up, with operations carried out in numbers and with relationships among numbers discovered. Furthermore, she was the only teacher observed to engage children in interactions, concerning behaviour and classroom procedures, as well as other non-mathematics topics which resulted in correspondingly less interactions on mathematics content. Over the year all teachers with the exception of Teacher D placed more emphasis on number than classification, shape and space, measurement of quantity and data handling.

In contrast to the first school studies of Bennett *et al.* (1984) and Desforges and Cockburn (1987), constraints of classroom organization did *not* lead to a predominance of monitoring of individual children, working largely alone on low-level, practice tasks. The choice and flexibility provided by three of the settings (of Teachers A, B and C) and the additional teaching staff available in the fourth (of Teacher D) allowed the provision of more intensive, teacher-led tasks which encouraged more group collaboration, active learning and joint problem solving. Whilst there was still much evidence of number and 2-D shape, and worksheet practice, teachers spent most of their time observing and assessing, coaching, guiding and correcting. In fact the greater the task demand the stronger was the need for instructing in, or informing of, procedures or making more explicit the strategies required for carrying out the task. Clearly teachers did not have time for lengthy diagnostic interviews but instead tasks presented allowed them to assess the extent to which children could answer questions about content and apply knowledge strategically. This illustrated the dynamic process of knowledge development in response to particular learning experiences and to situational demands. There was much evidence in classroom observations that teachers' scripts were flexible and dynamic, changing in response to feedback from children, with tasks being simplified, modified or extended, where necessary. In other words, task demand *changed* in the process of tutoring and guiding and in the 'scaffolding' of children's responses. This casts some doubt on a *static* notion of task demand and the matching of task to learner which ignores the dynamic role of social interaction between the experienced adult and the less experienced child in providing the impetus for learning. This finding is consistent with conclusions drawn in Chapter 4.

Observed lessons showed that within a mixed ability group there were many examples of teachers providing different levels and types of support and simplifying tasks in different ways for different children. This suggests an awareness on the part of these teachers of the *interaction* between assessment and instruction *and* a recognition that the teacher takes a lead in modelling cognitive strategies and in providing a temporary support to children's early efforts. Such practice has much in common with the cognitive strategy instruction described earlier in Chapter 3 and suggests that these teachers were providing children with the opportunity to construct meaning through their modification of tasks to take account of prior knowledge and, at the same time, 'scaffolding' extended responses through the provision of tutoring and guiding and 'talk aloud' strategies. If such processes are *unique* to learning and teaching mathematics in reception classrooms then they serve to provide a model of professional practice which warrants a wider dissemination to primary teachers.

The way teachers' perceptions of the attainments of individual pupils fed into their decision-making was less easy to access but, nevertheless, powerful. Both formally, in interview, and informally, in day-to-day discussion across the year, teachers offered contextualized accounts of young children's learning. This took the form of descriptions of children's unexpected responses to specific classroom tasks or anecdotes concerning their strategies and the outcomes of their activities. Rather than making use of the nursery records and assessment data mentioned by two, these teachers were accumulating rich, contextualized knowledge of children's attainments derived from close observation of the impact of particular experiences, in particular contexts, on particular children (see Table 8.2 for examples of teachers' observations).

The detailed consideration of what has been described as 'initiation–response–feedback' sequences by Sinclair and Coulthard (1975) and Edwards and Mercer (1987), or 'information questions' by Cazden (1988), which elicit information from children about topics for which the teacher already has the answer, showed that such interactions served a variety of educational purposes. Teacher D, for instance, used questions to check knowledge, to remind, to invite involvement in a demonstration, to stimulate prediction, to model, to encourage generation of 'self questions', to support children's actions, to review a sequence of procedures, to stimulate a choral response, to clarify, to summarize, to extend and to challenge. There were occasions when unhelpful and persistent questions signalled teaching had broken down through the 'mismatch' of teacher demand and the child's capacity to respond but these were in the minority. Unhelpful elicitations did not occur, as Edwards and Mercer (1987) suggested, because of teachers' mistaken belief that children should 'discover' or that knowledge should be seen to 'emerge' spontaneously from the child. These teachers did *not* believe children could learn by discovery as the interviews showed. They occurred, instead, when teachers misjudged the task which was set and the response which could be obtained. It happened, for instance, when Teacher A pressed a child to go beyond visual comparison of the length of two items and co-ordinate this with numerical comparison (how much longer) which many 7-year olds find difficult. Such situations arose less from an over-reliance on cued elicitation than from gaps or misconceptions in teachers' subject knowledge for teaching. In addition, they indicate the importance of using what is known about the development of *children's* mathematical ideas as a basis for sequencing topics for instruction.

Practice among the different teachers, as well as the practice of one teacher

Table 8.2: Teachers' Observations on Children's Learning in Groups

Teacher A	Teacher B	Teacher C	Teacher D
I usually do keep them all together. If you have all the Rachels (a special needs child) together you get very little feedback from them, whereas they'll spark off from one another, you know. If you have them (special needs children) altogether it's hard work.	How do you find out what children learn? Well, it's been a useful exercise this because it's made me think . . . I was thinking . . . what do I do . . . observation and indirect questioning, isn't it? That's why I have had to sit and think you see, well, what do I do? And then I've thought it out and I've pictured myself sitting and I thought, yes, it's by observation and indirectly . . . and it's in a practical situation because if you did it face-to-face they would just clam up, wouldn't they, and you wouldn't . . . In a group situation because they almost, sometimes they do . . . they answer you without looking at you. They are still busy doing it and, you know, they're not being rude. They are so engrossed but they still answer . . . Yes, they have got to talk about it, haven't they? Not just talk . . . I remember saying that to a student . . . don't be afraid to let them talk about it. They need to, don't they, otherwise how do they get it all together? It's like you asking me these questions. I thought, well, what do you	Asking how do they know or understand . . . ? You listen to how they explain it back to the teacher and build on that. It's difficult to explain how and why if you don't understand. You listen . . . how the child who grasps, the high achiever. Children worry more about mathematics than English. They learn from watching others. There is a need to get back confidence. It's very relaxed with children working together, isn't it? I mean taking part in an activity together. It's a fairer judgment of the child, then . . . of his real capabilities . . . observing games and joining in. In my own experience of learning . . . you were always faced 'head on' with something and asked questions . . . or a sharp test put in front of you. If you didn't know it, that was it, you didn't know it. There was no way that it was considered that you might know it because no-one had ever bothered to give you real practical experience and observe your communication with anyone else of your own age. There's quite a large number of children who only learn from 'hands on' and the 'doing'. Early years maths has to be more in	Separate groups work at separate tables with separate tasks. I watch and listen. It's interesting to see if there is a correlation between attainments in mathematics and English. I wouldn't have thought there was at 6 or 7 years. Able children? I try to get them separately and talk to them a little more. And, yes, give appropriate tasks. I also try really to watch and listen because it's very easy to think 'Oh, bright girl . . .' and there's probably someone else who can't read and is not interested in writing but actually very quick with maths.

Table 8.2: Cont'd

Teacher A	Teacher B	Teacher C	Teacher D
	do . . . it makes you . . . sort of think, doesn't it? I think it was last year. I had this child who I could never catch out. He would always know how many there were in the class . . . 25 in the class and 2 absent today . . . He'd get it right all the time. And you only need one like that and it triggers the others off and they'll have a go and eventually . . . but it doesn't come so naturally as it does to that one child. No, but it's amazing how a challenge . . . Do they surprise you? Yes, they do, don't they? You shouldn't ever under-estimate them, should you? I sat there with these questions and it just did me a power of good. I just sort of wrote and wrote and I read it back afterwards and I thought, gosh! I didn't realize . . . so it helps sometimes to get questions put in front of you.	smaller groups. I wouldn't always want to group them rigidly because I think it's . . . I know sometimes a very able child will want especially to practise, want always to tell rather than explain or . . . ask the less able child what the problem is . . . I still think there's a lot that children pick up from each other . . . There again, it's from personal experience . . . the ability of the able child to tell the less average child something in a more understandable way . . . It is expertise. They are on that level. They can see, they are able . . . they are not necessarily putting themselves into the less able child's place but they can see more quickly what the problem is. Possibly something they've more recently experienced themselves . . . in a nice, relaxed way. They'd rather aim to be as good as another child . . . rather than wanting to be as good as a teacher. The teacher is an adult. They would say, 'I don't know as much as they do' . . . 'they always know better' . . . 'they always have more to say'. They do model themselves on . . . know who's best at number or reading in the whole class . . . and they judge by that. And the less able often works on that model unfortunately.	

across lessons, varied in terms of the mathematical content introduced, its representation in tasks, in the support provided and, consequently, in the quality of instruction offered. This diversity in observed practice raises important issues with respect to teachers' pedagogical subject knowledge and, more specifically, to its influence on the content and processes of mathematical instruction. As noted already, the sources and development of teachers' subject knowledge are subtle and complex and, as yet, by no means perfectly understood. Whilst there is now a nationally prescribed school mathematics curriculum there is less certainty about what constitutes an effective mathematics teacher education curriculum. In fact, we know considerably more about the way young children learn mathematics than we know about how much mathematics students teachers need to learn, how much teaching mathematics and how much learning to teach mathematics should be provided. Mathematical concepts and competences develop over time so, as Vergnaud (1982) noted, conceptual fields such as additive structures form slowly from 3 to 14 years and beyond. The same case could be made for spatial measures, multiplicative structures, dynamics, classes, classification and boolean operations. It seems reasonable to suppose that *all* primary teachers should have a good grounding in these conceptual fields. In a recent study of subject matter knowledge in mathematics of primary post-graduate student teachers during training, Carré and Ernest (1993) noted that mathematical subject matter knowledge was not taught specifically on the course and that, in general, change in subject matter knowledge of mathematics was small, and not significant. Student teachers relied, instead, as the experienced teachers in this project appeared to do, on recalling their own school learning in order to plan and teach mathematics or 'study it on the job'.

In order to broaden our understanding of learning to teach Shulman (1986a) has argued that prospective teachers should have a case literature which catches and exemplifies the wisdom of practice. Whilst this phase of the project has concentrated on taking sample lessons from each of four teachers over children's first year in school a further phase is now considering whole sequences of lessons which introduce and develop the same topic over time with different teachers, as well as different topics with the same teacher. The aim is to provide a broader base of case knowledge to add to the practical knowledge available to teachers and students in training, through the construction of a body of knowledge on reception class processes related to teaching and learning mathematics. This knowledge is intended to provide teachers and students in training with the opportunity to consider how other teachers solve the same or similar, practical classroom problems that *they* meet and to consider how these might apply to their own practice. Building such a case literature from the practice of seven further experienced reception teachers, which has now been completed, will be one way to increase our understanding of subject knowledge for teaching and the development of professional practice.

Conclusion

The intention of this chapter has been to complete the reporting of the empirical phases of the project. The final goal is to provide the clear, analytical story with a specification of the relationships among categories. Accordingly the last chapter of the book will review the aims of the project and the key issues, conceptual and empirical, which emerged from the literature. It will set the context for re-assessing the role of teachers' subject knowledge in the analytic story. This will lead to the critical consideration of the research design and, finally, to an outline of the main implications of the project.

Notes

1   The frequent readjustments to observation times which were made, in fact, increased the writer's confidence in the representativeness of the samples obtained over the year.
2   t significant at the 5 per cent level.

9   Towards a Deeper Understanding of Pedagogical Subject Development

The Development of Learning and Teaching: The Context to the Project

Introduction

As noted in Chapter 1 teachers' knowledge of subjects and the effective deployment of this knowledge in classroom teaching has been promoted by policy makers as a key factor in the debate concerning the raising of standards in teaching. New lines of enquiry both conceptual and empirical have stimulated the interest of researchers in investigating the nature and substance of teachers' subject knowledge and, in particular, its transformation in classroom teaching.

Before examining the substantive and methodological issues, it was necessary first to consider some of the underlying assumptions, understandings and beliefs which have helped to influence knowledge production and utilization, to define legitimate problems and, hence, to shape the direction of policy and research.

Clearly subject matter content is fundamental to teaching. This has been accepted by researchers and policy-makers alike. As Ball (1990) observed, knowledge of subject content, in this case mathematics, is obviously fundamental to being able to help someone to learn. The notion that subject knowledge could be separated into a variety of components for examination marked a shift in thinking about teaching and a fresh interest in the way subject knowledge was developed. The name of Shulman (1986a) is widely associated with the identification of distinct components of teachers' subject knowledge, more specifically, his distinction of subject content knowledge from pedagogical content knowledge and curriculum knowledge. Subject knowledge, he argued, had already received extensive attention yet beyond subject content lay pedagogical subject knowledge where learning and teaching of subjects in ways compelling to young children converged in subject-specific pedagogy. Moreover it was hard to discuss representation of subject matter content without recourse to specific curriculum material and resources which exemplified that content. The attention drawn to the role of subject knowledge in teaching by Schulman stimulated new enquiry, conceptual and empirical, which has attempted to clarify the components of pedagogical subject matter. Investigation, however, is still in the early stages. As noted by Floden and Buchmann (1990), there has been surprisingly little investigation of the *connection* between teachers' subject matter knowledge and pupils' learning. In fact a central aim of the current project has been to explore the possible links between teachers' and pupils' subject knowledge and the nature of learning and teaching processes which occur in natural classroom settings.

Qualitative Enquiry on Teaching

Over the same period of time newer forms of enquiry on class teaching were being developed which led to theoretical and methodological innovation required in order to access qualitative aspects of learning and teaching. This has been characterized by Doyle (1990) as a shift in emphasis towards an understanding of context and situation, the focus being on domain-specific knowledge with explanation of events and actions being made within the context of purposes and meanings of teachers and pupils themselves. The new forms of enquiry, concerned with codifying and systematizing processes in natural settings, required a new paradigm which, in turn, influenced the way classroom practice was conceptualized and structured. This inductive process rendered traditional concepts of experimental approaches inadequate as noted by, for instance, Guba (1978; 1981) and later by Lincoln and Guba (1985).

Chapter 2 presented a justification for the use of an emergent design and its advantages with respect to enquiry into complex human interactions. This was described as a phenomenological approach which involves theoretical or purposive sampling, a process of data collection, coding and analysis, which generates decisions about what data to collect next and where to find them, and leading to ideographic interpretation and tentative application. As noted in Chapter 2, whilst much theoretical work has been completed criteria for trustworthiness have been more recently developed. That said, formulating interpretations of data grounded in natural settings provides a powerful means for understanding teaching and learning subject knowledge which seemed appropriate to the present project.

Objectives for the Project

The objectives set for the project were to:

- investigate teachers' pedagogical subject knowledge in mathematics through observation and analysis of classroom discourse collected over children's first year in school and through teacher interview;
- collect data on children's informal knowledge in key areas of mathematics at school entry as a starting point for judging teachers' understanding of the way children, in particular, their own pupils know and think about mathematics. This objective was addressed specifically through the analysis of teachers' interviews and class observation considered in the light of children's informal knowledge, assessed at school entry and re-examined towards the end of the school year;

- explore the co-ordination and utilization of teacher and pupil knowledge within the processes of teaching through observation and analysis of the style and content of classroom discourse supplemented by field notes; and
- consider the implications of the project findings for a mathematics curriculum for children's first year at school.

This led first to a review of learning and teaching mathematics with understanding. As Hiebert and Carpenter (1992) noted:

> There is a persistent belief in the merits of the goal, but designing school learning environments that successfully promote understanding has been difficult. (Hiebert and Carpenter, 1992, p. 65)

Learning and Teaching with Understanding

With respect to the development of understanding in teaching and learning to teach subject matter, different theoretical frameworks have been utilized, among them models and constructs from cognitive science which assume knowledge is organized and stored in structures and there is a growing movement, as noted in Chapter 3, to consider cognition interactively situated in physical and social contexts. It is also assumed that the individual's knowledge structures and mental representations play a central role in their perceptions, thoughts and actions (Putnam, Lampert and Peterson, 1990). Just as children do teachers, themselves, attempt to understand and think about new situations and events in terms of what they know already, making connections between new information and existing systems or 'schemata' of knowledge, such as pedagogical problem-solving or decision-making. To understand learning to teach one must consider how these systems and their relationships develop and change with experience.

If characterization of understanding has implications for teaching, then, inevitably it has implications for accessing understanding for deployment in teaching. Development of good teaching for understanding requires corresponding models of good assessment of that higher order understanding and learning. Knowledge structures, connections and representations, however, are not observable or directly measurable as noted in Chapter 4 with respect to the issue of matching mathematical task to learner. As a result learning is *inferred*. Furthermore, on the one hand, understanding cannot be inferred on the basis of a response to a single task, on the other hand, the greater the variety of tasks undertaken the more time consuming and complex and, hence, unmanageable and unreliable becomes the assessment process used. Error analysis of, for instance, Brown and VanLehn's (1980) buggy algorithm provides evidence of faulty routines but is hardly likely to provide a rich picture of existing knowledge before teaching starts or an indication of its transformation in teaching. Errors *may* indicate lack of understanding, however, in the case of buggy algorithms lack of errors will *not* provide evidence of understanding.

Whilst multiple perspectives on learning and teaching exist, more attention is required to the quality of instruction which takes account of both the role of learner and teacher, in particular the question of whether teachers' conceptions and children's conceptions interact during teaching. Thompson (1992) has suggested that whilst teachers' conceptions are reflected in their teaching practices we know very little, in fact, about whether, if at all, these practices communicate teachers' conceptions to children.

> Furthermore since teachers are the primary mediators between the subject matter of mathematics and the children, it is also natural to infer that the teachers' conceptions are indeed communicated to children through practices in the classroom. This chain of inferences, however, remains to be empirically validated. There is a great deal that we can learn from the insightful analysis of the nature of that interaction. (Thompson, 1992, p. 141)

The lack of exploration of links between teachers' and pupils' subject knowledge had been observed already by Floden and Buchmann (1990) and it was hoped that some insights on this interaction might be forthcoming from the project. Accordingly analysis of data from the empirical investigation led towards the progressive focusing on the core category, teachers' pedagogical subject knowledge and its relationship with the sub-categories of pupils' informal mathematical knowledge, teachers' subject knowledge, knowledge of learning and teaching, and curriculum knowledge. This paved the way for consideration of the analytical story which will take place in the next section.

Re-assessing the Role of Teachers' Subject Knowledge in Early Years Mathematics Teaching

Introduction

It is the intention of this section to report the analytic story (Strauss and Corbin, 1990), that is, to examine the extent to which project teachers' mathematical subject knowledge and understanding contributed to the opportunities that they provided for their children to learn mathematics.

Chapter 7 (Phase 3) reported the results of what Strauss and Corbin (1990) have described as 'open coding': the process of breaking down, examining, comparing, conceptualizing and categorizing data. From this process emerged conceptual labels placed on teachers' moves and routines (described in Chapter 7 under sub-categories of task components) and the grouping and ordering of these sub-categories under three main sub-categories supporting: lesson organization and management; instruction; and independent practice or application. These main sub-categories, in turn, were ordered under the higher order category of lesson segment, the basic classroom task or lesson unit. Beyond open coding, however, lies 'axial coding': the process of putting data back together in new ways after open coding, again, by making connections among categories. This is done by utilizing a coding paradigm involving: *conditions, context, action/interaction strategies* and *consequences*. The focus is on specifying a category in terms of conditions which give rise to it; the context in which it is embedded; the action/interaction strategies by which it is handled, managed or carried out; and the consequences of these strategies. The process of breaking data apart in open coding was begun in Chapter 7 (Phase 3) with the analysis of classroom tasks mediated through classroom discourse and exemplifying pedagogical subject knowledge, and extended in Chapter 8 (Phase 4) through the examination of two of the most important influences on teachers' classroom practice, the category of teachers' mathematical subject knowledge and the category concerning knowledge of their young pupils' mathematical competence (accessed directly through teacher interview and pupil assessment and serving to triangulate findings from analysis of discourse). This can be depicted as follows:

- *Conditions*: these comprised the sources of the teachers' subject knowledge (their own learning, education and professional training);
- *Phenomenon*: pedagogical subject knowledge (knowledge of the subject for teaching particular topics to particular children of particular ages, knowing what curriculum materials to deploy and balancing content with what children know about the subject, accessed and utilized in teaching);
- *Context*: the classroom setting, the children, the resources of time and materials, and the school curriculum;
- *Intervening Conditions*: the balancing of lesson organization and learning to maintain pupils' engagement and to reach teaching goals;
- *Action/Interaction*: the classroom discourse mediating the task, through verbal representations interacting with concrete, pictorial, numerical and diagrammatical representations, utilizing a range of strategies and with responsive elaboration to suit individual pupil needs;
- *Consequences*: the pupils' response and learning, drawing on previous experience and prior knowledge.

As in open coding and axial coding, through a further process of making comparison and asking questions emerges the 'selective coding'. This is the process of selecting the core category, systematically relating it to other categories and validating these relationships, in other words, explicating the 'story line' about the central phenomenon, pedagogical subject knowledge, and its relationship to teachers' classroom practice. This was explored through the rich descriptions provided in Chapter 8. The final goal was to provide a clear analytic story.

Teachers' Subject Knowledge

Classroom discourse was used to exemplify teachers' pedagogical subject knowledge through the task components that emerged in Phase 3 and mediated through verbal representations interacting with children's responses by the use of concrete, pictorial, numerical and diagrammatic representations as shown in the analysis of teachers' strategies or routines, within the components in Phase 3 and Phase 4. These strategies or routines consisted of what each teacher typically said, did or demonstrated, in fact, how she generally arranged activities so children could construct understanding of the concept or procedure involved. Routines also concerned what the children said, did or showed. These activities could range from didactic, direct and teacher-led as in the case of Teacher D, to discovery-based and indirect as with Teacher C. Teachers might simply state the information to be learned as did Teacher D, on the other hand, and more usually, they provided experiences and then supported children's own developing efforts at understanding as Teacher B typically did. Consideration of the lesson or task segments and their components revealed how individual teachers wove lessons together from the routines in which they engaged with children. The task components, thus, provided the structure, or 'warp' of lessons. Furthermore the strategies within the components varied from teacher to teacher, as did the manner in which they were conducted. These strategies or routines provided the 'weft' of the lesson. Discourse was, thus, the means of mediating the task components and content by utilizing a range of strategies, determined by the goals set and the materials used and which monitored, at key points, pupils' response and the impact of teaching (see Figure 9.1).

In effective teaching discourse was dynamic and flexible, responsive to pupils' needs. The indications from Chapter 8 (Phase 4), and this is being confirmed by the writer's subsequent work, are that very different approaches to task design and representation of mathematical content may be equally effective.

By way of illustration Teacher D, the most recently trained and most secure in her knowledge and understanding of early years mathematics, designed all her own mathematics tasks, introducing new ideas systematically and linking them to children's activities through verbal, concrete, numerical and symbolic representation. Teacher B relied far more heavily on published material, allocating children to card and board games and constructional toys and then circulating informally, leading, encouraging and supporting. This activity was complemented by workbook and worksheet tasks and computer games which involved simple matching, ordering, comparing and counting. Whilst more telling and instructing in procedures took place, self-checking and providing peer support was still encouraged. Yet another teacher observed, Teacher C, provided tasks which lacked mathematical purpose, relying instead on counting, reading and writing number tasks and overlooking work on sets, relations between sets, shape and space and measurement.

The critical factor appeared to be the linking of suitable mathematical content through a clearly structured task to children's existing ideas and understanding. At the heart of teachers' pedagogical subject knowledge, then, lies subject content knowledge and knowledge of the competence of their pupils. The observed diversity among different teachers as well as among different topics taught by the same teacher poses questions with respect to the adequacy of primary teachers' subject knowledge. Chapters 7 and 8 demonstrated graphically the impact of teachers' knowledge (or lack of it) on practice. In the current context of critical attention to

Figure 9.1: Mathematical Task Design

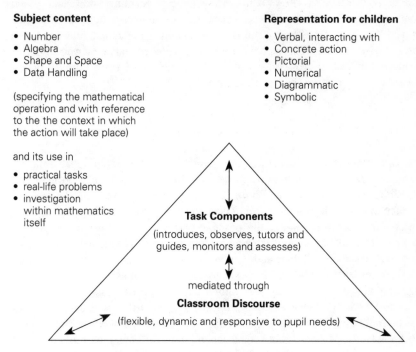

Subject content

- Number
- Algebra
- Shape and Space
- Data Handling

(specifying the mathematical operation and with reference to the the context in which the action will take place)

and its use in

- practical tasks
- real-life problems
- investigation within mathematics itself

Representation for children

- Verbal, interacting with
- Concrete action
- Pictorial
- Numerical
- Diagrammatic
- Symbolic

Task Components

(introduces, observes, tutors and guides, monitors and assesses)

mediated through

Classroom Discourse

(flexible, dynamic and responsive to pupil needs)

Teacher

utilizes a range of strategies

(telling, informing, questioning, repeating, talking aloud, eliciting, prompting, showing) reflecting:

- Subject content knowledge
- Knowledge of young children's competence
- Available curriculum materials

Pupil

actively constructs or deconstructs knowledge according to task demand and scaffolding provided

(shows, tells, repeats, comments, asks) reflecting:

- Prior knowledge
- Existing concepts and understanding
- Errors and misconceptions

the development of subject knowledge in initial training and, in particular, to the teaching of the basic subjects of English and mathematics these findings leave little room for complacency.

Wilson, Shulman and Rickert (1987) in investigating beginning secondary teachers' subject matter knowledge concluded that, whilst in the course of teaching, existing subject knowledge is transformed as beginning teachers evolve new understanding of subject matter when they begin to teach their subject to children, evidence is lacking that personal subject knowledge has grown. By focusing on experienced teachers the current project attempted to avoid taking too narrow a view on the learning of subject knowledge. There is, however, little evidence to suggest that the development of project teachers' subject matter through teaching occurred. The capacity to transform personal understanding, thus, depends on what teachers bring to the classroom. Whilst knowledge of learning and teaching and classrooms increases with experience, knowledge of subject content does not, as Wilson and Wineburg (1988) have shown. This suggests researchers may need now to consider ways to *increase* teachers' subject knowledge rather than to continue to document the lack of it. This issue has been addressed by a number of the experimental projects described in Chapter 3.

Teachers' Pedagogical Subject Knowledge for Teaching

With respect to knowledge concerning the development of children's mathematical ideas, teachers seemed quite unaware of the rich, informal knowledge brought into school. Whilst nursery records and informal assessment were mentioned there was no evidence that these informed teaching decisions. As Resnick (1987) noted, however, it is important to recognize the possible and practical relationship between formal knowledge of the school curriculum and informal practical knowledge of everyday, out-of-school contexts and how this could be managed in classroom contexts. This raises issues about children as learners, the role of assessment, the nature of judgments and issues covering the validity and appropriateness of evidence, as discussed in Chapter 3. What emerges from the project is that task demand is *not* static as teachers did adjust their tasks in relation to children's needs and responses, or prior knowledge. Mismatch between teachers' questions and children's response was due more to teachers' lack of subject knowledge than to beliefs about discovery learning, as suggested by a study of Edwards and Mercer (1987) and noted in Chapter 8. A further conclusion to be drawn is that assessment cannot be a 'bolt on' activity but must constitute an integral part of the teaching process. The interaction between the process of assessment of prior knowledge and instruction was demonstrated by the way in which teachers presented tasks and were able to assess the extent to which children could answer questions about content and apply knowledge strategically. The validity of teachers' judgments based upon accumulated knowledge built from the response of individual children to specific classroom tasks, however, would depend upon the quality of the task, in terms of its subject content and its relationship to the child's existing knowledge. These teachers' observed appreciation of the process of construction and deconstruction of situated knowledge which threaded in and out of classroom tasks does call into question the notion of assessment as a single event or occasion and the stable notion of match which, in the light of these findings, seems particularly outmoded. Furthermore, it provided empirical support for the critical conceptual analysis of matching by Davis (1993) identified in Chapter 3. The implications for teachers are that:

- they may need to access children's prior knowledge and ongoing cognitive processing in the course of instruction;
- the goals and, hence, task demand within and across lessons are likely to change and be adjusted as a result of children's response.

In order to work effectively in this manner, however, teachers would need to become more aware of the rich informal mathematical knowledge children bring to learning.

Views about Learning and Teaching

As noted by Desforges and Cockburn (1987) in respect of their first school teachers, two of the project teachers (Teachers B and C) did display in interview quite sophisticated views about children's learning which was depicted as socially shared work organized around joint accomplishment of tasks with features of apprenticeship, encouraging observation, commenting on the work of peers and fostering meaning construction and interpretation. This was not, however, transferred into the practice of Teacher C who clearly lacked subject content knowledge. Teacher B did scaffold children's responses in both informal games and in formal scheme book exercises as well as engage children in joint meaning construction. Whilst a distinction needs to be made between formal instruction and informal support of children's mathematical games, the teaching sequences observed did generally follow the stages of cognitive strategy instruction which have been found to encourage information processing, with modelling and self-instruction, cueing and correcting, thus, scaffolding and responsive elaboration according to the topic and to children's response was made. This provided children with the opportunity to integrate new knowledge with existing ideas, through action and interactive discourse. It seems likely that the scaffolded approaches observed were largely intuitive and, as demonstrated from a comparison of the practice of Teacher B and C, without a clear understanding of subject content neither sophisticated theories of children's learning nor scaffolded approaches will lead to effective teaching. The sensitive use made by Teacher B of published scheme material to guide her practice is worthy of comment. Ball and Feiman-Nemser (1988) have provided examples of student teachers learning subject content from textbooks though it must be borne in mind that Stodolsky (1988) has exposed the emphasis on procedural knowledge and calculation skill at the expense of central concepts and ideas which are often underdeveloped in written text books as a problem.

Limitations of the Research Design

Justification for the use of an emergent design for the current project in terms of its problem-determined boundaries and purposive sampling seemed sound. Qualitative enquiry can generate knowledge about classroom practices, uncover patterns and regularities in classroom events that occur in these contexts which lead to enhanced understanding of such processes. Data collection by qualitative methods such as unobtrusive observation of both verbal and non-verbal behaviour and interview in conjunction with the so-called 'human instrument' that allowed use of tacit as well as propositional knowledge in ascribing meaning to data as it emerged was appropriate to the exploratory nature of the main phase. The possibility of suspending a lifetime's experience of classroom observation in order to view events with fresh eyes, however, must be challenged and the influence of prior knowledge acknowledged. New ways of describing the structure of lessons, as noted in Chapter 7, are not limitless since teaching is a goal-directed enterprise, moving inevitably towards pre-planned outcomes within particular constraints of time, space and existing resources. This point leads back to the re-examination of the role of *a priori* theory which could not, and in any case it was not intended that it should, be eliminated from the investigation. Previous relevant research was not rejected and, in fact, provided an impetus to the generation of specific aims and the identification of key issues. The lack of previous investigation of the interaction of teacher and pupil subject knowledge or evidence for the influence of teachers' conceptions on children's and vice versa was, thus, a key stimulus to the present project. The intention, however, was to prevent *a priori* theory from constraining the study, so far as possible, and to ensure that theory emerged from, and was grounded in, the data.

At the heart of qualitative methodology is the process of data collection which occurs at different levels for different purposes. Typically data analysis takes place in the field as data are collected in order to guide subsequent data collection. In the present project classroom discourse was recorded over children's first year in school, subsequently transcribed and was, thus, potentially available for analysis. Once the decision had been taken to use a sample data handling lesson for each of the four teachers to generate the category system further transcripts were available for analysis until no new information emerged. This meant that time spent in data collection was extensive but allowed maximum variation in lessons recorded across the year.

The major drawback of the method used was the inordinate amount of time required to unitize and categorize data and to organize these under a taxonomy. Had tight time constraints been in operation this would have affected the quality of the analysis. Mature insights emerge very slowly over time and the requirements of rapidly prepared end-of-project reports of external funders do not encourage this process.

In terms of trustworthiness the procedures of Lincoln and Guba (1985) served to increase the confidence which could be placed in the project. Credibility (internal validity) was achieved by persistent observation (over the year), triangulation (with field notes and interviews) and member checks (with the teachers concerned). Achieving dependability (reliability) in the form of an external auditor whilst desirable was not possible, though an external consultant read draft papers. Acceptable professional practice, however, was judged by the scrutiny of colleagues and other academic peers at the end of each empirical phase through formal and informal seminar presentations at institutional, national and international level. Transferability (external validity) achieved through purposive sampling and thick description in report writing was less straightforward. Purposive sampling has been discussed above but thick description, as noted already, requires the report writer to tread a fine line between avoiding the trivial and commonplace whilst, at the same time, providing sufficient detail to substantiate the assertions made. To achieve this the decision was taken to report discretely each empirical phase in Chapters 5 to 8 with the appropriate level of descriptions and to provide a separate conceptual story in this final chapter where description could be kept to a minimum. This discussion serves to underline the lack of established conventions for report writing to support decisions about what to include and exclude and how to present data. It also serves to illustrate some of the difficulties faced in using a theoretical framework which is still being developed and which, moreover, has been developed in different ways by different groups of researchers. Lincoln and Guba's (1985) trustworthiness criteria make a real contribution to the objectivity of naturalistic research yet the simple unitizing and categorizing system they describe is strengthened by the use of the coding paradigm and the selection of core category advocated by Strauss and Corbin (1990) when attempting to capture the complexity of human interaction.

Inevitably the use of few schools and a small number of teachers in the main phase of the project was bound to lead to ideographic interpretation. This, however, allows the constructed realities of the participants, who worked with the writer for a long period of time while trust was established, to emerge. It requires, however, a tentative style of reporting which leaves the audience free to make the generalization, if justified.

The issues associated with validity, dependability and reliability of the mathematical tasks have been treated extensively in Chapter 3. The lack of extension tasks for appropriate use with high achieving pupils at the end of children's first year at school, it must be acknowledged, limited the extent to which progress over the year could be judged. Tasks were designed to be compatible with Level 1 of the National Curriculum (for 6-year-olds) and, thus, judged to be appropriate for 4 to 5-year-old children. At the time of design it was not anticipated that children would show such a range of competences. Whilst accepting that tasks designed should have extended beyond Level 1, however, it is salutary to note that the same children, with the exception of two, were judged to be functioning at Level 2, at which extension tasks would have been pitched, some two years later after completing the Key Stage 1 standard assessment tasks (SATs).

The progressive focusing on teachers' subject knowledge in the analysis of data inevitably meant that the responses of children, their telling, showing and commenting, was largely absent from analysis at Phase 4 though not, of course, from the raw data. A future task for the writer would be to re-analyse the data taking children's knowledge as the core category. In order to have captured the full richness of children's response it may be that video-tape recording would have been required. It is unlikely, however, that such obtrusive recording could have been maintained over a year. Finally, the cognitive orientation of the project may have led to insufficient attention being given to attitude and emotion and to the relationship of beliefs to cognitive processes of teachers and learners. As noted in Chapter 1 with respect to Shulman's model, unavoidably certain perspectives and arguments in this project, as in any other, have been highlighted whilst others have remained unexamined and its strength must be judged in terms of the areas it does illuminate.

Implications of the Project

Attention has been drawn to the role of subject knowledge in teaching and, in particular, to the components of teachers' subject knowledge that Shulman advocated as well as to the further enquiry that he stimulated. His system of components depended upon the distinctions drawn between categories and sub-categories and some criticisms levelled at the system were outlined in Chapter 1. In the ten years since his seminal paper was published a variety of conceptual and empirical enquiries have been carried out which have attempted to clarify the components of pedagogical subject knowledge. The findings of this project would suggest that pedagogical subject knowledge is the superordinate category which subsumes the sub-category of subject matter knowledge, on the one hand, and knowledge of young children's subject understanding, on the other, and incorporating curriculum knowledge which, in providing the means to represent this subject matter in ways which make sense to children, exemplifies teachers' pedagogical reasoning. Whether or not curriculum knowledge warrants a separate category remains uncertain.

This discussion, however, underlines the importance of mathematical understanding in the teacher's skilled teaching performance. In fact both children *and* teachers need to learn the interconnectedness of mathematical knowledge. In order to teach this to children teachers, themselves, *must* have rich and connected knowledge. Furthermore it is important for the teacher to appreciate the interrelationship between learning and teaching mathematics and, in the case of the current project this entailed attempting to make explicit emerging constructions concerning the ways mathematics were taught and learned. This was a gap identified in the knowledge base which the project attempted to address. Building a case literature of professional practice, as mentioned in Chapter 8, may be one way to create a practical knowledge base to stimulate reflection by teachers and students alike.

Although teachers' pedagogical subject knowledge is fundamental to effective practice as yet little empirical research has focused on its development in this country. One purpose of the project described here has been to offer a framework which may contribute to future research in this area. The intention has been to re-examine existing conceptions of pedagogical subject knowledge and, hopefully, to extend the knowledge base relating to this area.

As succeeding phases of the project have been published considerable interest has been shown in the documentation of children's informal mathematical knowledge, for example, *The Times Educational Supplement* (TES), 1993; the National Foundation for Research (NFER) *Topic* series, 1995; *Child Education*, 1995. This may simply reflect the sequence in which the project has been reported. If, however, it is an indication of a genuine engaged attention, a curiosity or a concern then the broader dissemination of the existing knowledge base concerning the development of children's mathematical concepts may be the most fruitful means for raising the quality of teachers' pedagogical subject knowledge. As noted in Chapter 3, experience of, for instance, the Calculator-Aware Number (CAN) curriculum (Shuard *et al.*, 1991) has demonstrated that experienced teachers' established practice can be transformed in order to enhance children's own inventiveness, problem solving and communication of strategies. Numerous overseas projects have confirmed this. In the Netherlands such principles underpin the realistic mathematics curriculum.

In response to this finding the writer is currently engaged in a project with the University of Ljubljana, Slovenia which aims to document children's informal methods of mental calculation across Key Stages 1 and 2, in the context of the development of number concepts and overall mathematics attainment. Already this is establishing that the rich inventiveness observed in 4-year-olds entering school is very little in evidence in children aged 6 to 11 years.

If the two most important influences on teachers' classroom practice are their knowledge of subject content and the knowledge of the competence of their pupils there is a good argument for focusing research and publication on the area in which interest has been spontaneously generated. Fennema, Carpenter and Peterson (1989) in their experimental study of cognitively guided instruction found that teachers provided with increased knowledge of children's early mathematical learning and thinking processes based their teaching on children's active involvement in mathematical problem solving. If any one of a variety of teaching styles may provide such a learning environment, enhancing teachers' knowledge of children's cognitions in specific content areas may be a fruitful way forward to increase teachers' subject knowledge. If, as ideas of situated knowledge and social cognition (Resnick, 1987) suggest, teachers, themselves, use pedagogical theories based on recollections of their own school experiences of learning rigid concepts and memorized procedures and, if, the development of mathematical understanding is, as cognitive theorists aver, a process of establishing relationships between existing and fresh knowledge, providing the means to help teachers develop a rich and better connected pedagogical knowledge may be the way forward. This finding has a particular resonance as the Teacher Training Agency (TTA, 1995) turns its attention to the quality and cost-effectiveness of continuing professional development of teachers.

Conclusion

The Value of the Project

What the project has sought to provide is a rich delineation of teachers' pedagogical subject knowledge through qualitative enquiry. This is an approach which is regarded as suitable for the examination of context- and curriculum-specific effects and can lead to the identification of specific conditions under which particular teaching practices may be appropriate. The method, thus, offered an apt means to generate enhanced understanding of teachers' pedagogical subject knowledge through the uncovering of patterns and regularities in classroom processes and, furthermore, it had the potential for exploring relationships such as those which might exist between teachers' and pupils' subject knowledge.

The analysis of classroom tasks which took place in the project, mediated by classroom discourse and exemplifying teachers' pedagogical subject knowledge, suggested that the two most important components of this pedagogical subject knowledge were teachers' own mathematical subject knowledge and knowledge of their pupils' mathematical competence. The critical skill involved appeared to be the linking of suitable mathematical content, through clearly structured tasks, to children's existing ideas and understanding. At the heart of teachers' pedagogical subject knowledge, in summary, lies subject content knowledge and knowledge of pupils' competence. Moreover, the observed diversity of practice among the project teachers, as well as among different topics taught by the same teacher, poses some questions regarding the adequacy of primary teachers' subject knowledge.

The teachers themselves, in interview described their own primary teaching experiences where they had worked largely alone in classrooms to memorize rules and narrow concepts. This knowledge is in some contrast to the rich, informal knowledge acquired in out-of-school settings observed to be brought into school by their pupils. Three of the four teachers went on to recall little further development of mathematical subject knowledge and concepts in college though one reported rich opportunities for growth of subject content. While knowledge of the curriculum and children's understanding of this *had* developed from their subsequent practice of teaching, the teachers seemed unaware of their pupils' existing competence in counting, recognition of numerals, representation of quantity, addition, subtraction and social sharing, appropriate language of measurement and selection of criteria to sort objects. In short, many children entered school with good mastery of Level 1 of the National Curriculum for mathematics. To take one striking example, teachers lacked awareness of children's existing capacity to solve simple addition and subtraction word problems. Phase 2 interviews revealed that teachers' introduction to children of addition and subtraction was determined by its particular position in the sequence of subject content in the published scheme of work being used.

Significantly, however, none of the lessons observed over the year by any of the teachers involved the operations of addition and subtraction. Whether, if recognized and accessed, this rich and diverse informal mathematical knowledge *could* have been utilized is another matter since teaching is a complex cognitive activity which involves the management of simultaneous and competing goals and high information-processing demands. This results, inevitably, in a selection of, and a reduction in, the number and range of stimuli which *can* be attended to at any one moment by the teacher.

In fact what the project clearly showed was the interactive nature of assessment of prior knowledge in the course of teaching through the process of presenting tasks and assessing children's capacity to answer questions about content and apply knowledge or skills strategically. The nature of teachers' own judgments, based upon accumulated knowledge of the response of individual children to specific classroom tasks, which carries an implicit recognition of the process of situated construction and deconstruction of knowledge in particular social situations, poses some challenge to traditional notions of 'task demand' and 'match'. HM Inspectors and educational researchers alike have repeatedly drawn attention to teachers' poor skills in matching tasks accurately to children's presumed need for new learning, or practice, revision and application of existing knowledge and skills. The flaw in the argument of researchers such as Bennett *et al.* (1984) and Desforges and Cockburn

(1987), however, is to assert, on the one hand, that the complex and shifting, moment-by-moment demands of teaching require teachers to select and *reduce* the number and range of stimuli that can be handled at any one time and, on the other hand, to propose that teachers should diagnose and take *more* account of complex and individualized needs of learners in the course of instruction. Furthermore, fundamental to the current, ten-subject National Curriculum and assessment system is the expectation that teachers' continuous assessment of individual children will inform their planning of the next stage of learning.

In observed lessons teachers provided different levels and types of support in mixed ability groups and modified tasks strategically for different children in different ways. This implicit awareness on the part of teachers of the interaction between assessment and instruction demonstrated that teachers could provide children with the opportunity to construct meaning in the course of teaching and provide temporary support to those in need. The validity of such judgments, however, would depend upon the quality of the task presented in terms of subject content, its relationship to children's existing knowledge and the effectiveness of its mediation.

In summary, the project findings re-emphasize the essential requirement of all primary school teachers to have sound conceptual knowledge of mathematics and a deeper awareness of the rich, informal mathematical knowledge children bring into school. Moreover the skill with which such knowledge is deployed in effective teaching appears to be considerably more complex than traditional notions of 'match' and 'task demand' would suggest.

Areas for Future Research

As noted in Chapter 8, the project described in this book concentrated on taking sample lessons from each of the four teachers over children's first year in school. The next stage was to follow a larger group of seven teachers through children's first year in school in order that whole sequences of lessons which introduced and developed the same topic over time with different teachers, as well as different topics with the same teacher, could be observed. Data for this stage have already been collected and analysis has begun. Shulman (1986b) called for a case literature to capture and exemplify the wisdom of practice. The aim of this further phase is to provide such a case knowledge which uncovers qualitative aspects of learning and teaching and seeks understanding of content and situation with a focus on domain-specific knowledge. Explanations of events and actions are, thus, made within the context of purpose and meaning of the teachers and pupils themselves. The intention is to stimulate teachers and students in training to reflect on the way other teachers construct meaning in particular classrooms in the light of their own distinctive educational backgrounds and professional experiences. Knowledge of teachers, as of their pupils, is constructed through the interaction of prior knowledge with current experience. Building a broader base of case knowledge from the practical and professional experience of seven further experienced teachers will be the next stage in increasing understanding of subject knowledge for teaching and the development of professional practice.

Appendix 1:
Extracts from Mathematical Assessment Tasks

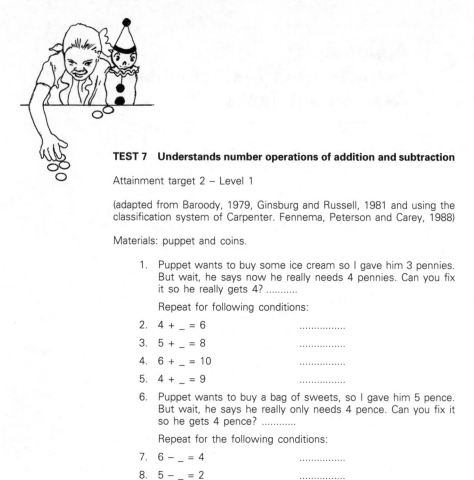

TEST 7   Understands number operations of addition and subtraction

Attainment target 2 – Level 1

(adapted from Baroody, 1979, Ginsburg and Russell, 1981 and using the classification system of Carpenter. Fennema, Peterson and Carey, 1988)

Materials: puppet and coins.

1. Puppet wants to buy some ice cream so I gave him 3 pennies. But wait, he says now he really needs 4 pennies. Can you fix it so he really gets 4? ....

   Repeat for following conditions:

2. 4 + _ = 6 ....
3. 5 + _ = 8 ....
4. 6 + _ = 10 ....
5. 4 + _ = 9 ....

6. Puppet wants to buy a bag of sweets, so I gave him 5 pence. But wait, he says he really only needs 4 pence. Can you fix it so he gets 4 pence? ....

   Repeat for the following conditions:

7. 6 − _ = 4 ....
8. 5 − _ = 2 ....
9. 8 − _ = 4 ....
10. 9 − _ = 4 ....

Tick the correct responses and note any interesting comments or behaviour.

Record the score, computed by counting the number of times the child produces the correct response to addition tasks and the number of times the child produces the correct response to subtraction tasks, with a total of 5 for each.

TOTAL SCORE
(*addition*)

TOTAL SCORE
(*subtraction*)

TEST 8   a) Division as Sharing

Attainment target 2 – Beyond Level 1

(adapted from Desforges and Desforges, 1980), with two items related to

b) Multiplication as continuous addition

a) Materials: 3 bears, sweets

1. (4 sweets, 2 bears) Say: Can you share these sweets between these bears?
    Prompt (once): . . . so it's fair.

    ....

2. (6 sweets, 3 bears) Can you share these sweets among these bears?
    Prompt (once): . . . so it's fair.

    ....

3. (9 sweets, 3 bears) Can you share these sweets among these bears?
    Prompt (once): . . . so it's fair.

    ....

4. (5 sweets, 2 bears) Can you share these sweets between these bears?
    Prompt (once): . . . so it's fair.

    ....

5. If the child identifies that there is one over, ask: What can you do to make it fair to the bears?

    ....

Tick for correct sharing. Note strategies – dealing sweets out in ones or groups, method of dealing with remainders at 5 and any other noteworthy behaviour.

Record correct responses out of 5.

b) Materials: do not draw attention to bears but leave on the table
1. Say: How many legs have two teddies got?
    Prompt (once): One teddy has two legs, so . . .

    ....

2. How many legs have three teddies got?

    ....

Record replies and any noteworthy behaviour. Tick correct responses and record, out of possible 2.

TOTAL SCORE
(*division*) [ ]

TOTAL SCORE [ ]

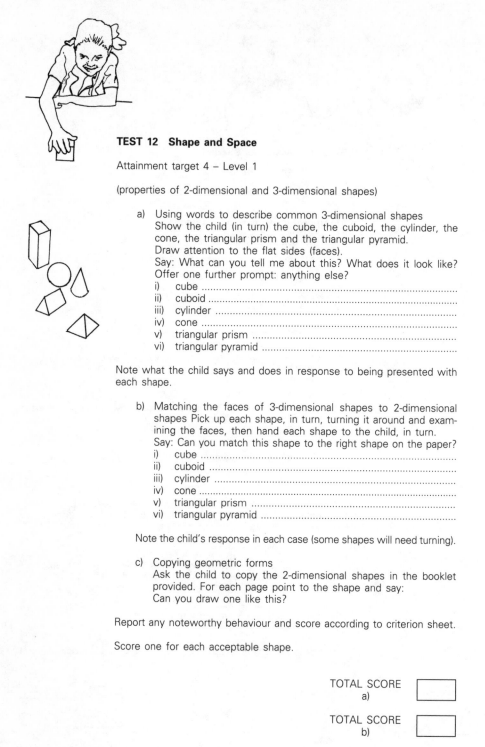

TEST 12   Shape and Space

Attainment target 4 – Level 1

(properties of 2-dimensional and 3-dimensional shapes)

a) Using words to describe common 3-dimensional shapes
Show the child (in turn) the cube, the cuboid, the cylinder, the cone, the triangular prism and the triangular pyramid.
Draw attention to the flat sides (faces).
Say: What can you tell me about this? What does it look like?
Offer one further prompt: anything else?
  i)   cube ....
  ii) cuboid ....
  iii) cylinder ....
  iv) cone ....
  v)   triangular prism ....
  vi) triangular pyramid ....

Note what the child says and does in response to being presented with each shape.

b) Matching the faces of 3-dimensional shapes to 2-dimensional shapes Pick up each shape, in turn, turning it around and examining the faces, then hand each shape to the child, in turn.
Say: Can you match this shape to the right shape on the paper?
  i)   cube ....
  ii) cuboid ....
  iii) cylinder ....
  iv) cone ....
  v)   triangular prism ....
  vi) triangular pyramid ....

Note the child's response in each case (some shapes will need turning).

c) Copying geometric forms
Ask the child to copy the 2-dimensional shapes in the booklet provided. For each page point to the shape and say:
Can you draw one like this?

Report any noteworthy behaviour and score according to criterion sheet.

Score one for each acceptable shape.

TOTAL SCORE [   ]
    a)

TOTAL SCORE [   ]
    b)

Appendix 2:
Copy of Field Notes Schedule

FIELD NOTES

School:

Teacher:

Date:

Topic/Title/Theme:

Plan of Classroom showing main activities/areas:

Lesson segments observed:

i) Introduction
    (Review, recap, exposition, activity)

    ....

ii) Development

    ....

iii) Conclusion
     (Summary, discussion)

    ....

Deployment of Adults
(Parents, Teachers, Ancillary help)

....

Pupil Grouping
(Number, Nature)

Role of Adults:
Tell, show, demonstrate
Elicit child's concepts
Facilitate child's construction
Guide, support, lead

....

Role of Pupils:
Choose, explore
Predict, explain
Investigate, discuss
Give facts, tell, answer, do
Describe results
Represent results
Apply everyday experience
Co-operate in small groups
Work independently
Work independently under guidance

....

Activities undertaken:
What children are doing

Emphasis:
Conceptual
Factual/Recall
Practice
Investigate

Comments:
Accuracy
Developmental appropriateness

....

Content: Mathematics involved, National Curriculum ATs/levels
(What children are intended to learn)

....

Materials used:
Equipment
(Diagrams if necessary)

Outcomes:
(e.g. Displays produced)

Comments on
Other existing Displays:

Additional Comments:

Other mathematical activities which have taken place this week:

Is there *one* significant event or incident with respect to mathematics learning/teaching during the week which springs to mind?

Appendix 3:
Copy of Teacher Interview Schedule for Phase Four

We should be glad to hear your ideas about maths teaching in the reception class. The following questions give some indication of the things we are particularly interested in, but please feel free to include anything else.

A General

Many adults are uneasy about maths.
What do you feel about maths and teaching maths in reception?
What people and events have influenced you?

B What maths should children learn?

Which are the key mathematical concepts and procedures to be taught in the reception class?
Is the National Curriculum a useful framework, an irrelevant complication or a restrictive imposition? For example, how should children 'use and apply' maths? Which areas of maths do children find particularly difficult or easy? Can you suggest why this might be so?

C How do children learn?

To what extent should children discover maths for themselves?
What place has direct teaching/exposition in reception maths?
How do you find out what children know/learn?
How do you assess new starters?
How do you find out the nature of children's problems?
How can the more able children be challenged?

D Planning and organization

What sources do you consult when planning lessons?
What are the advantages/disadvantages of commercial schemes?
What is your most valuable equipment for maths teaching?
How do you group children?
How many times a week do children do maths?
To give us an idea of the concepts presented to the children, please could we have a copy of any teaching plans (weekly, termly)?

E General

What advice would you give to a student teacher about teaching maths in the reception class?

If there were a really good in-service course available on maths what would you like it to deal with?

Do you think it is possible that young children can be underestimated in terms of maths knowledge? Do they ever surprise you?

Thank you for all your help.

Appendix 4:
Extracts from Teacher Interviews

A.	Teacher A	Teacher B	Teacher C	Teacher D
Own mathematical experience	School was formal.... there's a page of sums. Sit and do them, sort of thing.... You know? (of primary education) Secondary? I coped with what we did. I didn't get a fantastic pass at 'O' level but I passed. At college I don't think we did a lot. I mean, we had maths lectures but I don't know.... Oh dear it's so long ago.	Primary schooling? Very very formal, no practical experience at all.... all written in books, no practical experience. I enjoyed it. I took it to 'O' level and no way would I have taken it further. I did not enjoy it when it divided out into geometry and algebra. I enjoyed algebra. I used to get 100 per cent in algebra, lovely. Geometry I loved, you see, but once it got a bit further than that I sort of lost interest. I think it must have got beyond me. Recollections of college? Not at all.... very general and you hoped on your teaching practice you got a good teacher.... and that's more or less where you picked it up.	From my own experience.... learning or not learning? There was so much whole class teaching which didn't mean a thing to me.... so formal.... one teacher and the whole class. There was no practical way of working it out or asking or even any feedback from each other. Even at secondary school that was happening. Show you one method, scribble on the board, leave you to get on with it. Maths to understand came from my brother who went to the secondary modern. I trained for secondary schooling.	I enjoyed mathematics and was good at it in the primary school. I became less interested in the secondary school. I got GCE and enjoyed it. My own experiences as a parent have been important. I let mathematics slip and did a Cambridge Extension College mathematics course. At college I had x and y. This experience was extremely informative. Very practical but there was thinking of the ideas behind it.

B.

	Teacher A	Teacher B	Teacher C	Teacher D
What children should learn	They need a lot of work on the basic things: number concepts and that. Especially in a reception class because if they don't grasp it then you're going to have problems further up the school. I do a lot of work on number, probably more than shape and that sort of thing.	Relationships . . . the sorting, the ordering, the counting . . . sets and then very much later the recognizing and the writing numbers. And again the little work books . . . they are almost an assessment consolidating.	Counting accurately 'careful counting' that's the one-to-one, orderly counting . . . in rows, across, down . . . It's logical to order. I am keen to get them to understand 0–10, *never* forgetting 0, more than, less than. Once they have grasped *that* it is easy to go into tens. The zero is important. If it isn't understood when it is introduced in the scheme suddenly children are thrown. It has real meaning in mathematics, especially when you come to algebra and minus values. Mathematics should be related to everyday activities: to registration. How many are present or absent? Spatial mathematics depends a lot on experience . . .	I think of all the mathematical concepts which are relevant and deal with each in a practical way. I put a lot of things out, talk about things and let children explore, to remember.

C.	Teacher A	Teacher B	Teacher C	Teacher D
Children's learning	They definitely need a lot of practical work. I think when I was at school it was the case of 'this is the fact and that's it. . .' Yes they need to discover it for themselves but some of them would take forever. It has to be both. You know there's always maths things around. Basic arithmetic things . . . I do a lot of work on that . . . they need it. I don't assume they get anything much at home.	It just becomes a natural process in reception. How children learn? Should they discover maths for themselves? Yes, they should but it's got to be directed. The practical experiences *need* direction and organisation. They find ordering numbers difficult: fourth . . . fifth . . . Also at a certain point it becomes more abstract. You assess . . . in a practical situation . . . or they just clam up.	Children learning? At school we are always 'head on' with something. You might know it but nobody had bothered to give you real practical experience. You observe and communicate with someone else of your own age. There's a time for formal instruction. I still feel quite large numbers of children only learn from 'hands on' and 'doing'. Children learn from other children by observing and listening . . . they are relaxed taking part in an activity together.	It all hinges on the way it is put over at the beginning. Direct teaching has a place, we always start with 'carpet time' to introduce new work but concentration varies. I believe in teaching, not children 'finding out for themselves'.

D.	Teacher A	Teacher B	Teacher C	Teacher D
Planning Organization	The National Curriculum makes sure you're going in the right direction. Assessment? I do some sort of number recognition and colour recognition . . . see if they can build a tower . . . sequence and pattern. They stay in mixed groups . . . Sometimes they'll spark off one another . . . if you have them all together it's hard work. I try to make sure they all do the maths activity in a day . . . at least three times a week . . . Sometimes you manage every day. We use the Heinemann scheme and Maths Chest and Story Maths.	Data handling comes out of the theme they are following. The National Curriculum is a useful framework . . . to be aware of what's in the programmes of study . . . when you are choosing a new theme. My favourite is . . . they have to talk about it, haven't they? They stay in mixed ability groups for the first two terms. The more able ones get more out of the topic. I don't do a lot of work with the whole class together . . . just five or ten minutes grouping or counting. . . . And again the little IMP workbooks.	Early years has to be in groups, I think. From my own experience . . . there was so much whole class teaching. I think there is a natural grouping of ability. I wouldn't want to do it rigidly. A clever child might want to *tell* but the 'less able' child needs a 'less able' adult person to tell them, explain in a more relevant way. They model themselves on who is best in the class. Resources? Multilink from basic number to spatial work. Dominoes.	It's fine if there are two members of staff. With one this work would take a week to do, rotating the activities. The work would be on-going – time, number, with supporting activities. The National Curriculum keeps us on target. We do get nursery records and we have our own little assessment of number, colour. . . . Separate groups at separate tables with appropriate tasks. I watch . . . I design my own tasks. In year 1 we use the Ginn Scheme. I like solid shapes, textured ones to draw round, multilink, unifix, cards for sequencing. I wish I had more things to weigh, more scales. Able children? I try to talk to them a little more.

E.	Teacher A	Teacher B	Teacher C	Teacher D
General	Advice to a student? I think that on the whole they sort of plan too hard and expect too much. Recording . . . well so many of them . . . they can't really. INSET? I suppose it would be 'early years'. I've just been on one. Well, apart from telling me that what I was doing was alright. . . . It wasn't anything different, really.	Students feel they should be moving on each week and a lot of it with reception is so much repetition, but repetition in a different way. But I think that's what they find hard, don't they? I've always thought it would be nice to have a course just for 'early years'. Not that I've been on many maths courses but they seem to jump into National Curriculum Level 1 and I wish somebody would do 'Towards the National Curriculum'.	Advice to a student? Never say it's wrong to a child. I don't think they would nowadays, would they? Never assume a child doesn't know much. Find out about their experiences. INSET? I am lacking in computer experience.	I think my advice would be to begin in a very practical way and to reinforce all the time. Professional development. Gosh, that's hard. I would take one of the practical sessions that I had on my PGCE course. Any one really, where there's lots and lots of ways of exploring one concept. Because I think that's, perhaps, what some people haven't really done.

References

ALEXANDER, R. (1992) *Policy and Practice in Primary Education*, London, Routledge.

ALEXANDER, R., ROSE, J. and WOODHEAD, C. (1992) *Curriculum Organisation and Classroom Practice in Primary Schools: A Discussion Paper*, London, HMSO.

ANDERSON, J.R. (1987) 'Skill acquisition: Compilation of weak-method problem solutions', *Psychological Review*, **94**, 2, pp. 192–210.

ANDERSON, R. (1984) 'Role of the reader's schema in comprehension, learning and memory', in ANDERSON, R., OSHAM, J. and TIERNEY, R. (Eds) *Learning to Read in American Schools: Basal Readers and Content Texts*, Hillsdale, NJ, Lawrence Erlbaum, pp. 243–57.

ANGHILERI, J. (1995) 'Children's finger methods for multiplication', *Mathematics in School*, **24**, 1, pp. 40–5.

ANTELL, S.E. and KEATING, D.P. (1983) 'Perception of numerical invariance in neonates', *Child Development*, **54**, pp. 695–701.

ASKEW, M. and WILIAM, D. (1993) *Recent Research in Mathematics Education 5–16*, London, OFSTED.

AUBREY, C. (1994) *The Role of Subject Knowledge in the Early Years of Schooling*, London, Falmer Press.

AUBREY, C. (1995) 'The mathematical knowledge of school entrants and what teachers should do about it', *Topic*, Autumn, pp. 1–22.

AUSUBEL, D.P. (1986) *Educational Psychology: A Cognitive View*, New York, Holt, Rinehart and Winston.

BALACHEFF, N. (1987) 'Processus de preuve et situations de validation', *Educational Studies in Mathematics*, **18**, pp. 147–76.

BALL, D.L. (1988) 'Prospective teachers' understanding of mathematics: What do they bring with them to teacher education', Paper presented at the annual meeting of the American Educational Research Association, New Orleans.

BALL, D.L. (1990) 'The mathematical understandings that prospective teachers bring to teacher education', *Elementary School Journal*, **90**, pp. 449–66.

BALL, D.L. (1991) 'Research on teaching mathematics: Making subject-matter knowledge part of the equation', in BROPHY, J. (Ed) *Advances in Research on Teaching* (Vol. 2), Greenwich, Connecticut, JAI Press Inc., pp. 1–48.

BALL, D.L. and FEIMAN-NEMSER, S. (1988) 'Using textbooks and teachers' guides: A dilemma for beginning teachers and teacher educators', *Curriculum Inquiry*, **18**, pp. 401–23.

BAROODY, J.A. (1979) 'The relationship among the development of counting, number, conservation and basic arithmetic abilities', Unpublished PhD, Cornell

University, Cited in SAXE, G.B., GUBERMAN, S.R. and GEARHART, M. *Social Processes in Early Development*, Monograph of the Society for Research in Child Development, **52**, 2, Serial No. 216.

BAROODY, J.A. (1984) 'Children's difficulties in subtraction: Some causes and questions', *Journal for Research in Mathematics Education*, **15**, pp. 203–13.

BATTISTA, M.T. and CLEMENTS, D.H. (1988) 'A case for a logo-based elementary geometry curriculum', *Arithmetic Teacher*, **2**, 3, pp. 11–17.

BEGLE, E.G. (1979) *Critical Variables in Mathematics Education: Findings From a Survey of Empirical Research*, Washington, DC, Mathematics Association of America and the National Council of Teachers of Mathematics.

BEGLE, E.G. and GEESLIN, W. (1972) *Teacher Effectiveness in Mathematics Instruction: National Longitudinal Study of Mathematical Abilities Reports*, Washington, DC, Mathematics Association of America and the National Council of Teachers of Mathematics.

BEHR, M. (1976) *The Effects of Manipulatives in Second Graders' Learning of Mathematics* (Technical Report Vol. 1, No. 11), Tallahasse, FL, PMDC.

BENNETT, B. and KELL, J. (1989) *A Good Start? Four Year Olds in Infant Schools*, Oxford, Blackwell.

BENNETT, N. (1976) *Teaching Styles and Pupil Progress*, London, Open Books.

BENNETT, N., DESFORGES, C., COCKBURN, A. and WILKINSON, B. (1984) *The Quality of Pupil Learning Experiences*, London, Lawrence Erlbaum.

BORKO, H. and LIVINGSTON, C. (1990) 'High school mathematics review lessons: Expert–novice distinctions', *Journal for Research in Mathematics Education*, **21**, 5, pp. 372–87.

BRANSFORD, J.D., SHERWOOD, R., VYE, Y. and RIESER, J. (1986) 'Teaching thinking and problem solving: Research foundations', *American Psychologist*, **41**, 10, pp. 1078–89.

BRIARS, D.J. and LARKIN, J.H. (1984) 'An integrated model of skill in solving elementary word problems', *Cognition and Instruction*, **1**, pp. 245–96.

BROPHY, J.E. (1988) 'Research on teacher effects: Uses and abuses', *Elementary School Journal*, **89**, pp. 3–21.

BROPHY, J.E. (Ed) (1989) *Advances in Research on Teaching* (Vol. 1), Greenwich, CT, JAI Press.

BROPHY, J.E. (Ed) (1991) *Advances in Research on Teaching* (Vol. 2), Greenwich, CT, JAI Press.

BROPHY, J.E. and GOOD, T.L. (1986) 'Teacher behaviour and student achievement', in WITTROCK, M.C. (Ed) *Handbook of Research on Teaching*, New York, Macmillan, pp. 328–75.

BROWN, A.L. (1978) 'Knowing when, where and how to remember: A problem of metacognition', in GLASER, R. (Ed) *Advances in Instructional Psychology* (Vol. 1), Hillsdale, NJ, Lawrence Erlbaum, pp. 77–168.

BROWN, A.L., BRANSFORD, J.D., FERRARA, R.A. and CAMPIONE, J.C. (1983) 'Learning, remembering and understanding', in MUSSEN, P.H. (Ed) *Handbook of Child Psychology*, New York, Wiley, pp. 77–166.

BROWN, A.L. and PALINCSAR, A.S. (1982) 'Inducing strategic learning from texts by means of informed, self-control training', *Topics in Learning and Learning Disabilities*, **12**, 1, pp. 1–18.

BROWN, A.L. and PALINCSAR, A.S. (1984) 'Reciprocal teaching of comprehension: Fostering and monitoring activities', *Cognition and Instruction*, **1**, 2, pp. 175–7.

BROWN, A.L. and PALINSCAR, A.S. (1988) 'Guided, co-operative learning and individual knowledge acquisition', in RESNICK, L.B. (Ed) *Knowing, Learning and Instruction: Essays in Honor of Robert Glaser*, Hillsdale, NJ, Lawrence Erlbaum.

BROWN, J.S. and VANLEHN, K. (1980) 'Repair theory: A generative theory of bugs in procedural skills', *Cognitive Science*, **2**, pp. 379–426.

BRUNER, J.S. (1960) *The Process of Education*, Cambridge, MA, Holt, Rinehart and Winston.

BRUNER, J.S. (1966) *Towards a Theory of Instruction*, Cambridge, MA, Belkap Press.

BUCHMANN, M. (1982) 'The flight away from content in teacher education and teaching', *Journal of Curriculum Studies*, **14**, 1, pp. 61–8.

BUCHMANN, M. (1984) 'The priority of knowledge and understanding in teaching', in KATZ, L. and ROTH, J. (Eds) *Advances in Teacher Education* (Vol. 1), Norwood, NJ, Ablex, pp. 29–50.

BURGHER, W.F. and SHAUGHNESSY, J.M. (1986) 'Characterising the van Hieles levels of development in geometry', *Journal for Research in Mathematics Education*, **17**, 1, pp. 31–48.

CALDERHEAD, J. (Ed) (1987) *Exploring Teachers' Thinking*, London, Cassell.

CARLSEN, W.S. (1991) 'Subject-matter knowledge and science teaching: A pragmatic perspective', in BROPHY, J. (Ed) *Advances in Research on Teaching* (Vol. 2), Greenwich, CT, JAI Press, pp. 115–44.

CARPENTER, T.P. (1976) 'Analysis and synthesis of existing research on measurement', in LESH, R.A. (Ed) *Number and Measurement: Papers from a research workshop*, Columbus, OH, ERIC Clearinghouse for Science, Mathematics and Environmental Education.

CARPENTER, T.P. and MOSER, J.M. (1983) 'The acquisition of addition and subtraction concepts', in LESH, R. and LANDAU, M. (Eds) *Acquisition of Mathematical Concepts and Processes*, New York, Academic Press.

CARPENTER, T.P. and MOSER, J.M. (1984) 'The acquisition of addition and subtraction concepts in grades one through three', *Journal for Research in Mathematics Education*, **15**, pp. 179–202.

CARPENTER, T.P. and PETERSON, P.L. (Eds) (1988) 'Learning through instruction: The study of students' thinking during instruction in mathematics', *Educational Psychologist*, **23**, pp. 79–85.

CARPENTER, T.P., FENNEMA, E. and PETERSON, P.L. (1987) 'Teachers' pedagogical content knowledge in mathematics', Paper presented at the Annual Meeting of the American Educational Research Association, Washington, DC.

CARPENTER, T.P., FENNEMA, E., PETERSON, P.L. (1989) 'Teachers' pedagogical content beliefs in mathematics', *Cognition and Instruction*, **6**, 1, pp. 1–40.

CARPENTER, T.P., FENNEMA, E., PETERSON and CAREY, D.C. (1988) 'Teachers' pedagogical content knowledge of students problem solving in elementary arithmetic', *Journal for Research in Mathematics Education*, **19**, pp. 385–401.

CARPENTER, T.P., FENNEMA, E., PETERSON, P.L., CHIANG, C. and LOEF, M. (1988) 'Using knowledge of children's mathematical thinking in classroom teaching: An experimental study', Paper presented at the Annual Meeting of the American Educational Research Journal, New Orleans.

CARRÉ, C. and ERNEST, P. (1993) 'Performance in subject-matter knowledge in mathematics', in BENNETT, N. and CARRÉ, C. (Eds) *Learning to Teach*, London, Routledge, pp. 34–50.

CARRAHER, T.N., CARRAHER, D.W. and SCHLIEMANN, A.D. (1985) 'Mathematics in the streets and in schools', *British Journal of Developmental Psychology*, **3**, pp. 21–9.

CARTER, K. and DOYLE, W. (1987) 'Teachers' knowledge structures and comprehension processes', in CALDERHEAD, J. (Ed) *Exploring Teachers' Thinking*, London, Cassell, pp. 147–60.

CASE, R. (1982) 'General developmental influences on the acquisition of elementary concepts and algorithms in arithmetic', in CARPENTER, T.P., MOSER, J.M. and ROMBERG, T.A. (Eds) *Addition and Subtraction: A Cognitive Perspective*, Hillsdale, NJ, Erlbaum.

CASE, R. (1985) *Intellectual Development: Birth to Adulthood*, San Diego, CA, Academic Press.

CAZDEN, C.B. (1988) *Classroom Discourse*, Portsmouth, NH, Heinemann.

CHILD EDUCATION (1995) 'Research focus on mathematics', *Child Education*, August, pp. 15–18.

CLARK, C. and YINGER, R. (1979) 'Teachers' thinkings', in PETERSON, D.L. and WALBERG, H. (Eds) *Research on Teaching: Concepts, Findings and Implications*, Berkeley, McCutchan.

CLARK, C.M. and PETERSON, P.L. (1986) 'Teachers' thought processes', in WITTROCK, M.W. (Ed) *Handbook of Research in Teaching*, New York, Macmillan, pp. 255–96.

CLARK, C.M. and YINGER, R.J. (1987) 'Teacher planning', in CALDERHEAD, J. (Ed) *Exploring Teachers' Thinking*, London, Cassell, pp. 84–103.

CLEMENTS, D.H. and BATTISTA, M.T. (1992) 'Geometry and spatial reasoning', in GROUWS, D. (Ed) *Handbook of Research on Teaching and Learning*, Reston, VA, National Council of Teachers of Mathematics, pp. 420–64.

COBB, P. (1988) 'The tension between theories of learning and instruction in mathematics education', *Educational Psychologist*, **23**, 2, pp. 87–103.

COBB, P., WOOD, T., YACKEL, E. and MCNEAL, B. (1992) 'Characteristics of classroom mathematics traditions: An interactional analysis', *American Educational Research*, **29**, 3, pp. 573–604.

COBB, P., WOOD, T., YACKEL, E., NICHOLLS, J., WHEATLEY, G., TRIGATTI, B. and PERLWITZ, M. (1991) 'Assessment of a problem-centred second-grade mathematics project', *Journal for Research in Mathematics Education*, **22**, 1, pp. 3–29.

COCKCROFT, W.M. (1982) *Mathematics Counts: Report of Committee of Inquiry into the Teaching of Mathematics*, London, HMSO.

COOPER, R.G. JR. (1984) 'Early number development: Discovering number space with addition and subtraction', in SOPHIA, C. (Ed) *Origins of Cognitive Skills: The Eighteenth Annual Carnegie Symposium on Cognition*, Hillsdale, NJ, Erlbaum, pp. 157–92.

COXFORD, A. (1978) 'Research directions in geometry', in LESH, R. (Ed) *Recent Research Concerning the Development of Spatial and Geometric Concepts*, The Ohio State University, ERIC Clearinghouse for Science, Mathematics and Environmental Education.

DAVIS, A. (1993) 'Matching and assessment', *Journal of Curriculum Studies*, **25**, 3, pp. 267–79.

DAVIS, A. (1995) 'Criterion-referenced assessment and the development of knowledge and understanding', *Journal of Philosophy of Education*, **29**, 2, pp. 3–22.

DEARING, R. (1994) *The National Curriculum and its Assessment: Final Report*, London, School Curriculum and Assessment Authority.

DENVIR, B. and BROWN, M. (1987) 'The feasibility of class administered diagnostic assessment in primary mathematics', *Educational Research*, **29**, 2, pp. 95–107.

DENZIN, N.K. (1978) *Sociological Methods*, New York, McGraw-Hill.

DES (1983) *Quality Teaching*, London, HMSO.

DES (1984) *Organisation and Content of the 5–16 Curriculum*, London, HMSO.

DES (1985a) *Quality Schools*, London, HMSO.

DES (1985b) *Science 5–16: A Statement of Policy*, London, HMSO.

DES (1985c) *The Curriculum from 5 to 16*, London, HMSO.

DES (1988) *Education Reform Act*, London, HMSO.

DES (1989) *Circular 24/89: Initial Teacher Training, Approval of Courses*. London, DES.

DES (1991) *Mathematics in the National Curriculum*, London, HMSO.

DESFORGES, A. and DESFORGES, C. (1980) 'Number-based strategies of sharing in young children', *Educational Studies*, **6**, 2, pp. 97–109.

DESFORGES, C. and COCKBURN, A. (1987) *Understanding the Mathematics Teacher*, London, Falmer Press.

DEWEY, J. (1904–64) 'The relation of theory to practice in education', National Society for the Scientific Study of Education, Third Year Book, Part 1, Reprinted in ARCHAMBAULT, R.D. (Ed) *John Dewey on Education: Selected Writings*, Chicago, University of Chicago Press.

DFEE (1993) *Circular 14/93: The Initial Training of Primary School Teachers. New Criteria for Course Approval*. London, Sanctuary Buildings.

DIENES, Z.P. (1960) *Build Up Mathematics*, London, Hutchinson Educational Ltd.

DONALDSON, M. (1978) *Children's Minds*, London, Fontana.

DOYLE, W. (1986) 'Classroom organisation and management', in WITTROCK, M.C. (Ed) *Handbook of Research on Teaching*, New York, Macmillan, pp. 392–431.

DOYLE, W. (1990) 'Themes in teacher education research', in HOUSTON, W.R. (Ed) *Handbook of Research on Teacher Education*, New York, Macmillan, pp. 3–24.

DOYLE, W. and CARTER, K. (1984) 'Academic tasks in classrooms', *Curriculum Inquiry*, **14**, pp. 129–49.

DUNKIN, M.J. and BIDDLE, B.J. (1974) *The Study of Teaching*, New York, Holt, Rinehart and Winston.

DURKIN, K., SHIRE, B., RIEM, R., CROWTHER, R. and RUTTER, D. (1986) 'The social and linguistic context of early number word use', *British Journal of Developmental Psychology*, **4**, pp. 269–88.

EDWARDS, D. and MERCER, N. (1987) *Common Knowledge: The Development of Understanding in the Classroom*, London, Methuen.

EISNER, E.W. (1975) 'The perceptive eye: Towards the reformation of education evaluation', Occasional Papers of the Stanford Evaluation Consortium, Stanford, CA, Stanford University, (mimeo).

ERNEST, P. (1989) 'The knowledge, beliefs and attitudes of the mathematics teacher: A model', *Journal of Education for Teaching*, **15**, 1, pp. 13–33.

EVANS, L., PACKWOOD, A., ST. J. NEILL, S.R. and CAMPBELL, R.J. (1994) *The Meaning of Infant Teachers' Work*, London, Routledge.

FEIMAN-NEMSER, S. and BUCHMANN, M. (1986) 'The first year of teacher preparation: Transition to pedagogical thinking?', *Journal of Curriculum Studies*, **18**, pp. 239–56.

FEIMAN-NEMSER, S. and BUCHMANN, M. (1987) 'When is student teaching teacher education?', *Teaching and Teacher Education*, **3**, pp. 255–73.

FENNEMA, E., CARPENTER, T.P. and PETERSON, P.L. (1989) 'Learning mathematics with understanding: Cognitively guided instruction', in BROPHY, J. (Ed) *Advances in Research on Teaching* (Vol. 1), Greenwich, Connecticut, JAI Press, pp. 195–222.

FENSTERMACHER, G.D. (1986) 'Philosophy of research on teaching: Three aspects', in WITTROCK, M.C. (Ed) *Handbook of Research on Teaching*, New York, Macmillan, pp. 37–49.

FLAVELL, J.H., FRIEDRICKS, A.G., HOYT, J.D. (1970) 'Developmental changes in memorization processes', *Cognitive Psychology*, **1**, pp. 324–40.

FLODEN, R.E. and BUCHMANN, M. (1990) 'Philosophical inquiry in teacher education', in HOUSTON, W.R. (Ed) *Handbook of Research in Teacher Education*, New York, Macmillan, pp. 42–58.

FUSON, K. (1982) 'An analysis of the counting-on solution procedure in addition', in CARPENTER, T.P., MOSER, J.M. and ROMBERG, T.A. (Eds) *Addition and Subtraction: A Cognitive Perspective*, Hillsdale, New Jersey, Lawrence Erlbaum.

FUSON, K. (1988) *Children's Counting and Concepts of Number*, New York, Springer-Verlag.

FUSON, C.K. and KWON, Y. (1992) 'Korean children's single-digit addition and subtraction: Numbers structured by ten', *Journal for Research in Mathematics Education*, **23**, pp. 148–65.

GAGE, N.L. (Ed) (1976) *The Psychology of Teaching Methods* (75th Yearbook of the National Society for the Study of Education (Part 1), Chicago, University of Chicago Press.

GAGE, N.L. (1978) *The Scientific Basis of the Art of Teaching*, New York, Teachers' College News.

GAGE, N.L. (1985) *Hard Gains in the Soft Sciences: The Case of Pedagogy*, Bloomington, IN, Center of Evaluation, Development and Research, Phi Delta Kappan.

GAGNÉ, R.M. (1965) *The Conditions of Learning*, New York, Holt, Rinehart and Winston.

GALTON, M., SIMON, P. and CROLL, P. (1980) *Inside the Primary Classroom*, London, Routledge and Kegan Paul.

GEARY, D.C. and BOW-THOMAS, C.C. (1992) 'Numerical cognition: Loci of ability differences comparing children from China and the United States', *Psychological Science*, **3**, pp. 180–5.

GELMAN, R. and BROWN, A.L. (1986) 'Changing competence in the young', in SMELSER, N.J. and GERSTEIN, D.R. (Eds) *Behavioural and Social Science: Fifty Years of Discovery*, Washington, DC, National Academic Press, pp. 175–209.

GELMAN, R. and GALLISTEL, C.R. (1978) *The Child's Understanding of Number*, Cambridge, MA, Harvard University Press.

GINSBURG, H.P. (1977) *Children's Arithmetic: The Learning Process*, New York, Van Nostrand.

GINSBURG, H.P. and RUSSELL, R.L. (1981) *Social Class and Racial Influence on Early Mathematical Thinking*, Monograph of the Society for Research in Child Education, **46**, 6, Serial No. 193.

GLASER, B. (1978) *Theoretical Sensitivity*, Mill Valley, CA, Sociology Press.

GLASER, B. and STRAUSS, A. (1967) *The Discovery of Grounded Theory*, Chicago, Aldine.

GLASER, R. (Ed) (1986) 'Special Issue: Psychological science and education', *American Psychologist*, **40**, 10, pp. 1–157.

GLASER, R. and BASSOCK, M. (1989) 'Learning theory and the study of instruction', *Annual Review of Psychology*, **40**, pp. 631–66.

GOOD, T.L. and GROUWS, D.A. (1979) 'The Missouri mathematics effectiveness project: An experimental study in fourth grade classrooms', *Journal of Educational Psychology*, **71**, pp. 355–62.

GOOD, T.L., GROUWS, D.A. and EBMEIER, H. (1983) *Active Mathematics Teaching*, New York, Longman.

GRAVEMEIJER, K., VAN DEN HEUVEL, M. and STREEFLAND, L. (1990) *Context Free Productions Tests and Geometry in Realistic Mathematics in Education*, Utrecht Research Group for Mathematical Education and Educational Computer Centre.

GREEN, T.F. (1971) *The Activities of Teaching*, New York, McGraw.

GREENO, J.G., RILEY, M.S. and GELMAN, R. (1984) 'Conceptual competence and children's counting', *Cognitive Psychology*, **16**, pp. 94–134.

GROEN, G.T. and RESNICK, L.R. (1977) 'Can preschoolers invent addition algorithms?', *Journal of Educational Psychology*, **69**, pp. 645–52.

GROSSMAN, P.L. (1987) 'A tale of two teachers: The role of subject matter orientation in teaching', Paper presented at the Annual Meeting of the American Educational Research Association. Washington, DC.

GROSSMAN, P.L. (1990) 'When what you know doesn't work: A re-analysis of methods and findings', Paper presented at the Annual Meeting of the American Educational Research Association, Boston.

GROSSMAN, P.L. and RICKERT, A.E. (1986) 'Unacknowledged knowledge growth: A re-examination of the effects of teacher education', Paper presented at the Annual Meeting of the American Educational Research Association, San Franscisco.

GROSSMAN, P.L., WILSON, S.M. and SHULMAN, L.S. (1989) 'Teachers of substance: Subject matter knowledge for teaching', in REYNOLDS, M.C. (Ed) *Knowledge Base for the Beginning Teacher*, Oxford, Pergamon, pp. 23–36.

GUBA, E.G. (1978) *Towards a Methodology of Naturalistic Inquiry in Educational Evaluation*, Monograph 8, Los Angeles, UCLA Centre for the Study of Evaluation.

GUBA, E.G. (1981) 'Criteria for assessing the trustworthiness of naturalistic inquiries', *Educational Communication and Technology Journal*, **29**, pp. 75–92.

GUBA, E.G. and LINCOLN, Y.S. (1981) *Effective Evaluation*, San Francisco, Jossey-Bass.

HAMMERSLEY, M. (1993) 'Opening up the quantitative–qualitative divide', Paper presented at ESRC Seminar, University of Warwick, September, 1993.

HARLEN, W. and QUALTER, A. (1991) 'National Curriculum assessment: Increasing the benefit by reducing the burden in education and change in the 1990s', *Journal of the Educational Research Network of Northern Ireland*, 5, February, pp. 3–19.

HARLEN, W., GIPPS, C., BROADFOOT, P. and NUTTALL, D. (1992) 'Assessment and the improvement of education', *The Curriculum Journal*, **3**, 3, pp. 215–29.

HART, F. (1934) *Teachers and Teaching: By Ten Thousand High School Seniors*, New York, Macmillan.

HMI (1978) *Primary Education in England: A Survey by HM Inspectors of Schools*, London, HMSO.

HMI (1991) *Mathematics Key Stages 1 and 3, A report by HM Inspectorate on the first year 1989–90*, London, HMSO.

HMI (1992) *Mathematics, Key Stages 1, 2 and 3, A report by HM Inspectorate on the second year, 1990–91*, London, HMSO.

HIEBERT, J. and CARPENTER, T.P. (1992) 'Learning and teaching with understanding', in GROUWS, D.A. (Ed) *Handbook of Research on Mathematics Teaching and Learning*, New York, Macmillan, pp. 65–100.

HOFFER, A. (1983) 'Van Hiele-based research', in LESH, R. and LANDAU, M. (Eds) *Acquisition of Mathematics Concepts and Processes*, New York, Academic Press, pp. 205–27.

HOFFER, A. (1988). 'Geometry and visual thinking', in POST, T.R. (Ed) *Teaching Mathematics in Grades K-8*, Boston, Allyn and Bacon.

HUGHES, M. (1981) 'Can pre-school children add and subtract?', *Educational Psychology*, **1**, 3, pp. 207–19.

HUGHES, M. (1986) *Children and Number Difficulties in Learning Mathematics*, Oxford, Basil Blackwell.

INHELDER, B. and PIAGET, J. (1958) *The Growth of Logical Thinking from Childhood to Adolescence*, London, Routledge and Kegan Paul.

JACKSON, P.W. (1968) *Life in Classrooms*, New York, Holt, Rinehart and Winston.

JANVIER, C. (Ed) (1987) *Problems of Representation in the Teaching and Learning of Mathematics*, Hillsdale, NJ, Lawrence Erlbaum.

KAMII, C.K. (1985) *Young Children Reinvent Arithmetic: Implications of Piaget's Theory*, New York, Teachers' College, Columbia University.

KAMII, C.K. (1989) *Young Children Continue to Reinvent Arithmetic 2nd Grade: Implications of Piaget's Theory*, New York Teachers' College, Columbia University.

KAPUT, J.J. (1987) 'Representation systems as mathematics', in JANVIER, C. (Ed) *Problems of Representation in the Teaching and Learning of Mathematics*, Hillsdale, NJ, Erlbaum, pp. 159–95.

KIDDER, L.H. (1981) 'Qualitative research and quasi-experimental frameworks', in BREWER, M.B. and COLLINS, B.E. (Eds) *Scientific Inquiry and the Social Sciences*, San Francisco, Jossey-Bass.

KILPATRICK, J. and WIRSZUP, I. (1966–77) *Soviet Studies in Psychology of Learning and Teaching Mathematics*, School of Mathematics Study Group, Vol. 1–20, University of Chicago.

KLEIN, A. and STARKEY, P. (1988) 'Universals in the development of early arithmetic cognition', in SAXE, G.B. and GEARHART, M. (Eds) *Children's Mathematics*, San Francisco, Jossey-Bass Inc., pp. 5–26.

KOUNIN, J.S. (1970) *Discipline and Group Management in Classrooms*, New York, Holt, Rinehart and Winston.

KOZULIN, A. (1986) *Thought and Language, Ley Vygotsky*, Cambridge, MA, Harvard University Press.

LAMPERT, M. (1985) 'How do teachers manage to teach? Perspectives on problems in practice', *Harvard Education Review*, **53**, 2, pp. 178–94.

LAMPERT, M. (1987) 'Attending to students' thinking in mathematics classes: Teachers' perspectives', Paper presented at the Annual Meeting of the American Educational Research Association, Washington, DC.

LAMPERT, M. (1988) 'Connecting mathematical teaching and learning', in FENNEMA, E., CARPENTER, T.P. and LAMEN, S.J. (Eds) *Integrating Research on Teaching and Learning Mathematics*, Madison, WI, University of Wisconsin, Wisconsin Centre for Education Research, pp. 132–67.

LAMPERT, M. (1990) 'When the problem is not the question and the solution is not the answer: Mathematical knowing and teaching', *American Educational Research Journal*, **27**, 1, 1, pp. 29–63.

LAMPERT, M. (1992) 'Teaching and learning long division for understanding in school', in LEINHARDT, G., PUTNAM, R. and HATTRUP, R.A. (Eds) *Analysis of Arithmetic for Mathematics Teaching*, Hillsdale, NJ, Lawrence Erlbaum Associates, pp. 221–82.

LAVE, J. (1988) *Cognition in Practice: Mind, Mathematics and Culture in Everyday Life*, Cambridge, Cambridge University Press.

LAVE, J. (1991) *Situated Learning: Legitimate Peripheral Participation*, Cambridge, Cambridge University Press.

LAZERSON, M., McLAUGHLIN, J.B., McPHERSON, B. and BAILEY, S. (1985) *An Education of Value: The Purposes and Practices of Schools*, Cambridge, Cambridge University Press.

LEINHARDT, G. (1983) 'Routines in expert math teachers' thoughts and actions', Paper presented at the Annual Meeting of the American Research Association, Montreal.

LEINHARDT, G. (1987) 'Development of an expert explanation: An analysis of a sequence of subtraction lessons', *Cognition and Instruction*, **4**, 4, pp. 225–82.

LEINHARDT, G. (1989) 'Math lessons: A contrast of novice and expert competence', *Journal for Research in Mathematics Education*, **20**, 1, pp. 52–75.

LEINHARDT, G. (1993) 'On teaching', in GLASER, R. (Ed) *Advances in Instructional Psychology* (Vol. 4), Hillsdale, NJ, Lawrence Erlbaum, pp. 1–54.

LEINHARDT, G. and GREENO, J.G. (1986) 'The cognitive skill of teaching', *Journal of Educational Psychology*, **78**, 2, pp. 75–95.

LEINHARDT, G. and SMITH, D.A. (1985) 'Expertise in mathematics instruction: Subject matter knowledge', *Journal of Educational Psychology*, **77**, 3, pp. 247–71.

LEINHARDT, G., PUTNAM, R.T., STEIN, M.K. and BAXTER, J. (1991) 'Where subject knowledge matters', in BROPHY, J. (Ed) *Advances in Research on Teaching* (Vol. 2), Greenwich, CT, JAI Press, pp. 87–113.

LEONT'EV, A.N. (1981) 'The problem of activity in psychology', in WERTSCH, J.V. (Ed) *The Concept of Activity in Soviet Psychology*, Armonk, NY, M.E. Sharpe.

LESH, R., POST, T. and BEHR, M. (1987) 'Representation and translations among representations in mathematics learning and problem-solving', in JANVIER, C. (Ed) *Problems of Representation in the Teaching and Learning of Mathematics*, Hillsdale, NJ, Erlbaum, pp. 33–58.

LINCOLN, Y.S. and GUBA, E.G. (1985) *Naturalistic Inquiry*, London, Sage Publications.

MANSFIELD, H. (1985) 'Points, lines and their representations', *For the Learning of Mathematics*, **5**, 3, pp. 2–5.

MARKS, P.R. (1990) 'Pedagogical content knowledge: From a mathematical case to a modified conception', *Journal of Teacher Education*, **41**, 4, pp. 3–11.

McDIARMID, G.W., BALL, D.L. and ANDERSON, C.W. (1989) 'Why staying one chapter ahead doesn't really work: Subject-specific pedagogy', in REYNOLDS, M.C. (Ed) *Knowledge Base for the Beginning Teacher*, Oxford, Pergamon, pp. 193–206.

McLAUGHLIN, J.B., McPHERSON, B. and BAILEY, S. (1985) *An Education of Value: The Purposes and Practices of Schools*, Cambridge, Cambridge University Press.

McNamara, D. (1991) 'Subject knowledge and its application: Problems and possibilities for teacher educators', *Journal of Education for Teaching*, **17**, 2, pp. 113–27.

Medley, D. (1979) 'The effectiveness of teachers', in Peterson, P.L. and Walberg, H. (Eds) *Research on Teaching: Concepts, Findings and Implications*, Berkeley, CA, McCutchan, pp. 11–26.

Merrtons, R. and Vass, J. (1991) 'Assessing the Nation: Blue prints without tools', *Primary Teaching Studies*, **5**, 3, pp. 222–39.

Miles, M.B. and Huberman, A.M. (1984) *Qualitative Data Analysis: A Sourcebook of New Methods*, London, Sage Publications.

Miller, K., Perlmutter, M. and Keating, D. (1984) 'Cognitive arithmetic: Comparison of operations', *Journal of Experimental Psychology: Learning, Memory and Cognition*, **10**, pp. 46–60.

Munn, P. (1994) 'The early development of literacy and numeracy skills', *European Early Childhood Education Research Journal*, **2**, 1, pp. 5–18.

Murray, H. and Olivier, A. (1989) 'A model of understanding two-digit numeration and computation', in Vergnaud, G., Rogalski, J. and Artique, M. (Eds) *Proceedings of the Thirteenth International Conference for the Psychology of Mathematics Education* (Vol. 3), Paris, France, pp. 3–10.

Murray, H., Olivier, A. and Piet, H. (1991) 'Young children's division strategies', in Furinghetti, F. (Ed) *Proceedings of the Fifteenth International Conference for the Psychology of Mathematics Education* (Vol. 3), Assissi, Italy, pp. 49–56.

Murray, H., Olivier, A. and Piet, H. (1993) 'Voluntary interaction groups for problem-centred learning', in Hirayashi, I., Nohda, N., Shigematsu, K. and Lin, F. (Eds) *Proceedings of the Seventeenth International Conference for the Psychology of Mathematics Education* (Vol. 2), Tsukuba, Japan, pp. 73–80.

Murray, H., Olivier, A. and Piet, H. (1994) 'Young children's free comments as sources of information on their learning environment', in da Ponte, J.P. and Matos, J.F. (Eds) *Proceedings of the Eighteenth International Conference for the Psychology of Mathematics Education* (Vol. 3), Lisbon, Portugal, pp. 328–35.

National Curriculum Council (NCC) (1991) *National Curriculum Council Consultation Report on Mathematics*, September, 1991, York, NCC.

National Curriculum Council (NCC) (1993) *The National Curriculum at Key Stages 1 and 3*, York, NCC.

Nelson, N. and Frobisher, L. (1993) 'Assessing mathematics', in Shorrocks, D., Frobisher, L., Nelson, N., Turner, L. and Waterson, A. *Implementing National Curriculum Assessment in the Primary School*, London, Hodder and Stoughton.

Nunes, T., Schliemann, A.D. and Carraher, D.W. (1993) *Street Mathematics and School Mathematics*, Cambridge, Cambridge University Press.

Office for Standards in Education (OFSTED) (1993) *The Teaching and Learning of Number in Primary School National Curriculum Mathematics*, London, HMSO.

OFFICE FOR STANDARDS IN EDUCATION (OFSTED) (1995) *Mathematics: A Review of Inspection Findings*, London, HMSO.

PALINSCAR, A.S. and BROWN, A.L. (1984) 'Reciprocal teaching of comprehension-fostering and monitoring activities', *Cognition and Instruction*, **1**, pp. 117–75.

PETERS, R.S. (1977) *Education and the Education of Teachers*, London, Routledge and Kegan Paul.

PETERSON, D.L. (1979) 'Direct instruction reconsidered', in PETERSON, D.L. and WALBERG, H. (Eds) *Research on Teaching: Concepts, Findings and Implications*, Berkeley, McCutchan, pp. 57–69.

PETERSON, P.L. (1988) 'Teachers' and students' cognitional knowledge for classroom teaching and learning', *Educational Researcher*, **17**, 5, pp. 5–14.

PETERSON, P.L. and SWING, S.R. (1982) 'Beyond time on task: Students' reports of their thought processes during classroom instruction', *Elementary School Journal*, **82**, pp. 481–91.

PETERSON, P.L. and SWING, S.R. (1983) 'Problems in classroom implementation of cognitive strategy instruction', in PRESSLEY, M. and LEVIN, J.R. (Eds) *Cognitive Strategy Research: Educational Applications*, New York, Springer-Verlag, pp. 267–84.

PETERSON, P.L., FENNEMA, E. and CARPENTER, T.P. (1991) 'Teachers' knowledge of students' mathematical problem solving knowledge', in BROPHY, J.E. (Ed) *Advances in Research on Teaching* (Vol. 2), Greenwich, CT, JAI Press, pp. 49–86.

PETERSON, P.L., FENNEMA, E., CARPENTER, T.P. and LOEF, M. (1989) 'Teachers' pedagogical content beliefs in mathematics', *Cognition and Instruction*, **6**, 1, pp. 1–40.

PIAGET, J. and INHELDER, B. (1956) *The Child's Conception of Space*, London, Routledge and Kegan Paul.

PIAGET, J. and INHELDER, B. (1958) *The Growth of Logical Thinking from Childhood to Adolescence*, London, Routledge and Kegan Paul.

PIAGET, J. and INHELDER, B. (1969) *The Psychology of the Child*, New York, Basic Books, (original book published 1966).

PIAGET, J., INHELDER, B. and SZEMINSKA, A. (1960) *The Child's Conception of Geometry*, London, Routledge and Kegan Paul (original book published in 1948).

PUTNAM, R.T. (1987) 'Structuring and adjusting content for students: A study of live and simulated tutoring of addition', *American Educational Research Journal*, **24**, pp. 13–48.

PUTNAM, R.T., LAMPERT, M. and PETERSON, P.L. (1989) 'Alternative perspectives on knowing mathematics in elementary schools', in CAZDEN, C. (Ed) *Review of Research in Education* (Vol. 16), Washington, DC, American Educational Research Association, pp. 57–149.

RESNICK, L.B. (1982) 'Syntax and semantics in learning to subtract', in CARPENTER, T.P., MOSER, J.M. and ROMBERG, T.A. (Eds) *Addition and Subtraction: A Cognitive Perspective*, Hillsdale, NJ, Lawrence Erlbaum, pp. 136–55.

RESNICK, L.B. (1985) 'Learning in school and out', *Educational Researcher*, **16**, 9, pp. 13–20.

RESNICK, L.B. (1986) 'The development of mathematical intuition', in PERLMUTTER, M. (Ed) *Perspectives on Intellectual Development*, The Minnesota Symposium on Child Development (Vol. 19), Hillsdale, NJ, Lawrence Erlbaum, pp. 159–94.

RESNICK, L.B. (1987) *Education and Learning to Think*, Washington, DC, National Academic Press.

RILEY, M.S., GREENO, J.G. and HELLER, J.I. (1983) 'Development of children's problem-solving ability in arithmetic', in GINSBURG, H.P. (Ed) *The Development of Mathematical Thinking*, New York, Academic Press.

ROMBERG, T.A. (1983) 'A common curriculum for mathematics', in FENSTER-MACHER, G.I. and GOODLAD, J.J. (Eds) *Individual Differences and the Common Curriculum*, Chicago, National Society for Science Education, pp. 121–59.

ROMBERG, T.A. and CARPENTER, T. (1986) 'Research on teaching and learning mathematics: Two disciplines of scientific inquiry', in WITTROCK, M.C. (Ed) *Handbook for Research on Teaching*, New York, Macmillan, pp. 850–73.

ROMBERG, T.A., HARVEY, J., MOSER, J. and MONTGOMERY, M. (1974, 1975 and 1976) *Developing Mathematics Processes*, Chicago, IL, Rand McNally.

ROSENSHINE, B. (1976) 'Classroom instruction', in GAGE, N.L. (Ed) *The Psychology of Teaching Methods* (77th Yearbook of the National Society for the Study of Education, Part 1) Chicago, University of Chicago Press, pp. 335–71.

RYLE, G. (1952) *The Concept of Mind*, London, Hutchinson.

SAXE, G.B. (1977) 'A developmental analysis of national counting', *Child Development*, 48, pp. 1512–20.

SAXE, G.B. (1988) 'Candy selling and maths learning', *Educational Researcher*, **17**, 6, pp. 14–21.

SAXE, G.N., GUBERMAN, S.R. and GEARHART, M. (1987) *Social Processes in Early Number Development*, Monograph of the Society for Research in Child Development, **52**, 2, Serial No. 216.

SCARDAMALIA, M., BEREITER, C. and STEINBACK, R. (1984) 'Teachability of reflective processes in written composition', *Cognitive Science*, **8**, 2, pp. 173–90.

SCHAEFFER, B., EGGLESTON, V.H. and SCOTT, J.L. (1974) 'Number development in young children', *Cognitive Development*, **5**, pp. 357–79.

SCHOENFELD, A.H. (1985) *Mathematical Problem Solving*, New York, Academic Press.

SCHOENFELD, A.H. (1986) 'On having and using geometric knowledge', in HIEBERT, J. (Ed) *Conceptual and Procedural Knowledge: The Case of Mathematics*, Hillsdale, NJ, Lawrence Erlbaum, pp. 225–64.

SCHON, D. (1983) *The Reflective Practitioner: How Professionals Think in Action*, New York, Basic Books.

SCHOOLS EXAMINATION and ASSESSMENT COUNCIL (SEAC) (1989) *A Guide to Teacher Assessment: Pack C: A Source Book for Teacher Assessment*, London, SEAC/Heinemann Educational.

SCHWAB, J.J. (1964) 'Structure of the disciplines: Meanings and significance', in FORD, G.W. and PUGNO, L. (Eds) *The Structure of Knowledge and the Curriculum*, Chicago, Rand McNally, pp. 6–30.

SCHWAB, J.J. (1978) 'Education and the structure of the disciplines', in WESTBURY, I. and WILKOF, N.J. (Eds) *Science, Curriculum and Liberal Education*, Chicago, University of Chicago Press, pp. 229–72.

SHORROCKS, D., FROBISHER, L., NELSON, N., TURNER, L. and WATERSON, A. (1993) *Implementing National Curriculum Assessment in the Primary School*, London, Hodder and Stoughton.

SHUARD, H., WALSH, A., GOODWIN, V. and WORCESTER, G. (1991) *The Calculator-Aware Number (CAN) Curriculum. Calculators. Children and Mathematics*, London, Simon Schuster for NCC.

SHULMAN, L.S. (1986a) 'Those who understand: Knowledge growth in teaching', *Educational Researcher*, **15**, 2, pp. 4–14.

SHULMAN, L.S. (1986b) 'Paradigms and research programs in the study of teaching: A contemporary perspective', in WITTROCK, M.C. (Ed) *Handbook of Research on Teaching*, New York, Macmillan.

SHULMAN, L.S. (1987) 'Knowledge and teaching: Foundations of the new reform', *Harvard Educational Review*, **57**, pp. 1–22.

SCHULMAN, L.S. and GROSSMAN, P.L. (1988) *Knowledge Growth in Teaching: A Final Report to the Spencer Foundation*, Stanford, CA, Stanford University.

SIEGLER, R.S. (1983) 'Information processing approaches to development', in MUSSEN, P. and KASSEN, W. (Eds) *Manual of Child Development*, New York, Wiley.

SIEGLER, R.S. (1986) 'Child as the measurer of all things: Measurements procedures and the development of quantitative concepts', in SOPHIAN, C. (Ed) *Origins of Cognitive Skills: The Eighteenth Annual Carnegie Symposium on Cognition*, Hillsdale, NJ, Erlbaum, pp. 193–228.

SILBERT, J., CARNINE, C. and STEIN, M. (1981) *Direct Instruction Mathematics*, Columbus, OH, Charles Merrill.

SINCLAIR, J.M. and COULTHARDT, R.M. (1975) *Towards an Analysis of Discourse: The English Used by Teachers and Pupils*, London, Oxford University Press.

SKRTIC, T.M. (1985) 'Doing naturalistic research into educational institutions', in SKRTIC, T.M., GUBA, E.G. and KNOWLTON, H.E. *Interorganisational Special Education Programming in Rural Areas: Technical Report on the Multisite Naturalistic Field Study*, Washington, DC, National Institute for Education.

SLAVIN, R. (1983) *Co-operative Learning*, New York, Longman.

SMYTH, J. (Ed) (1987) *Educating Teachers: Changing the Nature of Pedagogical Knowledge*, London, Falmer Press.

SOCKETT, H.T. (1987) 'Has Shulman got the strategy right?', *Harvard Educational Review*, **57**, 2, pp. 208–19.

STARKEY, P. and GELMAN, R. (1982) 'The development of addition and subtraction abilities prior to formal schooling in arithmetic', in CARPENTER, T.P., MOSER, J.M. and ROMBERG, T.A. (Eds) *Addition and Subtraction: A Cognitive Perspective*, Hillsdale, NJ, Erlbaum.

STEFFE, L.P., COBB, P. and VAN GLASERSFELD, E. (1988) *Construction of Arithmetical Meanings and Strategies*, New York, Springer-Verlag.

STEFFE, L.P., THOMPSON, P.W. and RICHARDS, J. (1982) 'Children's counting in arithmetic problem-solving', in CARPENTER, T.P., MOSER, J.M. and ROMBERG, T.A. (Eds) *Addition and Subtraction: A Cognitive Perspective*, Hillsdale, New Jersey, Lawrence Erlbaum.

STEIN, M.K., BAXTER, J.A. and LEINHARDT, G. (1990) 'Subject-matter knowledge and elementary instruction: A case from functions and graphing', *American Education Research Journal*, **27**, pp. 639–63.

STEINBERG, R.M. (1985) 'Instruction on derived facts strategies in addition and subtraction', *Journal for Research in Mathematics Education*, **16**, 5, pp. 337–55.

STEPHENSON, H.W., LEE, S.Y., CHEN, C., STIGLER, J.W., HSU, C.C. and KITAMURA, S. (1990) 'Contexts of achievement: A study of American, Chinese and Japanese children', *Monographs of the Society for Research in Child Development*, **55**, 1–2. Serial No. 221.

STIERER, B. (1990) 'Assessing children at the start of school: Issues dilemmas and current developments', *The Curriculum Journal*, **1**, 2, pp. 155–69.

STIGLER, J.W. and PERRY, M. (1988) 'Mathematics learning in Japanese, Chinese and American Classrooms', in SAXE, G.B. and GEARHART, M. (Eds) *Children's Mathematics: New Directions for Child Development*, **41**, San Francisco, Jossey-Bass Inc., pp. 27–54.

STODOLSKY, S. (1988) *The Subject Matters: Classroom Activity in Mathematics and Social Science*, Chicago, University of Chicago.

STRAUSS, A. (1987) *Qualitative Analysis for Social Scientists*, Cambridge, Cambridge University Press.

STRAUSS, A. and CORBIN, J. (1990) *Basics of Qualitative Research. Grounded Theory, Procedures and Techniques*, London, Sage Publications.

STREEFLAND, L. (Ed) (1991) *Realistic Mathematics Education in Primary School*, Utrecht, The Netherlands, Freudenthal Institute, Research Group on Mathematics Education, Centre for Science and Mathematics Education.

SUGGATE, J., AUBREY, C. and PETTITT, D. (1996) *The Knowledge of 4–5 Year Olds at School Entry and at the End of the First Year* (In Submission).

SUYDAM, M.N. and WEAVER, J.F. (1975) 'Research on mathematics learning', in PAYNE, J.N. (Ed) *Mathematics Learning in Early Childhood*, Reston, VA, National Council of Teachers of Mathematics.

TAMIR, P. (1988) 'Subject matter and related pedagogical knowledge in teacher education', *Teaching and Teacher Education*, **4**, 2, pp. 99–110.

TEACHER TRAINING AGENCY (TTA) (1995) *The Continuing Professional Development of Teachers*, London, TTA.

THE TIMES EDUCATIONAL SUPPLEMENT (TES) (1993) 'Maths picked up before school', *TES*, 9 April, p. 8.

THOMPSON, A. (1992) 'Teachers' beliefs and conceptions: A synthesis of the research', in GROUWS, D.A. (Ed) *Handbook of Research on Mathematics Teaching and Learning*, New York, Macmillan, pp. 127–46.

Tizard, B. and Hughes, M. (1984) *Young Children Learning: Talking and Thinking at Home and at School*, London, Fontana.

Tizard, B., Blatchford, P., Burke, J., Farquahar, C. and Plewis, I. (1988) *Young Children Growing Up in the Inner City*, London, Lawrence Erlbaum.

Tom, A.R. (1987) 'Replacing pedagogical knowledge with pedagogical questions', in Smyth, J. (Ed) *Educating Teachers: Changing the Nature of Pedagogical Knowledge*, London, Falmer Press, pp. 9–17.

Valli, L. and Tom, A.R. (1988) 'How adequate are the knowledge base frameworks in teacher education?', *Journal of Teacher Education*, 39, pp. 5–12.

Van Hiele, P. and M. (1959) 'La Pensée de l'enfant et la géometrie', *Bulletin de l'Association des Professeurs de Mathématiques de l'Enseignement Public*, **38**, pp. 199–205.

VanLehn, K. (1983) 'On the representation of procedures in repair theory', in Ginsburg, H.P. (Ed) *The Development of Mathematical Thinking*, Hillsdale, NJ, Lawrence Erlbaum, pp. 3–17.

Vergnaud, G. (1982) 'Cognitive and developmental psychology and research in mathematics education: Some theoretical and methodological issues', *For the Learning of Mathematics*, **3**, 2, pp. 31–41.

Vergnaud, G. (1983) 'Multiplicative structures', in Lesh, R. and Landau, M. (Eds) *Acquisition of Mathematics Concepts and Processes*, New York, Academic Press.

Wang, M.C. and Palincsar, A.S. (1989) 'Teaching students to assume an active role in their learning', in Reynolds, M.C. (Ed) *Knowledge Base of the Beginning Teacher*, Oxford, Pergamon Press, pp. 71–85.

Wells, G. (1973–8) *Language at Home and at School*, Bristol, Bristol Language Development Project.

Wells, G. (1985) *Language, Learning and Education*, Windsor, NFER-Nelson.

Wertsch, J. (1979) 'From social interaction to high psychological processes: A clarification and application of Vygotsky's theory', *Human Development*, **22**, pp. 1–22.

Willes, M. (1983) *Children into Pupils: A Study of Language in Early Schooling*, London, Routledge and Kegan Paul.

Williams, E. and Shuard, H. (1988) *Primary Mathematics Today: Third Edition for the Age of the Calculator*, Harlow, Essex, Longman.

Wilson, J. (1975) *Education Theory and the Preparation of Teachers*, Windsor, NFER.

Wilson, S.M. and Wineburg, S. (1988) 'Peering at history through different lenses: The role of disciplinary perspectives in teaching history', *Teachers College Record*, **89**, pp. 525–39.

Wilson, S.M., Shulman, L.S. and Rickert, A.E. (1987) '150 different ways of knowing: Representations of knowledge in teaching', in Calderhead, J. (Ed) *Exploring Teachers' Thinking*, London, Cassell, pp. 104–24.

Wineburg, S.S. and Wilson, S.M. (1988) 'Models of wisdom in the teaching of history', *Phi Delta Kappan*, **70**, 1, pp. 150–8.

WOOD, D.J., BRUNER, J.S. and ROSS, G. (1976) 'The role of tutoring in problem-solving', *Journal of Child Psychology and Psychiatry*, **17**, 2, pp. 89–100.

WOOD, T., COBB, P. and YACKEL, E. (1990) 'The contextual nature of teaching: Mathematics and reading instruction in one second-grade classroom', *The Elementary School Journal*, **90**, 5, pp. 497–513.

WYNN, K. (1992) 'Addition and subtraction by human infants', *Nature*, **358**, pp. 749–50.

YOUNG-LOVERIDGE, J.M. (1987) 'Learning mathematics', *British Journal of Developmental Psychology*, **5**, pp. 155–67.

YOUNG-LOVERIDGE, J.M. (1991) *The Development of Children's Number Concepts from Ages Five to Nine: Early Mathematics Learning Project: Phase 11* (Vol. 1: Report of Findings), New Zealand, University of Waikato.

Index